Lecture Notes in Computer Science   13855

Founding Editors

Gerhard Goos
Juris Hartmanis

Editorial Board Members

The series Lecture Notes in Computer Science (LNCS), including its subseries Lecture Notes in Artificial Intelligence (LNAI) and Lecture Notes in Bioinformatics (LNBI), has established itself as a medium for the publication of new developments in computer science and information technology research, teaching, and education.

LNCS enjoys close cooperation with the computer science R & D community, the series counts many renowned academics among its volume editors and paper authors, and collaborates with prestigious societies. Its mission is to serve this international community by providing an invaluable service, mainly focused on the publication of conference and workshop proceedings and postproceedings. LNCS commenced publication in 1973.

Maryam Mehrnezhad · Simon Parkin
Editors

Socio-Technical Aspects in Security

12th International Workshop, STAST 2022
Copenhagen, Denmark, September 29, 2022
Revised Selected Papers

 Springer

Editors
Maryam Mehrnezhad
Royal Holloway University of London
Surrey, UK

Simon Parkin
Delft University of Technology
Delft, The Netherlands

ISSN 0302-9743   ISSN 1611-3349 (electronic)
Lecture Notes in Computer Science
ISBN 978-3-031-83071-6   ISBN 978-3-031-83072-3 (eBook)
https://doi.org/10.1007/978-3-031-83072-3

This Springer imprint is published by the registered company Springer Nature Switzerland AG
The registered company address is: Gewerbestrasse 11, 6330 Cham, Switzerland

If disposing of this product, please recycle the paper.

Message from the Programme Chairs

The 12th International Workshop on Socio-Technical Aspects in Security (STAST 2022) aimed to create an exchange of research and ideas relating to how real-world systems can be designed to be secure where users and technologies interact. The term "socio-technical" then refers to the relationship between technology and people. The 2022 workshop focused especially on the interplay of technical and human factors in achieving or breaking computer security, privacy, and trust, in both organizational and individual settings.

Typically for STAST, the workshop received a wide range of inter-disciplinary submissions with a number of distinct methodologies.

The peer-review was organized as a double-blind process, with a strong conflict-of-interest management system. Each submission received a minimum of three reviews. Submissions with appreciable variance in review scores were assigned a fourth review as tie-breaker. The peer-review process included an active discussion phase, facilitated by a designated discussion lead for each submission, who subsequently summarized the discussion outcome and, when needed, agreed conclusions in a meta-review.

All of the 20 papers initially submitted to the workshop were retained by the chairs for peer-review after an initial check against the stipulations of the call for papers. Eventually, we accepted 8 submissions for publication in this volume (6 full paper submissions and 2 work-in-progress papers), yielding an acceptance rate of 40%.

Thomas Groß was recognized with the STAST 2022 Best Paper Award for the paper *Why Most Results of Socio-Technical Security User Studies Are False – And What to Do About it*.

Overall, we were very pleased with the quality of STAST's 12th volume. We are grateful for the high-quality work of the authors involved and for the invaluable contributions of the 25 program committee members and one additional reviewer, whose dedication and attention to detail enabled this volume. We thank Xengie Doan, Emre Koçyiğit, and Borče Stojkovski for their help with the publicity for the workshop and the workshop's web site.

February 2023

Maryam Mehrnezhad
Simon Parkin

Message from the Workshop Organizers

STAST has a solid foothold in its second decade, reaching its twelfth edition this year. It has become common knowledge that security stems from two main types of measures at present, namely technical measures and organisational measures.

All complex computer programs to thwart attacks clearly are technical measures. The definition of appropriate roles, policies and procedures for an institution, also with the aim of preserving security, translate into various organisational measures. Elements such as human awareness, predisposition to bias, avoidance of mental effort as well as deception (by the self or induced) form the so-called human factor*s* (plural form is intentional here), which dramatically affect both types of measures. For example, while coding errors may demolish the benefits of an entire software suite, a loose application of relevant procedures may baffle an institution faced with a security incident.

STAST has been promoting research, at both theoretical and applied levels, to tackle the human factor as it is outlined above. We are confident that, as a result, security in its various incarnations of computer security, internet security, IoT security, cyber security, etc., is better and better understood as a requirement concerning modern, computerised technologies as well as their human users. This has various useful consequences in our daily lives. One is a more enlightened interpretation of attacks (which, unfortunately, continue to occur every minute). For example, if ransomware containment is theoretically impossible, preventing it by a backup and disaster recovery site is wise. However, if the ransomware exploited a vulnerability that had been known for years, its root cause is carelessness, which inherently is of human origin.

We are therefore delighted to welcome the reader to the proceedings of the 2022 edition of STAST, the premier workshop on such pivotal topics!

February 2023

Giampaolo Bella
Gabriele Lenzini

Organization

General Chairs

Giampolo Bella   University of Catania, Italy
Gabriele Lenzini   University of Luxembourg, Luxembourg

Program Committee Chairs

Maryam Mehrnezhad   Royal Holloway University of London, UK
Simon Parkin   Delft University of Technology, The Netherlands

Programme Committee

Panagiotis Andriotis	University of the West of England, UK
Kalliopi Anastasopoulou	Greek Ministry of Health, 7th Health Region of Crete, Greece
Ingolf Becker	University College London, UK
Zinaida Benenson	University of Erlangen-Nuremberg, Germany
Jan-Willem Bullee	University of Twente, The Netherlands
Kovila Coopamootoo	King's College London, UK
Lynne Coventry	Northumbria University, UK
Rosario Giustolisi	IT University of Copenhagen, Denmark
Thomas Groß	Newcastle University, UK
Pieter Hartel	Singapore University of Technology and Design, Singapore
Markus Jakobsson	Artema Labs, USA
Laura Kocksch	Ruhr University Bochum, Germany
Shujun Li	University of Kent, UK
Jean Everson Martina	Universidade Federal de Santa Catarina, Brazil
Masakatsu Nishigaki	Shizuoka University, Japan
Norbert Nthala	Google LLC, USA
Saša Radomirović	University of Surrey, UK
Karen Renaud	University of Strathclyde, UK
Peter Y. A. Ryan	University of Luxembourg, Luxembourg
Diego Sempreboni	King's College London, UK
Ehsan Toreini	Durham University, UK

Kerry-Lynn Thomson	Nelson Mandela Metropolitan University, South Africa
Luca Viganò	King's College London, UK
Daniel Woods	University of Innsbruck, Austria
Konrad Wrona	NATO Communications and Information Agency, The Netherlands and Military University of Technology-Warsaw, Poland

Additional Reviewer

Gerard Buckley

Publicity and Web Site Chairs

Xengie Doan	University of Luxembourg, Luxembourg
Emre Koçyiğit	University of Luxembourg, Luxembourg
Borče Stojkovski	University of Luxembourg, Luxembourg

Fonds National de la Recherche Luxembourg

securityandtrust.lu

UNIVERSITÀ degli STUDI di CATANIA

UNIVERSITÉ DU LUXEMBOURG

Contents

Work in Progress: Considering Human Factors in Collaborative Decision Making for Secure Architecture Design

Brahim Hamid[1]([⊠])[iD] and Jason Jaskolka[2][iD]

[1] Institut de Recherche en Informatique de Toulouse (IRIT), University of Toulouse, UT2, Toulouse, France
brahim.hamid@irit.fr

[2] Systems and Computer Engineering, Carleton University, Ottawa, ON, Canada
jason.jaskolka@carleton.ca

Abstract. Developing large and complex software systems requires the collaboration of teams of developers, architects, managers, and more. These teams often work together during the design phase to make architectural design decisions that can impact many different system qualities including security. Thus, it is important to consider the human factors including levels of expertise and experience, as well as different attitudes and behaviors towards securing the system that impact the decision-making process of the team members individually and as a whole. This paper presents a work in progress that describes a conceptual framework to consider human factors in collaborative decision-making for secure architecture design. The framework is based on a combination of model-driven engineering techniques and human science approaches. We describe a design scenario with which we illustrate the usage of the proposed framework from the development team perspective. This work aims to enhance the understanding of how collaborative decisions are made and to provide better traceability of decisions impacting system security to gain confidence in the decisions taken by a team of diverse members.

Keywords: human factors · decision making · security · architecture

1 Introduction

The development of secure, large, and complex software systems requires the collaboration of many team members with varying levels of experience and expertise. As a result, it is necessary to consider the role played by human factors in secure architecture design. *Human factors* can be understood very broadly to include individual, institutional, and societal dimensions. Hence, a study of the human factors for developing secure systems must not only consider individual human behaviors, but also the social structures that enable collective action by groups and communities of various sizes.

Collaborative processes are usually defined as a structured or unstructured process where two or more stakeholders work together to fulfill a shared,

M. Mehrnezhad and S. Parkin (Eds.): STAST 2022, LNCS 13855, pp. 1–13, 2025.
https://doi.org/10.1007/978-3-031-83072-3_1

collective, and bounded goal. The various decision stakeholders differ in their distribution of physical teams (local, distributed), domain knowledge and expertise (security policies, business rules, regulations, etc.), and responsibilities (project manager, architect, developer, etc.). This situation is especially true for secure software development processes and particularly in the processes of collaborative software architecture design, where the software architecture is used as a means for coordination and a repository of common understanding between the different stakeholders. Resolution of design errors and conflicts at this level will reduce considerably the presence of errors and conflicts in the next phases. Architectural decisions are commonly used as the primary means for designing, describing, and documenting the software architecture, the collaboration in the process of architecture decision-making becomes one of the most important activities of software architecture design.

Supporting collaboration and improving security awareness of development teams involved in building secure systems, have been noted as key elements contributing to more effective security assurance for software-dependent systems [14]. Existing approaches studying collaborative architectural decision-making processes tend to focus on consensus-based approaches and do not consider the constraints of the team members (i.e., human factors) in the decision-making process. To address these issues, this paper describes a work in progress in developing a conceptual framework that takes into account human factors related to the expertise and experience of the team members involved in collaborative decision-making processes when developing secure software architectures. This work combines the technical, organizational, and human factors of designing secure software architectures to achieve security objectives. The proposed framework aims to enhance our understanding of collaborative decision-making processes when designing secure software architecture and to better support the traceability to gain confidence in the decisions impacting system security. We use Model-Driven Engineering (MDE) to describe these artifacts and add more formality to improve parts of the system design.

The rest of this paper is organized as follows. Section 2 describes the state-of-the-art in understanding human factors and collaborative decision-making in secure software and systems development. Section 3 presents our conceptual framework. Section 4 illustrates the development team workflow within the proposed framework using an illustrative example. Section 5 discusses the next steps of our research activities. Lastly, Sect. 6 concludes.

2   State-of-the-Art

Existing methods and tools for collaborative architectural decision-making (e.g., [8,9,17,19–21,27]) focus mainly on sharing and reusing knowledge, making trade-offs, and achieving consensus. These works argue that design decisions must carefully consider domain-specific security objectives and policies, data control and processing requirements, business rules, regulations, etc., in addition to technical resource limitations, exceptional circumstances, and other non-technical factors. However, they do not explicitly account for the different levels of expertise, experience, and awareness of the individual team members tasked with collaborating to arrive at an acceptable decision. The need for measuring the human factor of cybersecurity was expressed in [4] and [12]. The goal was to propose ways to quantify the security posture of human organizations especially within large corporations and government agencies. Since then, several works have aimed at understanding human factors in cyber security context by exploring the skills, knowledge, and behaviors of those involved in developing secure systems [2,23] and comparing the practices of security and non-security experts [6,13]. Other foundational works have explored more generally how human reasoning, judgments, and decisions [5,7]. Conversely, some works have studied ways to address security issues in software architecture design [15,24]. In recent work, Gaubatz et al. [10] began to merge these ideas by exploring the development of frameworks for understanding collaboration architectural decision making. However, this work primarily focuses only on roles and on consensus-based approaches and does not consider the constraints on the roles (or more broadly, profiles) of the team members participating in the decision-making process.

To address these issues, we aim to develop a framework that takes in account human factors related to the expertise, experience, and awareness of the team members involved in collaborative decision-making processes when developing secure software architectures. More broadly, we seek to further the understanding of how collaborative decisions are made and provide better traceability of decisions impacting system security to gain confidence in the decisions taken by a team of diverse members.

3   Proposed Approach and Conceptual Framework

This section describes the fundamental ideas behind our proposed approach and our progress in developing a conceptual framework. Earlier, we noted the need for having an explicit interpretation of security at the architecture design stage by the different stakeholders involved in the system development process. In addition, today it is well accepted by the community that models are a useful tool for designing secure system architectures. From our opinion, human factors should be specified in the form of models following the MDE fashion as first-class citizens to develop software systems through a design philosophy. We achieve this in the first step of our approach through the creation of a conceptual view of intended framework as an ecosystem of models. Figure 1 highlights the general idea of the intended framework.

As part of the development process, the software architect will build several models including those described below.

Human Factors Model which characterizes the development team based on their awareness with respect to factors such familiarity, capability, riskiness, etc. with respect to technical security mechanisms, policies and procedures, and the adoption of security best practices, for example. One way in which to build the human factors model is to create a set of development team profiles using the

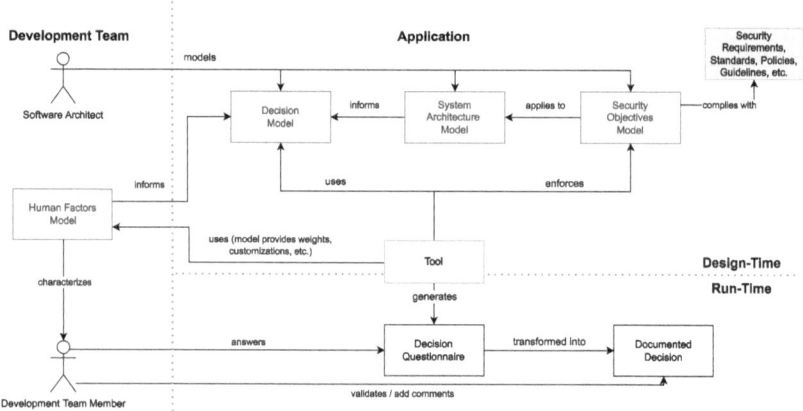

Fig. 1. An overview of the proposed approach and conceptual framework

results of questionnaires completed by the development team members involved in the project. The development of this model in our framework is a work in progress. We are currently exploring the use of fuzzy trace theory [7] combined with measurements of attributes related to Knowledge (what you know), Attitudes (what you think) and Behavior (what you do), referred to as *KAB* [18], assessed through questionnaires to create development team profiles.

Security Objectives Model which describes the specific security objectives for the software system. For example, a software system may have security objectives related to authentication and authorization of components to perform certain actions, accountability of components for the actions they perform, confidentiality, integrity, and availability of data in transit, in processing, and at rest, etc. The security objectives must comply with any relevant standards, policies, and guidelines for the given system context. In our current progress, these objectives are defined in a manner similar to [25].

System Architecture Model which describes the software system architecture. For example, the architect may use a component-port-connector model to describe a software system that aims to provide secure communications for components. In our current progress, we are conforming to the component-port-connector architecture metamodel described in [26] to specify the structure and behavior of the software architecture.

Decision Model which is informed by the system architecture models and the human factors model characterizing the development team. The decision model captures a collection of architectural design decisions (ADDs) that need to be made collaboratively by the development team to achieve the security objectives. For example, an ADD may be: "How to provide authentication for components?" The decision may be parameterized by several parameters. For example, it may be necessary to know which component(s) require authentication, what kinds of connections each component handles, and what kinds of data each component handles. The development of the decision model is current a work in progress.

To build these models we are exploring the use of a Domain Specific Modeling Language (DSML) to express ADDs and the associated parameters that influence the decision. The use of a DSML will enable the development of reusable elements that can be selected based on the application-specific context, security objectives and requirements, and architectural constraints, as well as the human factors characterized in the human factors model. The *design-time* models will serve as the inputs to a software tool (to be developed). The *software tool* will use the human factors model to generate *Decision Questionnaires* to be completed by the development team at *run-time*. The generated questionnaires will be based on the decision model developed by the software architect. By additionally enforcing the constraints in the security objectives model, the generated questionnaires will provide weights and customization for ADD parameters for individual team members based on their profile. Once complete, the software tool will use a decision resolution algorithm to suggest decisions based on the development team's responses.

4   Illustration of the Approach Through an Example

To better understand our collaborative security design decision-making framework with models, we provide a description of one usage scenario.

Consider a development team that is developing a college library web application [22]. Note that in this paper, we adapt this example system which was described in the context of secure engineering design with models and patterns in [11] to demonstrate aspects of the proposed framework. The application provides online services to students, staff, and librarians for searching and requesting books. Librarians can also add books and add users. The application must ensure that all internal and external connections to the web server are subject to appropriate authentication and authorization mechanisms. For example, the application must clearly define the user types and the access rights for said users. Further, the application must ensure that no sensitive data or authentication credentials are transmitted in the clear either internally or externally.

The development team is tasked with designing a secure architecture for the college library web application. There are several alternatives that can be considered, and several ADDs need to be made to ensure that the security objectives and requirements outlined in the design scenario described above are satisfied. Once the framework is established, the anticipated flow of system development follows the steps shown in Fig. 2.

Step 1: Development Team Completes Profiling Studies. For a software project, a development team consisting of a collection of team members, often with a variety of knowledge, experience, and security awareness is formed. At the outset of the project, team members are expected to answer a profile questionnaire or participate in an observation study with several scenarios to characterize their individual expertise, attitudes, and behaviors which are captured by the development team profiles. Note that this step is performed once for a set of applications, although improvement of the team over time should be considered.

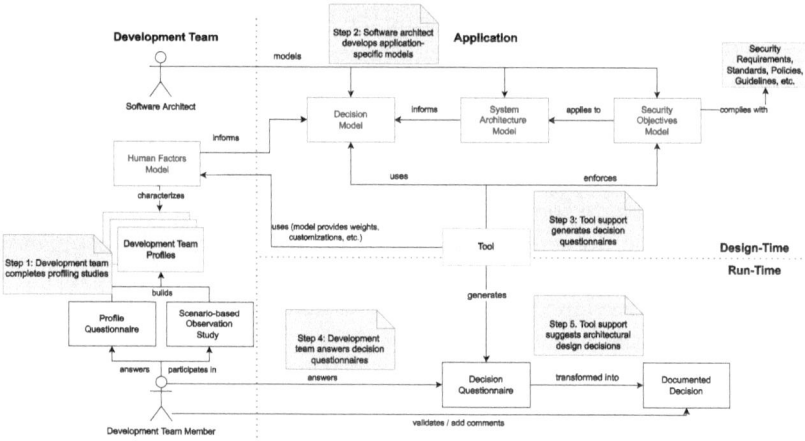

Fig. 2. Instance of use cases and involved stakeholders as proposed by our approach

Table 1. Sample answers to the Profile Questionnaire by three development team members for the college library web application

Team Member	Q1	Q2	Q3	Q4	Q5
D1	4	4	4	4	4
D2	2	3	3	2	3
D3	4	4	4	5	5

For the college library web application, this step establishes the human factors model for the assembled development team that will be used in subsequent steps of the framework. The following items present an excerpt of a Profile Questionnaire to present to the development team, who are asked to rate their skills on a Likert-like scale. In the context of this example, we have defined a scale from 1 to 5, 1 being the lowest value of mastering the presented concepts (not at all) and 5 being the highest value of mastering the presented concepts (expert-level).

Q1. How familiar are you with user authentication?
Q2. How familiar are you with database authentication?
Q3. How familiar are you with server authentication?
Q4. How capable are you to identify internal/external component connections?
Q4. How capable are you to identify sensitive information within a system?

The answers of each development team member will inform the decision model and be used in the decision resolution process. For the purpose of illustration suppose that we have a three development team members (**D1, D2** and **D3**) which have provided the responses shown in Table 1 to the sample Profile Questionnaire given above. Based on the results, it can be determined that **D1** and **D3** are similar in their expertise, experience, and awareness, and therefore

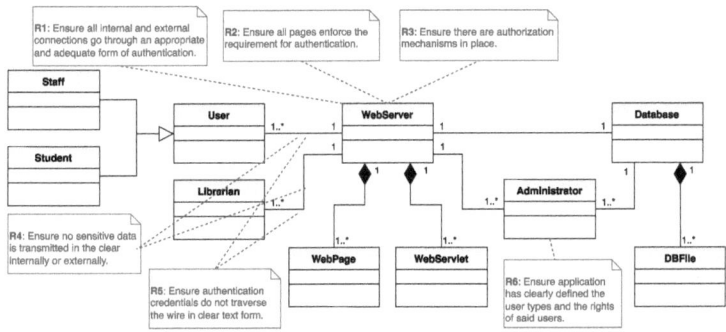

Fig. 3. Security objectives model of the college library web application

can belong to the same profile labelled as *Proficient*, whereas **D2** may belong to a different profile labelled as *Competent*.

Step 2: Software Architect Develops Application-Specific Models. The software architect develops several models for the specific application associated with the software project. For the college library web application, suppose that the software architect provides the system architecture model, security objectives model, and decision model as described below.

Figure 3 shows the system architecture model and the security objectives model. The *System Architecture Model* is provided as a UML class diagram where software components are represented by classes and relationships between the components are represented by associations. The *Security Objectives Model* documents the security objectives using model annotations to describe a set of security requirements (blue boxes) to achieve the desired security objectives.

The *Decision Model* is informed by the system architecture model and the security objectives model. Based on the security objectives (annotated on the model in Fig. 3), the development team has to collaboratively make several ADDs to ensure the satisfaction of the security objectives. For example, with specific consideration to the authentication objective for the college library web application, the decision model will consist of the following ADDs and associated questions to determine the decision parameters (*P*):

> *ADD1.* How to provide authentication for components?
>   *P1.* Which component?
>   *P2.* What kind of connections does the component handle?
>   *P3.* What kind of data does the component handle?
> *ADD2.* How to provide authentication for connections?
>   *P1.* Which connector?
>   *P2.* What kind of connections does the connector handle?
>   *P3.* What kind of data does the connector handle?

In the context of our work, the solutions for ADDs will be provided in the form of suggestions using patterns as in [11] or abstract representations of security mechanisms providing authentication at the level of components (in the case

Table 2. Sample choices from the Decision Questionnaire by three development team members for the college library web application

Team Member	P1	P2	P3
D1	WebServer	Both	Both
D2	WebServer	Internal	Both
D3	WebServer	Both	Both

of *ADD1*) or connectors (in the case of *ADD2*) considering the parameter values. For instance, authentication for a component C handling internal and external connections and sensitive and non-sensitive data could be achieved using an authorization pattern composed of an authorization component linked to C and to the set of components with respect to C's potential external connections.

Additional architectural decision decisions may be derived for the given system architecture with respect to other security objectives such as confidentiality, authorization, etc.

Step 3: Tool Support Generates Decision Questionnaires. The proposed tool support is used, taking the decision model, security objectives model, and human factors model as inputs, to generate a *Decision Questionnaire* for the development team members involved in the collaborative decision-making process. For the college library web application, the decision questionnaire will be populated with specific choices for the ADD parameters from the decision model, considering the security objectives model and human factors model. For instance, the decision questionnaire for the college library web application would contain:

> *ADD1.* How to provide authentication for components?
> > *P1.* Which component? (*weight* $= w_{11}$)
> > > – *Choices populated from the system architecture model (see Fig. 3) and include:* WebServer, Database, Administrator, etc.
> > *P2.* What kind of connections does the component handle? (*weight* $= w_{12}$)
> > > – *Choices include:* Internal/External/Both
> > *P3.* What kind(s) of data does the component handle? (*weight* $= w_{13}$)
> > > – *Choices include:* Sensitive/Non-sensitive/Both/None
> *ADD2.* How to provide authentication for connections?
> > *P1.* Which connector? (*weight* $= w_{21}$)
> > > – *Choices populated from the system architecture model (see Fig. 3) and include:* User–WebServer, WebServer–Administrator, WebServer–Database, etc.
> > *P2.* What kind of connections does the connector handle? (*weight* $= w_{22}$)
> > > – *Choices include:* Internal/External/Both
> > *P3.* What kind of data does the connector handle? (*weight* $= w_{23}$)
> > > – *Choices include:* Sensitive/Non-sensitive/Both/None

With consideration to the human factors model, the generated decision questionnaire will have associated with it specific weights for each decision parameter (see w_{xy} in the example above where x and y correspond to the *ADD* and parameter P identifiers respectively) to inform the decision resolution process.

Step 4: Development Team Answers Decision Questionnaires. Each development team member completes the decision questionnaire, selecting the specific choices for each parameter associated with an ADD. For example, for *ADD1* for the college library web application, the three development team members may make the choices as shown in Table 2.

As described above, because each team member will have different human factors affecting their decision-making and the selections to the questionnaires, the weights of each choice will be considered when resolving the decision in Step 5. For illustration and simplicity, suppose that team members in the *Proficient* profile (i.e., **D1** and **D3**) have weights $w_{xy} = 4$ for all x, y and team members in the *Competent* profile (i.e., **D2**) have weights $w_{xy} = 3$ for all x, y.

Step 5: Tool Support Suggests Architectural Design Decisions. After each team member completes their decision questionnaire, the proposed software tool suggests a decision based on its decision resolution algorithm. The suggested decision will, of course, be informed by the specific choices made by each development team member's decision questionnaire and their associated weights. It will also be further validated, perhaps with additional comments added to yield a documented ADD.

For example, for *ADD1* in the college library web application, we can consider a very simple decision resolution algorithm where we add the weights from each development team member for each choice of parameter. Because all development team members chose `WebServer` for *P1* and `Both` for *P3*, the resolution is obvious. However, both **D1** and **D3**, members of the *Proficient* profile, chose `Both` for *P2* so their profile weights are considered, and the total is $4 + 4 = 8$. **D2**, on the other hand, a member of the *Competent* profile, chose `Internal` for *P2*, so the profile weights are considered, and the total is simply 3. Therefore, because the total is higher for `Both`, this is the decided value for *P2*. Now, with the input *P1* = `WebServer`, *P2* = `Both`, *P3* = `Both`, a suggested decision for *ADD1* may be to add an *Authorization* component connected to the WebServer, Database, and Administrator that can help satisfy *R1*, *R2*, *R3*, and *R6* (see Fig. 3) because the choices provided in the decision questionnaires in Step 4 suggested that the WebServer which handles both internal and external connections, and sensitive and non-sensitive data requires an authentication and authorization solution.

A similar procedure would take place for *ADD2* and, as a result, a suggested decision for *ADD2* may be to add a *SecureCommunication* component between the Users (Staff, Students, Librarians) and the WebServer to help satisfy *R4* and *R5* (see Fig. 3). Additional ADDs and parameters may further suggest that the *SecureCommunication* component consist of an *Authenticator*, a *SecureChannel*, and considering the confidentially objectives, provide encryption services using TLS, for example.

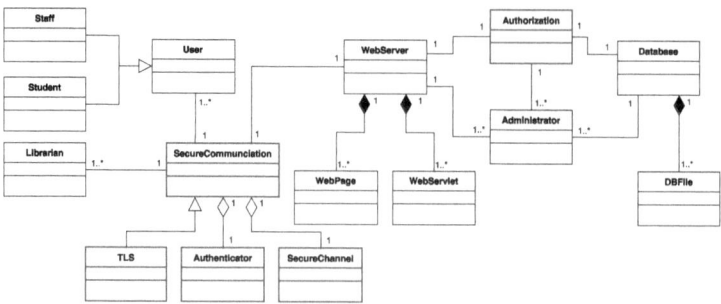

Fig. 4. Solution model based on the architectural design decisions

Expected Outcome. The proposed approach is expected to give a set of documented ADDs in an appropriate architectural decision template such as the
one proposed in [28]. The documented designs would lead to a solution model
as shown in Fig. 4 where the decisions are realized in the system architecture
model. For example, the solution incorporates an *Authorization* component and
a *SecureCommunication* component which correspond to the documented decisions described above.

5   Next Steps and Anticipated Challenges

Moving forward with the development of the proposed framework, we will investigate a cybersecurity development methodology based on technology, organizational culture, and security culture [30]. Related facets beyond technological
solutions such as human factors that affect the design choices should be addressed
at both the development team member and organizational levels. Regarding the
developers team interactions, considerations about what they need to use as
knowledge when performing the corresponding tasks, how they traverse the software architecture across components and layers, and what tools they use can
play a significant role in better understand the relationships between the human
factors model and the decision model in the proposed framework. We plan to
perform a similar study as in [3] to identify appropriate patterns of developer
behaviors during the secure system development with a focus on architecture
design. This can further extend to studying how the core and peripheral roles
played by the developers in a software project affect design decisions [16]. Implications resulting from this abstract classification may be used during the definition of weights for each decision parameter and during the decision resolution
process.

From another perspective, in the context of security development, Wang and
Nagappan [29] examined communication patterns between developers within the
"Hero Developers" classification [1]. This study contributes to characterizing the
nature of developer interactions in security development helping developers and
architects to understand how vulnerabilities are introduced in designs and how

to mitigate them under these interactions. Similarly, the fulfillment of security objectives resulting from collaborative design choices should be considered with respect to the social and human interactions of different software developers.

6   Concluding Remarks

Collaborative decision-making plays an integral role in developing secure software architectures for large and complex systems. In this paper, we presented our work in progress on developing a conceptual framework that combines the technical, organizational, and human factors of designing secure software architectures to achieve system security objectives. The proposed framework uses a combination of MDE techniques and human science approaches to account for human factors related to the expertise, experience, and awareness of the team members involved in collaborative decision-making processes when developing secure software architectures. We illustrated the development team workflow within the proposed framework using an example design scenario for a college library web application.

We expect that continuation of this work and elaboration of the presented ideas can lead to significant advances in the state-of-the-art in the tools and methods for taking human factors into account in collaborative decision-making processes for building secure software architectures. Among other benefits, the proposed approach will yield documented decisions with traceability to how and why those decisions were made, improving the confidence in the resulting design.

References

1. Agrawal, A., Rahman, A., Krishna, R., Sobran, A., Menzies, T.: We don't need another hero?: the impact of "heroes" on software development. In: Paulisch, F., Bosch, J. (eds.) ICSE (SEIP), pp. 245–253. ACM (2018)
2. Alshaikh, M.: Developing cybersecurity culture to influence employee behavior: a practice perspective. Comput. Secur. **98**, 102003 (2020)
3. Astromskis, S., Bavota, G., Janes, A., Russo, B., Di Penta, M.: Patterns of developers behaviour: a 1000-hour industrial study. J. Syst. Softw. **132**, 85–97 (2017)
4. Bowen, B.M., Devarajan, R., Stolfo, S.: Measuring the human factor of cyber security. In: 2011 IEEE International Conference on Technologies for Homeland Security (HST), pp. 230–235 (2011)
5. Brust-Renck, P.G., Weldon, R.B., Reyna, V.F.: Judgment and decision making. Oxf. Res. Encycl. Psychol. (2021)
6. Compagna, L., Khoury, P.E., Massacci, F., Thomas, R., Zannone, N.: How to capture, model, and verify the knowledge of legal, security, and privacy experts: a pattern-based approach. In: 11th International Conference on Artificial Intelligence and Law, ICAIL 2007, pp. 149–153. ACM, New York (2007)
7. Corbin, J.C., Reyna, V.F., Weldon, R.B., Brainerd, C.J.: How reasoning, judgment, and decision making are colored by gist-based intuition: a fuzzy-trace theory approach. J. Appl. Res. Mem. Cogn. **4**(4), 344–355 (2015)

8. Dasanayake, S., Markkula, J., Aaramaa, S., Oivo, M.: Software architecture decision-making practices and challenges: an industrial case study. In: 2015 24th Australasian Software Engineering Conference, pp. 88–97 (2015)

9. Falessi, D., Cantone, G., Kazman, R., Kruchten, P.: Decision-making techniques for software architecture design: a comparative survey. ACM Comput. Surv. **43**(4) (2011)

10. Gaubatz, P., Lytra, I., Zdun, U.: Automatic enforcement of constraints in real-time collaborative architectural decision making. J. Syst. Softw. **103**, 128–149 (2015)

11. Hamid, B., Weber, D.: Engineering secure systems: models, patterns and empirical validation. Comput. Secur. **77**, 315–348 (2018)

12. Handley, H.A.H., Smillie, R.J.: Architecture framework human view: the NATO approach. Syst. Eng. **11**(2), 156–164 (2008)

13. Ion, I., Reeder, R., Consolvo, S.: "...No one can hack my mind": comparing expert and non-expert security practices. In: 11th USENIX Conference on Usable Privacy and Security, SOUPS 2015, pp. 327–346. USENIX Association, USA (2015)

14. Jaskolka, J.: Recommendations for effective security assurance of software-dependent systems. In: Arai, K., Kapoor, S., Bhatia, R. (eds.) SAI 2020. AISC, vol. 1230, pp. 511–531. Springer, Cham (2020). https://doi.org/10.1007/978-3-030-52243-8_37

15. Jasser, S.: Enforcing architectural security decisions. In: 2020 IEEE International Conference on Software Architecture (ICSA), pp. 35–45 (2020)

16. Joblin, M., Apel, S., Hunsen, C., Mauerer, W.: Classifying developers into core and peripheral: an empirical study on count and network metrics. In: 39th International Conference on Software Engineering, pp. 164–174. IEEE/ACM (2017)

17. Jugel, D., Schweda, C.M., Zimmermann, A.: Modeling decisions for collaborative enterprise architecture engineering. In: Persson, A., Stirna, J. (eds.) CAiSE 2015. LNBIP, vol. 215, pp. 351–362. Springer, Cham (2015). https://doi.org/10.1007/978-3-319-19243-7_33

18. Kaur, J., Mustafa, N.: Examining the effects of knowledge, attitude and behaviour on information security awareness: a case on SME. In: 2013 International Conference on Research and Innovation in Information Systems (ICRIIS), pp. 286–290 (2013)

19. Nowak, M.: Collaborative software architecture decisions: structure and dynamics. Ph.D. thesis, USI Faciulty fo Informatics (2014)

20. Nowak, M., Pautasso, C.: Team situational awareness and architectural decision making with the software architecture warehouse. In: Drira, K. (ed.) ECSA 2013. LNCS, vol. 7957, pp. 146–161. Springer, Heidelberg (2013). https://doi.org/10.1007/978-3-642-39031-9_13

21. Nowak, M., Pautasso, C., Zimmermann, O.: Architectural decision modeling with reuse: challenges and opportunities. In: 2010 ICSE Workshop on Sharing and Reusing Architectural Knowledge, SHARK 2010, pp. 13–20. ACM, New York (2010)

22. OWASP: Threat modeling process (2020). https://owasp.org/www-community/Threat_Modeling_Process. Accessed June 2022

23. Oyetoyan, T.D., Jaatun, M.G.G., Cruzes, D.S.: Measuring developers' software security skills, usage, and training needs. In: Exploring Security in Software Architecture and Design. IGI Global (2019)

24. Rouland, Q., Hamid, B., Jaskolka, J.: Specification, detection, and treatment of STRIDE threats for software components: modeling, formal methods, and tool support. J. Syst. Architect. **117**, 102073 (2021)

25. Rouland, Q., Hamid, B., Bodeveix, J.P., Filali, M.: A formal methods approach to security requirements specification and verification. In: 24th International Conference on Engineering of Complex Computer Systems, pp. 236–241. ICECCS 2019 (2019)
26. Rouland, Q., Hamid, B., Jaskolka, J.: Formal specification and verification of reusable communication models for distributed systems architecture. Futur. Gener. Comput. Syst. **108**, 178–197 (2020)
27. Tofan, D., Galster, M., Avgeriou, P., Schuitema, W.: Past and future of software architectural decisions - a systematic mapping study. Inf. Softw. Technol. **56**(8), 850–872 (2014)
28. Tyree, J., Akerman, A.: Architecture decisions: demystifying architecture. IEEE Softw. **22**(2), 19–27 (2005)
29. Wang, S., Nagappan, N.: Characterizing and understanding software developer networks in security development. In: 2021 IEEE 32nd International Symposium on Software Reliability Engineering (ISSRE), pp. 534–545 (2021)
30. Wiley, A., McCormac, A., Calic, D.: More than the individual: examining the relationship between culture and information security awareness. Comput. Secur. **88**, 101640 (2020)

Hunting High or Low: Evaluating the Effectiveness of High-Interaction and Low-Interaction Honeypots

Yekta Kocaogullar[1]([✉]), Orcun Cetin[1], Budi Arief[2], Calvin Brierley[2], Jamie Pont[2], and Julio Hernandez-Castro[2]

[1] Sabanci University, Istanbul, Turkey
{ykocaogullar,orcun.cetin}@sabanciuniv.edu
[2] University of Kent, Canterbury, UK
{b.arief,c.r.brierley,j.pont,j.c.hernandez-castro}@kent.ac.uk

Abstract. Background. Honeypots are cybersecurity mechanisms that are set up as decoys in networks to lure and monitor attackers trying to compromise vulnerable systems. Two commonly used honeypot designs are high-interaction and low-interaction honeypots, which differ in the amount of interplay that the attackers are allowed to do. So far, the effectiveness of high-interaction and low-interaction honeypots has been understudied, making it difficult for security teams to choose between different honeypot technologies.
Aim. The aim of this paper is to compare the effectiveness of high-interaction and low-interaction honeypots through real-world data.
Method. We deployed multiple Elasticsearch honeypot implementations to collect data: a closed-source high-interaction honeypot developed by the authors, and three types of open-source low-interaction honeypots (namely Elastichoney, Delilah and Elasticpot). The collected data came from 48 instances of high-interaction honeypots and 111 instances of low-interaction honeypots, over a period of 14 days.
Results. We found that low-interaction honeypots captured only a fraction of the attacks that high-interaction honeypots can catch. On the other hand, low-interaction honeypots are simpler, more efficient to run due to their low usage of resources, and easier to deploy. In our dataset, high-interaction honeypots captured 76.12% of the total attack packets and attracted 70.61% of the unique attacker IPs. In comparison, low-interaction honeypots performed a lot worse in collecting attack data; they only managed to capture 23.88% of the total attack packets and attracted 29.39% of the unique attacker IPs.
Conclusions. In this paper, we present an experiment that evaluated and compared the effectiveness of high-interaction and low-interaction honeypots in terms of the amount and the type of information collected from attacks targeting them. It follows from our findings that it would be wiser to either concentrate solely on using high-interaction honeypots, or to increase the effectiveness of low-interaction ones by automatically changing each static value during deployment and/or by increasing the mimicking capabilities of low-interaction honeypots.

© The Author(s), under exclusive license to Springer Nature Switzerland AG 2025
M. Mehrnezhad and S. Parkin (Eds.): STAST 2022, LNCS 13855, pp. 14–30, 2025.
https://doi.org/10.1007/978-3-031-83072-3_2

Keywords: Security · honeypot · high-interaction · low-interaction · decision-making · comparative study

1   Introduction

Honeypots are one of those essential cybersecurity systems that can be useful in detecting network compromises, while learning the behaviour of the attackers at the same time. These systems are set up to mimic vulnerable assets that could be infiltrated by attackers. A honeypot typically has monitoring and logging capabilities that would allow security researchers (the honeypot operators) to gather information about attackers' behaviour, including the tools and exploits used by these attackers. In other words, a honeypot can be thought of as a "digital network bait" which is used to discover potential attackers - both insiders and remote [17] and to gather evidence about them.

Honeypots can serve as a valuable tool, as long as attackers interact with them [14]. In the simplest form, there are two different categories of honeypot interaction: high and low. High-interaction honeypots offer a fully functional decoy system that can be compromised by the attackers [20]. This allows high-interaction honeypots to collect more information regarding attackers' behaviour, as well as their attack tools [17]. However, high-interaction honeypots are harder to develop – and typically more resource-intensive – in comparison to low-interaction honeypots.

On the other hand, low-interaction honeypots provide attackers with minimal access – for example, they do not let attackers to access the operating system but instead they provide some minimalist implementation of a limited number of Internet protocols and services [14]. This limitation – while reducing the possibility of the honeypot getting completely compromised by the intruder – also restricts the honeypot's ability to emulate the full functionality of a vulnerable system [17]. Low-interaction honeypots are also usually easier to develop, deploy and maintain, as they require less computational resources.

Challenges and Motivation. Nowadays, some attackers are becoming increasingly aware of the presence of honeypots. As they try to navigate their way through their victim's devices, those attackers would keep an eye for honeypot-like features on the systems they hit, in order to avoid being monitored – or even worse, captured [30]. They would also like to avoid wasting their time and effort on not-real systems, and naturally, they do not want to give away valuable and incriminating information about themselves.

At the same time, security community knows remarkably little about which type of honeypot would attract more attackers, and how much of the attackers' data can be captured by using either the high- or low-interaction honeypots.

This means that any claims within the security community that high-interaction honeypots are outperforming low-interaction honeypots currently lack numerical evidence. Furthermore, the extent of such a proposed performance difference is currently unexplored. These observations provide the key challenges and motivation for the research we present in this paper.

Most importantly – and in relation to the socio-technical aspects of security – this gap in knowledge makes it difficult for practitioners (with varying degrees of expertise) to make decision whilst trying to build a secure system. This is especially true for real-world systems, in which diverse sets of needs would come up, due to different budgets, environments and demands. Furthermore, not knowing enough about how high- and low-interaction honeypots would perform in the real-world setting may lead to a false sense of security by the users of such systems. As a consequence, this false sense of security may increase the possibility of errors due to the human element.

To address the challenges above, this paper compares the effectiveness of high-interaction and low-interaction honeypots in terms of attracting attacks in a real-world setting. We conducted an experiment in which we contrasted network traffic data captured by one custom high-interaction honeypot group and three popular low-interaction ones, within a 14-day period. We deemed this 14-day observation period would be sufficient, since first and foremost, we were only interested in the initial and short term effects, rather than the long term and historic data of honeypot operations (the latter is a valuable research in its own right, but it is beyond the scope of the research we wanted to focus on here).

Contributions. The main contributions of our paper are:

– we analyse and compare the efficacy of high- and low-interaction honeypots based on the data we collected from our experiment;
– we provide some insights into the geographical spread of potential attackers;
– finally, we come up with a set of recommendations that may help security researchers in choosing the type of honeypots suitable for their work.

The rest of the paper is organised as follows. Section 2 provides some background information regarding the honeypot systems we used in our study, as well as our rationale in using Elasticsearch for this study. Section 3 focuses on our deployment methodology and our rule set for evaluating incoming attacks. Section 4 presents the results by (a) comparing the performances of high- and low-interaction honeypots, (b) comparing the three types of low-interaction honeypots we used with each other, and (c) analysing the geographical locations of the attackers. Section 5 outlines and briefly discusses related work, while Sect. 6 concludes our paper and provides several ideas for future research.

2   Elasticsearch Honeypots

Elasticsearch is a NoSQL database that can store, search, and analyse large amounts of data [22]. It currently has eight common vulnerabilities and exploits (CVEs) listed on the Exploit Database [5]. While six of these CVEs are from 2014 and 2015 and are currently legacy problems affecting older versions, two of them are relatively recent, from July 2021 [5].

In 2021, Paganini scanned 334,013 servers that used port 9200 and discovered that 9,202 were running instances of Elasticsearch and 5,740 were accessible without any authorisation [23]. Elasticsearch servers are heavily targeted by cyber criminals to steal and ransom victims' data. In another recent example, an attacker wiped and defaced more than 15,000 Elasticsearch servers and tried to pin the blame on Night Lion Security, a US cyber-security firm [10]. These vulnerabilities and recent attacks are the main reasons behind our decision to focus on Elasticsearch honeypots.

In order to respond to these threats, security community has designed various open-source honeypot implementations. Most of these are low-interaction, and their source code is available on GitHub. These honeypots usually provide an easy to set up and easy to use approach with ready-made default configurations. In addition to this, since low-interaction honeypots are less resource hungry, simply cloning a low-interaction Elasticsearch honeypot from GitHub and following the provided setup instructions is a cheap and effortless way of setting up honeypots. However, these low-interaction honeypots have several limitations, most notably the lack of useful information about the attackers' behaviour that can be collected.

2.1 Designing High-Interaction Elasticsearch Honeypot

In order to avoid the shortcomings of low-interaction honeypot implementations (and the lack of readily available high-interaction honeypots), we decided to construct our own high-interaction Elasticsearch honeypot, based on the latest version of the Elasticsearch services which we deployed into a Docker image. This allows our honeypot to return exactly the same responses that any compromised Elasticsearch servers would do. Moreover, in order to increase the decoy capabilities of our honeypot, we created random (yet believable) business and organisation, and related datasets to fill the indices of the Elasticsearch servers with realistic data. Moreover, index names were randomly selected from a list of 16 business-related database tables. Random indices data creation and name selection were performed every time a honeypot was deployed, to reduce the risk of potential attackers recognising "already seen" data.

Lastly, a `tcpdump` script was placed outside of the Docker image to record Internet traffic coming from all the visiting and attacking IP addresses. These traffic data were stored in packet capture (or `pcap`) files. These files were regularly parsed by automated scripts using the rule set mentioned in Sect. 3.2.

2.2 Low-Interaction Elasticsearch Honeypots

In comparison to high-interaction honeypots, low-interaction honeypots only allow attackers a limited access to the system [9, 27, 30].

This lack of freedom means that low-interaction honeypots use fewer resources than high-interaction honeypots. However, whilst easy to deploy and maintain, low-interaction honeypots do not behave like a real production system, and hence typically do not collect so much valuable data [27].

There are many open-source low-interaction Elasticsearch honeypots readily available on the Internet. For the purpose of our research, we selected widely-used low-interaction honeypots in the wild, taking into account their ease of deployment, as well as the clarity and availability of their documentation. These selection criteria would allow for the deployment of the chosen honeypots without demanding high technical knowledge or specific configurations.

For these reasons, we selected all three Elasticsearch honeypots (only the ones that are listed as database honeypots) that are being listed in popular honeypot lists [1,16,32]. These three honeypots are:

– *Elastichoney* is an open-source low-interaction Elasticsearch honeypot. It was "designed to catch attackers exploiting RCE vulnerabilities in Elasticsearch" [13]. It takes requests in the /, /_search and /_nodes endpoints and mimics an Elasticsearch database by replying with a JSON response that emulates what an actual vulnerable Elasticsearch instance would send [24]. Elastichoney keeps track of the attacks it receives and writes them into a log file. We deployed it with the default configuration in order to standardize our deployment process and capture the real world scenarios as more systems being deployed with default configurations rather than specific configurations.
– *Delilah* is another open-source low-interaction Elasticsearch honeypot that aims to catch attackers who are using the Elasticsearch Groovy vulnerability (CVE-2015-1427) [15,26]. Delilah mimics a vulnerable Elasticsearch instance and "detects and identifies attack commands, reconnaissance attempts, and download commands (specifically `wget` and `curl`)" [26]. Delilah is capable of downloading files an attacker is trying to insert into the system and it can also send email notifications to the managers of the system for real-time analysis.
– *Elasticpot* is an open-source low-interaction Elasticsearch honeypot that mimics a vulnerable Elasticsearch instance and stores the logs of incoming attacks [8]. It does not use Docker by default; however, deploying the honeypot into a Docker container is an option. This honeypot responds to an attacker by mimicking an old version of a vulnerable Elasticsearch server. However, it is possible to change the responses it gives to attackers if the honeypot owner would like the system to behave in a certain way (for instance, if they would like to focus on certain types of interaction), by editing the configuration file.

3   Methodology

We carried out a study design process to prepare the set up to be used for running our honeypots, as well as the strategy for collecting the data, and the rule set for examining the traffic behaviour.

3.1   Honeypot Deployment

Before starting the data collection, it is necessary to make critical decisions regarding the deployment process, which includes parameters such as deployment locations, cloud providers and the deployment period. In order to minimise

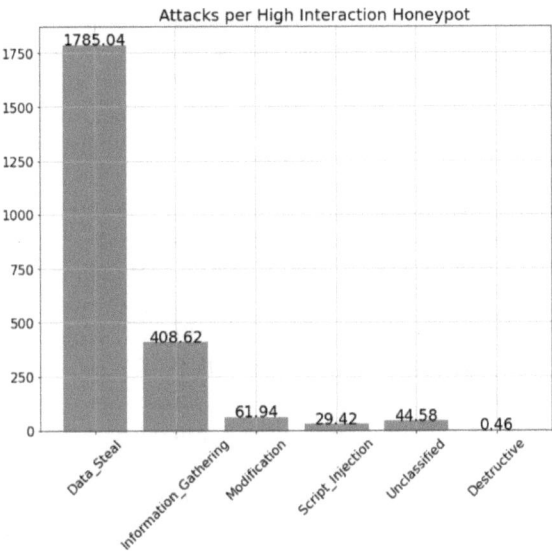

Fig. 1. The number of attacks for each of the six types of attack behaviour (high-interaction honeypot)

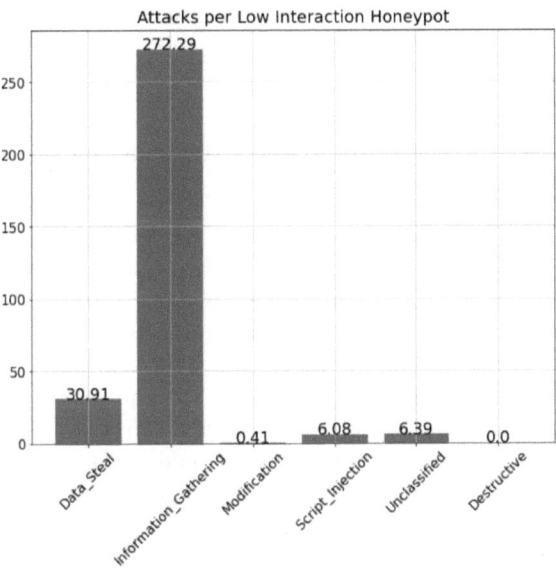

Fig. 2. The number of attacks for each of the six types of attack behaviour (low-interaction honeypot)

the chance of attackers identifying our honeypots collectively, the deployment process was randomised.

The deployment of our 48 high-interaction and 111 low-interaction honeypots was deployed consecutively, over a period of 14 days in order to understand initial and short term effects of fidelity and degree of honeypot interaction. Using this deployment strategy – instead of simultaneously deploying all our honeypots at once – ensured that the likelihood of attackers finding any link between our honeypots would be low.

We randomised the location of both high- and low-interaction honeypots to avoid any region-specific trends. The randomly selected regions for deployment were Europe, US, as well as some parts of Asia, Australia and Africa.

Furthermore, to avoid any cloud-provider-specific issue, we selected them randomly from a list of companies such as Alibaba, Amazon, Azure, Digital Ocean, Google Cloud, Hetzner, Linode and OVH. We selected well-known and widely-used cloud providers to include in this set in order to have our honeypots hosted at IP addresses that are commonly scanned and attacked by potential intruders. Additionally, the number of honeypots that we deployed was also randomised for the same reason (to avoid identification of all our honeypots as a collective). We restricted the randomisation of the number of instances in order to avoid widely different numbers of instances for each honeypot type. This process resulted in 48 high-interaction honeypots, 35 Elastichoney honeypots, 38 Delilah honeypots and 38 Elasticpot honeypots. We also conducted a "per honeypot type" analysis in Fig. 1 and Fig. 2 to mitigate the risk of having a different number of instances affecting the results.

3.2   Evaluation and Rule Set

We manually classified six different types of traffic behaviour towards our honeypots. We explain these below.

- *Data Steal.* We have classified data steal attacks as attempts to send a request to endpoints where reading critical information is possible. For example, a request sent to the /_search endpoint may access critical information inside the honeypot; thus, we classified such a request as a "data steal" attempt.
- *Information Gathering.* Information gathering consists of reconnaissance attempts, i.e. activities that are attempting to acquire information about the clusters and nodes of the system, rather than attempting to access the content inside of our honeypot. They normally precede an attack. So, requests that we classify as "information gathering" try to gain details about the system, rather than the information inside.
- *Data Modification.* This type of traffic behaviour includes POST and PUT requests that try to write data inside the honeypot, or attempt to alter existing data.
- *Script Injection.* Script injection attacks are associated with requests that abuse the known vulnerabilities of Elasticsearch to run malicious code or conduct a code injection into the server which allow attackers to gain full control of the compromised system.

– *Destructive.* We classified as "destructive" traffic behaviour requests that attempt to remove existing data in the server. These requests usually include the keyword `DELETE`.
– *Unclassified.* This traffic category is a catch-all type group, and consists of requests that do not fall easily into any of the other five categories above. For example, a request meant to target another service can fall into this category. Only 0.5% of the total packets we collected belong to this category.

4   Results

In this section, we discuss the efficacy of high- and low-interaction honeypots. First, we evaluated how the honeypots performed, in terms of their handling upon receiving attacks. After that, we analysed and evaluated the impact of honeypot locations. Lastly, we reported the possible origins of these attacks.

4.1   Efficacy of High-Interaction Honeypots

Honeypots are valuable tools in network security as long as they capture attacks. In this section of our paper, we analyse how good high-interaction honeypots are at capturing attacks compared to low-interaction honeypots.

First, we would like to determine whether using high-interaction honeypots would attract more attacks than low-interaction honeypots. Table 1 provides a statistical summary of the packets received for each type of attack, in relation to each type of honeypot. This table shows that the high-interaction honeypot received more packets than any of the low-interaction honeypots. For instance, high-interaction honeypots captured 1412 (67.66%) script injection attempts, compared to 253 (12.12%), 207 (9.92%) and 215 (10.30%) script injection attempts for those that belonged to Elastichoney, Delilah and Elasticpot, respectively. Similarly, high-interaction honeypots received 96% of the data steal attempts and 98% of data modification attempts. Moreover, only high-interaction honeypots received attacks designed to remove data from the database (this is typically associated with an effort to demand a ransom from the database owners).

We also investigated the number of unique IP addresses captured by the honeypots. Table 2 displays the number of unique IP addresses captured by each honeypot group, per attack type. Some IP addresses are involved in multiple attack types. For example, attackers often gather information about the database before performing data steal or modification attempts from the same IP. As shown in Table 2, high-interaction honeypots captured fewer unique IP addresses for data steal and information gathering attacks in comparison to two of the low-interaction honeypots. However, high-interaction honeypots captured significantly higher numbers of unique IP addresses for more involved attacks such as data modification, script injection and data removal. One way to interpret these results is that high-interaction honeypots received more attacks from more sophisticated attackers.

Table 1. A statistical summary of the types of attack behaviour, according to each honeypot group

Honeypots	#	# Packet captures	#Unique IP addresses	Data steal	Information Gathering	Modification	Script injection	Destructive
High-interaction	48	111843 (76.12%)	1578	85682 (96.15%)	19614 (39.36%)	2973 (98.51%)	1412 (67.66%)	22 (100%)
Elastichoney	35	10300 (7.01%)	1571	1109 (1.24%)	8711 (17.48%)	28 (0.93%)	253 (12.12%)	0
Delilah	38	12841 (8.74%)	1649	1486 (1.67%)	10911 (21.89%)	17 (0.56%)	207 (9.92%)	0
Elasticpot	38	11943 (8.13%)	1428	836 (0.94%)	10602 (21.27%)	0	215 (10.30%)	0
Total	159	146927 (100%)	3276 (100%)	89113 (100%)	49838 (100%)	3018 (100%)	2087 (100%)	22 (100%)

Table 2. The number of unique IP addresses based on the types of attack behaviour, according to each honeypot group

Honeypots	#	# Packet captures	# Unique IP addresses	Data steal	Information Gathering	Modification	Script injection	Destructive
High-interaction	48	111843 (70.61%)	1578	338	1353	31	102	4
Elastichoney	35	10300 (6.50%)	1571	379	1375	11	84	0
Delilah	38	12841 (8.11%)	1649	411	1430	5	73	0
Elasticpot	38	23419 (14.78%)	1428	303	1224	0	67	0

Working under the assumption that high-interaction honeypots are much harder to spot by attackers, we focused on studying if there was any evidence pointing towards attackers being able to detect and avoid low-interaction ones.

To get a better sense of whether attacker have shown any avoidance behaviour towards low-interaction honeypots, we investigated if IP addresses captured by high-interaction honeypots were also observed in low-interaction honeypots.

Table 3 shows how attackers that were captured by high-interaction honeypots behaved when they encountered low-interaction honeypots. Many attacking IP addresses captured by high-interaction honeypots were not seen at all by low-interaction honeypots. For example, only a handful of IP addresses engaging in modification attacks on high-interaction honeypots were also seen by low-interaction honeypots. This might be because these attackers use up-to-date blacklists that can be derived from using self-written scripts or publicly available honeypot detection tools to ignore low-interaction honeypots [3,4,25,28]. They only scan the homepage and two other pages (namely /_search and /_all/_mapping), which

Table 3. A statistical summary of some attack behaviour of IP addresses captured by the high-interaction honeypot, when they also hit low-interaction honeypot(s)

Categories	# of IPs captured by HIH	Elastichoney			Delilah			Elasticpot		
		Seen IPs	Used for the same purpose	Used for other purpose	Seen IPs	Used for the same purpose	Used for other purpose	Seen IPs	Used for the same purpose	Used for other purpose
Data steal	338	70	34	36	87	50	37	68	35	33
Modification	31	3	0	3	4	0	4	1	0	1
Script injection	102	21	21	0	22	22	0	24	24	0
Destructive	4	3	0	3	2	0	2	3	0	3

provide information about the database. By using the returned answers, these attackers might have detected and ignored the low-teraction honeypots.

The destructive attack category shows a similar picture, whereby known IP addresses are not used for gathering information about the database rather than deleting instances. Additionally, at most 24% of attacks in the script injection category was captured by single low-interaction honeypots. The rest of the attackers mght have used a blacklist or some other method to avoid low-interaction honeypots.

Interestingly, all the IP addresses captured in low-interaction honeypots were involved in script injection. This demonstrates that one quarter of attackers involved in script injection were not involved in any kind of low-interaction honeypot avoidance. Similarly, in data steal category, at most 25% of the attacks reported in high-interaction honeypots were captured by single low-interaction honeypots. More than half of these attackers were observed using queries for stealing data on low-interaction honeypots, as they did on high-interaction ones.

Our results show that attackers that conducted destructive and modification attacks clearly engaged in avoidance of low-interaction honeypots. Data stealing attackers display a somewhat similar behaviour. On the other hand, attackers involved in script injection did not exhibit this honeypot-evading behaviour.

Still, high-interaction honeypots captured five times more script injection attacks. This might be because script injection attacks only use blacklists to ignore low-interaction honeypots but no response-based avoidance is used. On the other hand, other attacker types seem to be using both response-based.

Furthermore, Fig. 3 shows the overlap of captured IP addresses for each honeypot group. We can see that a total of 415 IP addresses were captured by *all*

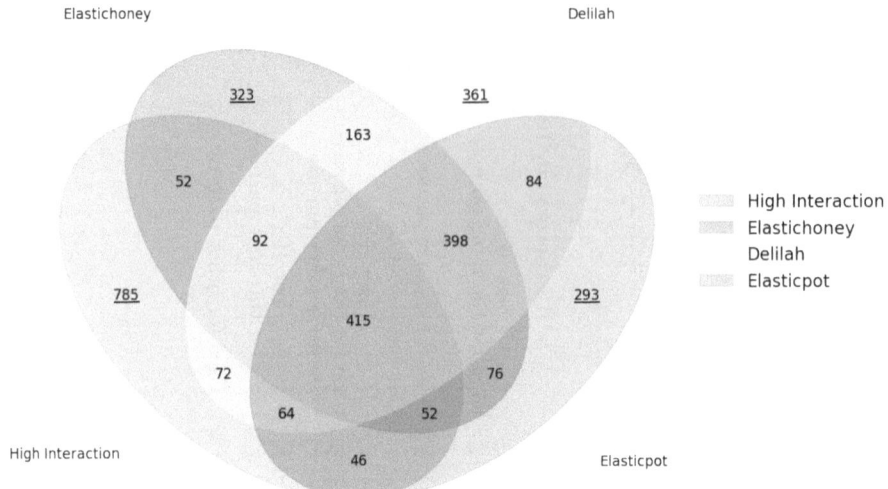

Fig. 3. A Venn diagram showing the distribution of the unique IP addresses captured for each honeypot group

honeypot groups. On the other hand, 785 IP addresses were only captured by high-interaction honeypots, while Elastichoney only captured 323 IP addresses, and Delilah only captured 361 IP addresses. Lastly, 293 IP addresses were only captured by Elasticpot which was less than all other honeypot groups. The total number of IP addresses exclusively attacking each honeypot group is shown as underlined in Fig. 3.

4.2   Efficacy of Different Low-Interaction Honeypots

In our study, the low-interaction honeypots (Elastichoney, Delilah, and Elasticpot) all performed badly in comparison to our high-interaction honeypot, both collectively and individually. Furthermore, the performance of these low-interaction honeypots did not differ notably, which suggests that the characteristics of any low-interaction honeypot would not lead to a meaningful difference in a real-world scenario.

Figure 4 presents the breakdown of the percentages of network traffic received by low-interaction honeypots based on their implementation. This figure shows that 36.6% of the total malicious network traffic were received by Delilah, compared to 34% and 29.4% for those received by Elasticpot and Elastichoney implementations respectively. These discrepancies in performances are most likely due to attackers' ability to identify low-interaction honeypots.

To understand whether our honeypots can be identified by external resources, we queried our IP addresses in the Shodan search engine [29]. Typically, Shodan can identify low-interaction honeypots by just scanning their metadata. Our search results found that Shodan identified none of the Delilah honeypots. However, all the Elastichoney and Elasticpot honeypots were correctly identified by

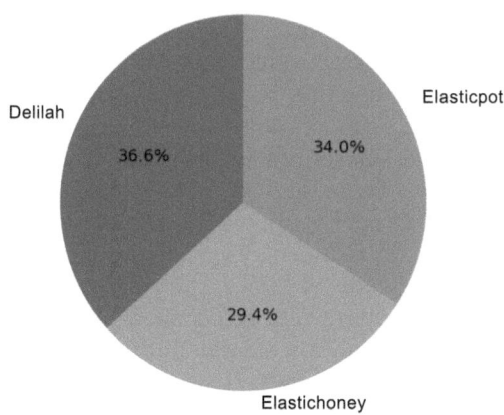

Fig. 4. The percentages of attacks captured by low-interaction honeypots for each of the three implementations used

Shodan. This success of detecting honeypots by Shodan might be the reason behind the slightly better overall performance of Delilah honeypots compared to the other low-interaction honeypots.

4.3   Analysing the Attackers

This subsection focuses on the source locations of the attacks that our honeypots had attracted. We used Maxmind GeoIP services to identify the origins of the attacks [2].

Table 4. The top-10 offending countries from which the IP addresses of the traffic to our honeypots came from

Total			High-Interaction		Low-Interaction	
Rank	Country	#	Country	#	Country	#
1	United States	2054	United States	978	United States	1569
2	China	316	China	152	China	240
3	United Kingdom	112	United Kingdom	53	United Kingdom	79
4	Germany	84	Netherlands	51	Germany	59
5	Netherlands	76	Germany	35	Netherlands	57
6	Canada	57	Canada	25	Canada	36
7	Singapore	51	Singapore	25	France	34
8	India	44	Lithuania	23	Singapore	31
9	Russian Federation	39	Russian Federation	20	Russian Federation	31
10	France	35	India	18	India	30

Table 4 shows the top-10 countries in terms of the number of attacking IP addresses per honeypot type. Our results cover IP addresses captured by both high-interaction and low-interaction honeypots. IP addresses were located in 60 different countries. The top-10 countries were United States, China, United Kingdom, Germany, Netherlands, Canada, Singapore, India, Russia and France. These 10 countries account for more than 91,4% of the total number of unique IP addresses. Moreover, United States alone accounts for more than 66.4% of the total number of attacking IP addresses. Typically, countries with larger hosting industries are present in this top-10 list.

The results from the Maxmind data do not show a clear difference in the top-10 countries in terms of the number of attacking IP addresses for different honeypot groups. These top-10 countries are very similar for both high-interaction and low-interaction honeypot groups. In fact, the top-3 countries were the same for both high- and low-interaction honeypots. Nine countries appeared in the top-10 of both groups, albeit at slightly different positions. The only major difference is that Lithuania appeared in the high-interaction list (at number 8) but not in the low-interaction list, while France appeared in the low-interaction honeypot (at number 7), but not in the high-interaction list.

5   Related Work

As far as we know, there is no prior research comparing the performances of high- and low-interaction honeypots through real-world data. This section will look at prior research under two subsections: Honeypot Detection and Comparison of Honeypots.

The studies that focus on detecting low-interaction honeypots are related to this research as the performance differences between high- and low-interaction honeypots are likely due to – at least in part – low-interaction honeypots getting detected more easily. However, these studies do not typically include high-interaction honeypots into their analysis. The scarce prior research in comparing honeypots is also related to our present research. However, previous work tends to compare low-interaction honeypots with each other, rather than drawing a comparison between high- and low-interaction honeypots [12,18,21].

5.1   Honeypot Detection

The ability to avoid detection is crucial for the performance of a honeypot. There are many attempted methods for detecting low-interaction honeypots. One such approach proposed by Aguirre-Anaya et al. is done by fingerprinting the low-interaction honeypots' static features [6]. In this method, using some features of a honeypot, such as "communication protocols, network services or specific environments", a fingerprint is obtained. Then, using this fingerprint, it is possible to distinguish a honeypot from a real system.

In addition to this, Morishita et al. discussed the detection of 14 open-source low-interaction honeypots [18]. This research is significant for our study, because we have used open-source low-interaction honeypots as well. In particular, Morishita et al. created 20 simple signatures to detect 19,208 honeypots across 637 autonomous systems. Furthermore, they found that low-interaction honeypots that use default configurations are more susceptible to getting identified.

Mukkamala et al. used some additional methods for honeypot identification [19]. In their research, detecting honeypots at the network level is explored, and they argue that, by looking at the network features of a system, low-interaction honeypots may be identified. Among other methods, fingerprinting is also discussed as a viable tool for identification in this paper.

In another paper that focuses on network-level detection, Defibaugh-Chavez et al. also argued that it is possible to identify low-interaction honeypots just by looking at their network features [11].

5.2   Comparison of Honeypots

Several studies have looked into comparing low-interaction honeypots. A paper by Abubakar Zakari et al. presents a comparative analysis among five widely used low-interaction honeypots, namely Honeyahole, Honeywall, Honeyd, Honeytrap, and Nepenthes [31]. Their study focused on literature analysis rather than real-world data. Through their work, they showed that almost all honeypots in question lack robustness or intelligence, and these limitations play negatively into their effectiveness.

In another work that evaluated honeypot technologies, we can see a comparison between open-source honeypots and commercial honeypot tools [21]. However, this study did not focus on real-world data based on network traffic, but instead compared their various features, such as services offered and platform support.

Finally, Alata et al. focused on the behaviour of attackers who have succeeded in entering the system [7]. Since this study used both high- and low-interaction honeypots, it is the one most closely related to our paper here. Alata et al. made an observation that their low-interaction honeypots have performed worse compared to high-interaction honeypots in terms of capturing attacks. However, since their experiment focused more on the attack behaviour and weak password attacks, their study did not offer anything more than an observation regarding the comparison of high- and low-interaction honeypots. Furthermore, the authors noted that this discrepancy was due to low-interaction honeypots not having the ssh service open, which means a lower number of attacks were being received.

6   Conclusion

Honeypots are heavily used by cybersecurity teams to collect indicators of compromise and other intelligence regarding cybercriminals. Some teams prefer to use high-interaction honeypots, which are designed so that they fully emulate a vulnerable system. Others use low-interaction honeypots that emulate only a few basic elements of a vulnerable system. There are good reasons to chose the latter, particularly because they consume less resources, are more readily available, and easier to deploy. Moreover, there are many open-source low-interaction honeypot projects to choose from, while there are very few high-interaction honeypots available freely.

In this paper, we present our study regarding the impact of the degree of interaction and fidelity in terms of capturing intelligence from attackers. For that purpose, we compared attack data collected by a high-interaction Elasticsearch honeypot with those collected by a group of three different low-interaction open-source honeypot projects.

We found a clear evidence that the high-interaction approach leads to gaining more volume and more pertinent intelligence from the attackers. Moreover, the difference is so significant that no combination of any of the three low-interaction honeypots can match the quantity or quality of the evidence gathered by the high-interaction one.

We recommend practitioners to use high-interaction honeypots where possible and limit the use of low-interaction ones to systems that, due to a chronic lack of resources, cannot afford to run the costlier high-interaction type.

There are several areas that merit further investigation. First, it would be interesting to explore if there is a link between the initial feature being hit by an attacker, and how long the attacker is likely to spend interacting with that honeypot. Second, investigating the possible use of blacklists (of already identified high-interaction and low-interaction honeypots) among attackers might reveal other strategies for improving the effectiveness of these honeypots. Finally, it would be valuable to explore ways to reduce the cost and the system requirements of high-interaction honeypots, while improving their usability and detection-avoidance rates.

References

1. Curated list of awesome lists. https://project-awesome.org/paralax/awesome-honeypots
2. GeoIP and GeoLite. https://dev.maxmind.com/geoip?lang=en
3. Honeypot or not? https://honeyscore.shodan.io/
4. nessus. https://www.tenable.com/products/nessus
5. nessus. Offensive security's Exploit Database Archive. https://www.exploit-db.com/
6. Aguirre-Anaya, E., Gallegos-Garcia, G., Luna, N.S., Vargas, L.A.V.: A new procedure to detect low interaction honeypots. Int. J. Electr. Comput. Eng. (IJECE) **4**(6) (2014)
7. Alata, E., Nicomette, V., Kaâniche, M., Dacier, M., Herrb, M.: Lessons learned from the deployment of a high-interaction honeypot. In: 2006 Sixth European Dependable Computing Conference, pp. 39–46. IEEE (2006)
8. Bontchev. Bontchev/elasticpot: An elasticsearch honeypot. https://github.com/bontchev/elasticpot
9. Campbell, R.M., Padayachee,K., Masombuka, T.: A survey of honeypot research: Trends and opportunities. In: 10th International Conference for Internet Technology and Secured Transactions (ICITST), pp. 208–212. IEEE (2015)

10. Cimpanu, C.: A hacker has wiped, defaced more than 15,000 elasticsearch servers (2020)
11. Defibaugh-Chavez, P., Veeraghattam, R., Kannappa, M., Mukkamala, S., Sung, A.H.: Network based detection of virtual environments and low interaction honeypots. In: Proceedings of the 2006 IEEE SMC, Workshop on Information Assurance, pp. 283–289 (2006)
12. Fan, W., Du, Z., Fernández, D., Villagra, V.A.: Enabling an anatomic view to investigate honeypot systems: a survey. IEEE Systems J. **12**(4), 3906–3919 (2017)
13. Jordan-Wright. Jordan-Wright/elastichoney: a simple elasticsearch honeypot. https://github.com/jordan-wright/elastichoney
14. Kambow, N., Passi, L.K.: Honeypots: the need of network security. Int. J. Comput. Sci. Inf. Technol. **5**(5), 6098–6101 (2014)
15. Xiphos Research Ltd. Elasticsearch - remote code execution (2015). https://www.exploit-db.com/exploits/36337
16. Maciej. Collection of honeypots (2019). https://iceburn.medium.com/collection-of-honeypots-a7ec6e446163
17. Mokube, I., Adams, M.: Honeypots: concepts, approaches, and challenges. In: Proceedings of the 45th Annual Southeast Regional Conference, pp. 321–326 (2007)
18. Morishita, S., et al.: Detect me if you oh wait. An internet-wide view of self-revealing honeypots. In: 2019 IFIP/IEEE Symposium on Integrated Network and Service Management (IM), pp. 134–143. IEEE (2019)
19. Mukkamala, S., Yendrapalli, K., Basnet, R., Shankarapani, M.K., Sung, A.H.: Detection of virtual environments and low interaction honeypots. In 2007 IEEE SMC Information Assurance and Security Workshop, pp. 92–98. IEEE (2007)
20. Mushtakov, R.E., Silnov, D.S.: New approach to detect suspicious activity using http-proxy honeypots. In: 2017 IEEE Conference of Russian Young Researchers in Electrical and Electronic Engineering (EIConRus), pp. 600–605. IEEE (2017)
21. Nagpal, B., Singh, N., Chauhan, N., Sharma, P.: CATCH: comparison and analysis of tools covering honeypots. In: 2015 International Conference on Advances in Computer Engineering and Applications, pp. 783–786. IEEE (2015)
22. Elastic NV. What is elasticsearch? https://www.elastic.co/what-is/elasticsearch
23. Paganini, P.: Data breaches tracker monitor unsecured Elasticsearch Servers Online (2021). https://securityaffairs.co/wordpress/115698/security/data-breaches-tracker-unsecured-elasticsearch.html
24. Jordan Wright's Picture, Jordan WrightSecurity Researcher, and San Antonio. Introducing Elastichoney - an Elasticsearch Honeypot (2015). https://jordan-wright.com/blog/2015/03/23/introducing-elastichoney-an-elasticsearch-honeypot/
25. Sanfilippo, S., et al.: Hping-active network security tool (2008). http://www.hping.org/
26. SecurityTW. SecurityTW/Delilah. https://github.com/SecurityTW/delilah
27. Seifert, C., Welch, I., Komisarczuk, P.: Taxonomy of honeypots (2006)
28. Send-Safe. Send-safe honeypot hunter download (2022). https://send-safe-honeypot-hunter.apponic.com/
29. Shodan. Shodan Search Engine. https://www.shodan.io
30. Tsikerdekis, M., Zeadally, S., Schlesener, A., Sklavos, N.: Approaches for preventing honeypot detection and compromise. In: 2018 Global Information Infrastructure and Networking Symposium (GIIS), pp. 1–6. IEEE (2018)

31. Zakari, A., Lawan, A.A., Bekaroo, G.: Towards improving the security of low-interaction honeypots: insights from a comparative analysis. In: International Conference on Emerging Trends in Electrical, Electronic and Communications Engineering, pp. 314–321. Springer (2016)
32. Zion3R. Collection of awesome honeypots (2015). https://www.kitploit.com/2015/12/collection-of-awesome-honeypots.html

Why Most Results of Socio-Technical Security User Studies are False
And What to Do About it

Thomas Groß[(⊠)]

School of Computing, Newcastle University, Newcastle upon Tyne, UK
thomas.gross@newcastle.ac.uk

Abstract. Background. In recent years, cyber security user studies have been scrutinized for their reporting completeness, statistical reporting fidelity, statistical reliability and biases. It remains an open question what strength of evidence positive reports of such studies actually yield. We focus on the extent to which positive reports indicate relations true in reality, that is, a probabilistic assessment. **Aim.** This study aims at quantifying overall strength of evidence in cyber security user studies. **Method.** Based on 431 coded statistical inferences in 146 cyber security user studies from a published SLR covering the years 2006–2016, we first compute a simulation of the *a posteriori* false positive risk based on parametrized prior probability, biases and effect size thresholds. Second, we establish the observed likelihood ratios for positive reports. Third, we compute the reverse Bayesian argument on the observed positive reports by computing the prior required for a fixed *a posteriori* false positive rate. **Results.** We obtain a comprehensive analysis of the strength of evidence of the field. The simulations show that even in face of well-controlled conditions and high prior likelihoods, only few studies achieve good *a posteriori* probabilities. **Conclusions.** This work constitutes a "What if?" analysis, which permits the reader to evaluate the consequences of their assumptions on the state of the field. One may stop short at the bleak conclusion that the strength of evidence of the field leaves something to be desired and that most positive reports are likely false. At the same time, the "What if?" analysis offers a way forward to sensitize researchers to the effects of investigating many relations and incurring biases. It, thereby, allows them to plan better ahead for future studies.

Keywords: User studies · SLR · Cyber security · Strength of Evidence

1 Introduction

Empirical user studies heave an important place in studying socio-technical security. They investigate user attitude and behaviors in face of security technologies

---

Open Science Framework: https://osf.io/7gv6h/.

M. Mehrnezhad and S. Parkin (Eds.): STAST 2022, LNCS 13855, pp. 31–51, 2025.
https://doi.org/10.1007/978-3-031-83072-3_3

as well as the impact of different interventions. They affect a wide range of topics in the field.

Aiming at advancing the quality of evidence in the field, cyber security user studies have been appraised for a number of factors in recent years: (i) their reporting completeness [3], (ii) their statistical reporting fidelity [9], and (iii) their statistical reliability [11].

The most recent of those analyses estimated effect sizes from reported statistical tests, simulated the statistical power of the studies from effect size thresholds, and showed a range of overall biases of the field. Specifically, that prior study observed that few studies achieved recommended power levels, highlighting the power failure of the field. These observations, however, do not quantify the strength of evidence of the studies in the field. Hence, we aim at estimating the magnitude of the strength of evidence found in the field. We ask the question: *"To what extent can positively reported results be trusted?"*

We understand as *strength of evidence* the probability of a reported relation being true in reality. Typically, we are most interested in *positive reports*, that is, relations that were reported as statistically significant. We will consider multiple metrics to evaluate that probability under different circumstances. First, we consider the *a posteriori* probability of a relation being true after the observations of the study were made. This is the *Positive Predictive Value* (PPV). The estimate of the PPV and its complement, the False Positive Risk (FPR), are dependent on knowing or assuming the prior probability of the relation under investigation and the bias incurred by the research design and execution.

The major crux of this proposed strength-of-evidence analysis, however, is that prior probability and bias are hard to estimate unknown quantities. They are neither easily nor reliably derived from the published papers after the fact. The first approach to overcome this problem is to parametrize the analysis by prior and bias and simulate the result.

In addition to this classical Bayesian approach, we seek to quantify the strength of evidence independent from prior knowledge. We achieve this with the *likelihood ratio* (LR), a measure to quantify the strength of evidence solely based on the ratio of probabilities for and against the result.

Finally, we investigate the prior probability one would have needed before the study to achieve a desired fixed false positive risk after the study. This approach constitutes reverse reasoning and establishes the *reverse Bayesian prior* (RBP). These three perspectives, though all drawn from Bayes' law, offer different lenses to appraise the strength of evidence of relevant user studies.

Clearly, the investigation of positive predicted value and related quantities is not entirely new. Most famously, Ioannidis [14] made a convincing case that most published results are false, in general. Others have added to this argument, considering false positive risks or replications in a range of fields [19,22] or promoted Bayesian views on statistical testing [1,2,13]. In fact, some of the inspiration for this work is drawn from Ioannidis bold proclamation [14] and Colquhoun's thoughts on strength of evidence [2]. In this study, however, we are the first to evaluate the strength of evidence in socio-technical security studies based on an empirical evaluation of a systematic sample from the field.

In addition, we are interested to what extent the field pays attention to the strength of evidence as a factor to make the decision to cite studies. We thereby ask to what extent the number of citations of studies in the field is correlated to the strength of evidence they provide.

Overall, the strength of evidence evaluation provided in this study offers an empirical scaffolding to make decisions on further studies in the field.

Our Contributions. We are the first to offer a systematic evaluation of the strength of evidence in socio-technical security user studies. We do this based on an empirical sample from a systematic literature review and coded statistical tests. This evaluation is informative and meaningful for the field as it raises awareness and manages expectations what can be achieved with particular study setups. While an awareness of statistical power is already present in the community, the impact of prior probability (influenced by the number of investigated relations of the study) and bias (influenced by research methods employed) is often neglected. Our work quantifies to what extent studies in the field would yield compelling evidence for the reported effects, considering those variables. Thereby, our work enables members of the community to make more informed decisions on the trust into existing reported results and on the setup of new studies.

2   Background

2.1   Null Hypothesis Significance Testing

Null Hypothesis Significance Testing (NHST) [8] is a statistical method commonly used to evaluate whether a null hypothesis H_0 can be rejected and an alternative hypothesis H_1 be considered plausible in its place. Recent reviews of the method include, for instance, the work by Lehmann and Romano [17]. Null hypothesis significance testing has often been criticized, in its own right as well as for how scientists have fallen for a range of fallacies [20]. Problems with the null hypothesis significance testing have led to a stronger endorsement of estimation theory, relying on effect sizes and their confidence intervals [7].

In broad strokes, the method computes a p-value, that is, the probability of how likely it is to make observations as extreme or more extreme than the observations made D, *assuming the null hypothesis H_0 to be true*. Hence, the p-value is a conditional probability:

$$p := \mathsf{P}\left[D \mid H_0\right].$$

Clearly, the p-value does *not* tell us how likely the alternative hypothesis is, after having made the observations of the study, $\mathsf{P}\left[H_1 \mid D\right]$ in mathematical terms. However, such misinterpretations of the p-value often lead to confusion.

2.2   Bayes' Law

Naturally, we are interested in how likely the hypotheses of a study are, after its observations are taken into account. We refer to the *a posteriori* probabilities $P[H_0 \mid D]$ and $P[H_1 \mid D]$ for null and alternative hypotheses, respectively. We can find *a posteriori* probabilities by consulting *Bayes' Law* [15], stated in a form of *odds*, conducive to our subsequent argument [2]:

$$\underbrace{\frac{P[H_1 \mid D]}{P[H_0 \mid D]}}_{\text{a posteriori odds}} = \underbrace{\frac{P[D \mid H_1]}{P[D \mid H_0]}}_{\text{likelihood ratio}} \times \underbrace{\frac{P[H_1]}{P[H_0]}}_{\text{prior odds}}.$$

The p-value $P[D \mid H_0]$ is the denominator of the likelihood ratio. $P[D \mid H_1]$ indicates the probability of observations as extreme or more extreme than the observations made, assuming the alternative hypothesis H_1 being true. This is the statistical power of the test $(1-\beta)$. The prior odds are typically unknown. In general, we subscribe to the Bayesian interpretation of Bayes' Law, in which a probability quantifies the belief in a hypothesis. Appendix A contains a summary of different interpretations of the p-value for likelihood-ratio computation for the interested reader.

Positive Predictive Value (PPV) and False Positive Risk (FPR). The first quantity we are interested in is *How likely is a positively reported result true in reality, considering the evidence of the experiment?* This question is answered in two metrics: (i) the positive predictive value (PPV) $P[H_1 \mid D]$ and (ii) the false positive risk (FPR) $P[H_0 \mid D]$. While first quantifies how likely the alternative hypothesis is true, the second one evaluates how likely the null hypothesis is true, that is, how likely we are left with a false-positive result.[1] Expressed in Bayes' Law, these probabilities can be derived as follows:

$$P_{\mathsf{PPV}} := P[H_1 \mid D] = \frac{P[H_1]\,P[D \mid H_1]}{P[H_1]\,P[D \mid H_1] + (1 - P[H_1])P[D \mid H_0]}$$

$$P_{\mathsf{FPR}} := P[H_0 \mid D] = \frac{(1 - P[H_1])P[D \mid H_0]}{P[H_1]\,P[D \mid H_1] + (1 - P[H_1])P[D \mid H_0]}$$

We note that the use of Bayes' Law depends on the prior probability $P[H_1]$, which is typically unknown and parametrized by the researcher.

Integrating Bias into Estimations. It is not sufficient to consider the *a posteriori* probabilities in their foundational form. This is because all experimentation

---

[1] Here, we use Colquhoun's terminology [2, A.1], who uses False Positive Risk (FPR) as term for the False Discovery Rate (FDR), $\mathsf{FPR} = \mathsf{FDR} = 1 - \mathsf{PPV}$.

exhibits a certain amount of bias that interferes with the pure probability deduction. In general, a bias is a challenge to the internal validity of an experiment. Ioannidis [14] defined *bias* as "the combination of various design, data, analysis, and presentation factors that tend to produce research findings when they should not be produced." The biases incurred by studies are many, for example (i) sampling and non-sampling biases, (ii) selection and self-selection biases, (iii) survivorship, attrition and assignment biases, (iv) experimenter-related biases (e.g., observer bias), (v) participant-related biases (e.g., self-serving bias, recall bias, Hawthorne effect), (vi) measurement and manipulation instrument biases, (vii) statistical biases, and (viii) biases rooted in researcher degrees of freedom. Ioannidis quantified biases as u, the proportion of tests that would not have been findings. We use Ioannidis' estimation for PPV under the influence of bias, where R refers to the pre-study odds, that is, the ratio of true relationships to not-true relationships:

$$\mathsf{P}_{\mathsf{PPV},u} := \frac{\mathsf{P}\left[D \mid H_1\right]R + u(1 - \mathsf{P}\left[D \mid H_1\right])R}{R + \mathsf{P}\left[D \mid H_0\right] - \mathsf{P}\left[D \mid H_1\right]R + u - u\mathsf{P}\left[D \mid H_0\right] + u(1 - \mathsf{P}\left[D \mid H_1\right])R}$$

When inspecting studies after the fact, the bias incurred by that study is not easily discernible. Ioannidis [14] calibrated biases with practical examples, which Table 1 takes as inspiration for the context of socio-technical studies.

Table 1. Practical examples of pre-study odds and biases, adapted from Ioannidis [14]

Pre-study odds R	Bias u	Practical Example
1:1	.10	RCT with very little bias and 1:1 pre-study odds
1:5	.20	Well-performed intermediary RCT
1:5	.30	Weak intermediary RCT
1:5	.80	Poorly performed intermediary RCT
1:10	.30	Exploratory study

Note: We added a bias $u = .30$ as "weak RCT" here for consistency with Table 2.

Likelihood Ratio (LR). The likelihood ratio measures the strength of evidence independent from prior probability and is given by

$$LR := \frac{\mathsf{P}\left[D \mid H_1\right]}{\mathsf{P}\left[D \mid H_0\right]}.$$

Because the LR is independent of prior odds, it is a useful tool to ascertain the strength of evidence a study yields.

Reverse Bayesian Argument. It is unfortunate that computations of the PPV and the FPR depend on the prior probability, as this probability is typically unknown. The *reverse Bayesian argument* aims to overcome this problem by considering the reverse line of reasoning: *For a desired false positive risk, how likely would the result need to be before the study?* This is achieved by computing the prior necessary to achieve a desired fixed false positive risk P^*_{FPR}. This method was originally proposed by Matthews [18] and endorsed by Colquhoun [2]. We compute the reverse Bayesian prior $P_{\mathsf{RBP}} = P^* [H_1]$ as follows:

$$P_{\mathsf{RBP}} := P^* [H_1] = \frac{P [D \mid H_0] (1 - P^*_{\mathsf{FPR}})}{P [D \mid H_0] (1 - P^*_{\mathsf{FPR}}) + P [D \mid H_1] P^*_{\mathsf{FPR}}}$$

3   Related Works

3.1   Strength of Evidence in Other Fields

That most published findings are likely false was prominently discussed by Ioannidis [14] in general terms and applicable to any field. That study focused on the estimation of the positive predictive value and offered estimation formula and thresholds for the inclusion of study biases. We adopt Ioannidis estimation methods in this study, as well.

Other studies considered false positive reporting probability and the impact of replications, where we cite two examples [19, 22] as context.

This study is also related to approaches to estimate likelihood ratios and reverse Bayesian prior. Colquoun [1, 2] offered such estimations in the discussion of the *p*-value null hypothesis significance testing and reproducibility. He promoted the use of the reverse Bayesian prior, where the use of the reverse Bayesian argument was originally proposed by Matthews [18].

3.2   Appraisals of Cyber Security User Studies

Cyber security user studies have received a range of appraisals in recent years. A first step was made by Coopamootoo and Groß [3], who conducted a systematic literature review of cyber security user studies from relevant venues in the years 2006–2016. That study included a coding of nine reporting completeness indicators [4], giving a qualitative overview of scientific reporting. The authors expanded upon said completeness indicators in a design and reporting toolkit [5].

Subsequently, Groß [9, 10] built on the same SLR sample to establish the fidelity of statistical reporting. This study re-computed *p*-values from published test statistics and parameters to find quantitative and decision errors.

Groß [11, 12] turned to estimating effect sizes and their confidence intervals of statistics tests in the papers obtained from the 2017 Coopamootoo-Groß-SLR. That work further established simulations of statistical power vis-à-vis specified effect size thresholds, highlighting a power failure. This power failure was deduced by comparison to typical expert recommendations of power thresholds, but did not quantify the actual strength of evidence. In addition, the study showed the presence of statistical biases, such as the publication bias or the winner's curse.

This paper, however, takes a different tack. Though based on the same SLR sample as previous work and considering the same statistical tests as extracted by Groß [11], this work focuses on strength of evidence and estimates false positive risk, likelihood ratio and reverse Bayesian prior for the statistical tests reported in papers of the SLR sample.

4 Aims

4.1 Strength of Evidence

RQ 1. (Strength of Evidence) *What is the distribution of the strength of evidence in the field of cyber security user studies?*

This study aims at investigating the strength of evidence measured in an empirical evaluation as (a) Positive Predictive Value (PPV) and its complement False Positive Risk (FPR) (based on assumed priors), (b) Likelihood Ratio (LR), and (c) Reverse-Bayesian Prior (RBP) for a fixed false positive probability.

4.2 Attention to Strength of Evidence

RQ 2. (Attention to Strength of Evidence) *To what extent is the attention studies receive (in citations) related to their strength of evidence?*

We investigate this question by evaluating the correlation between the strength of evidence and the number of citations, measured as Average Citations Per Annum (ACPA). We do so by testing the following hypotheses.

$H_{C,0}$: There is no correlation between the strength of evidence (in terms of Reverse Bayesian Prior) and the measured ACPA.

$H_{C,1}$: The strength of evidence (in terms of Reverse Bayesian Prior) and the measured ACPA are correlated.

5 Method

The statistical estimations are computed with R. Statistical tests are computed at a significance level $\alpha = .05$.

5.1 Sample

We obtained the sample for this study from prior work. Its original foundation is the 2016/17 Systematic Literature Review (SLR) by Coopamootoo and Groß [3]. The characteristics of the SLR are also documented by Groß [9].

In addition, this work is based on the effect size extraction achieved by Groß [11]. It contains t-, χ^2-, r-, one-way F-tests, and Z-tests. The effect sizes were extracted based on an automated evaluation by statcheck [21] as well as manual coding.

Table 2. Choice of parameters

(a) Effect Size		(b) Bias		(c) Prior Probability		
Case	Cohen's d	Case	Bias u	Case	Pre-Study odds R_{prior}	
small	0.3	well-run RCT	.20	confirmatory	1 : 1	.50
medium	0.5	weak RCT	.30	intermediate	1 : 4	.20
large	0.8	biased study	.80	exploratory	1 : 9	.10

5.2   Procedure

The study proceeded in the following fashion.

1. We have taken as input a table of coded p–values, standardized effect sizes, sample sizes, citations, and year of publication.
2. We set the parameters according to Table 2 with the rationale to cover a range of presumed effect size thresholds in reality, a range of possible biases from well-run random-controlled trials (RCTs) to biased studies and a range of pre-study odds. In that, we call "confirmatory" studies, which have pre-study odds of one-to-one of the relation under investigation being either true or false. We call "exploratory" studies, which have pre-study odds of one relation being true for nine relations under investigation being false.
3. We established a statistical power simulation based on the parametrized effect size thresholds, incl. a variant with multiple-comparison corrections.
4. Based on the actual p-values in the studies as well as their multiple-comparison adjusted variants, we computed the positive-predictive value (PPV), the false positive risk (FPR), and the reverse Bayesian prior (RBP).
5. We computed the likelihood ratio in the p-less-than interpretation from power and p-values.
6. To assess the relation between attention studies are receiving and their strength of evidence, we computed a hierarchical linear model on strength of evidence by Average Citations per Annum (ACPA), using the study ID as random-effect variable.

5.3   Pre-registration, Reproducibility and Replication Package

This study is pre-registered in the Open Science Framework[2]. This paper was compiled directly from the underlying data with knitR. We have prepared a **replication package**[3], which includes the SLR sample specification and list of papers used in the study, the underlying datasets, a Shiny app demonstrating the results and it source code as well as a **Binder environment**[4] to host the app.

---

[2] https://osf.io/7gv6h/.
[3] https://github.com/tgrncl/StrengthOfEvidenceReproducable.git.
[4] https://mybinder.org/v2/gh/tgrncl/StrengthOfEvidenceReproducable.git/master?urlpath=rstudio.

6   Results

6.1   Sample

The refined sample shown in Table 3 includes studies with extractable effect sizes as determined by Groß [11].

Table 3. Sample refinement on SLR papers (as reported in [11])

Phase	Excluded	Retained
Source SLR [3]		
Search results (Google Scholar)	—	1157
Inclusion/Exclusion	1011	146
Refinement in this study		
Empirical studies	2	144
With sample sizes	21	123
With extractable tests	69	54

The sample displayed in Table 4 includes statistical tests and their effect sizes that could be extracted from the papers in the sample. The final sample includes 431 statistical tests and their effect sizes.

Table 4. Sample refinement on extracted effect sizes (adapted from [11])

Phase	Excluded	Retained
Total effects extracted	0	650
statcheck automated extraction		252
Test statistic manual coding		89
Means & SD manual coding		309
Refinement in Groß [11]		
Violated reporting and assumptions	219	431

6.2   False Positive Risk and Positive Predictive Value

We examine the distribution of false positive risk, that is, the *a posteriori* probability that the alternative hypotheses of statistical tests are false. Subsequently, we consider the capacity to gain information with the Positive Predictive Value (PPV). We evaluate these probabilities, dependent on parametrized bias and prior probabilities.

False Positive Risk by Bias and Prior. In Appendix A.1, we discuss the false positive risk for a single parameter set of bias $u = .30$ and *prior* $= .20$ to illustrate how the graphs presented in this section can be used.

Figure 1 displays false positive risk graphs for three cases for bias and prior, respectively. The graphs are based on statistics with family-wise multiple-comparison corrections. The parameters are chosen according to Table 2.

First, we observe that the amount of bias present in the study depresses the capacity to reduce the false positive risk with additional power. For biased studies (bias $u = .80$), power in terms of increased sample size, is inconsequential to eliminate false positive risk. Second, different degrees of pre-study odds in terms of relations investigated offset the false positive risk, the more confirmatory a study is, the greater a prior a test operates against the less the false positive risk. Overall, we find that only confirmatory studies (*prior* $= .50$) that are either run as well-run RCT ($u = .20$) or weak RCT ($u = .30$) yield a false positive risk less than 50%.

Capacity to Gain Knowledge. In Figure 2, we take a different perspective from Fig. 1. Here we consider the simulation of *a posteriori* probability of the alternative hypotheses, as a heatmap faceted by bias and effect size threshold. This figure is organized by study and conveys the maximal Positive Predictive Value (PPV) the study can achieve with any test conducted. It is ordered by maximal PPV achieved.

Figure 2 shows as white a positive predictive value of 50%. Studies that achieve an upper-bound PPV greater than 50% are colored orange/red, studies that only yield an upper-bound PPV of less than 50% are colored blue. The figure can be read as follows: Assuming a certain effect size in the population (say medium, $d = 0.5$), assuming that studies in question were conducted as a weakly-run RCT, and assuming confirmatory studies with a great prior probability close to .50, we would select the centre facet of the plot. Here we observe that only two fifth (43%) of the studies reached a PPV equal or greater to 50% and only conditioned on a prior close to .50.

6.3   Strength Evidence of Positive Reports

In the following, we focus on positive reports, that is, relations studies reported as statistically significant. We include graphs giving an overview of these positive reports in Appendix B.

Likelihood Ratio. We consider the strength of evidence of positive reports quantified as likelihood ratio, that is, the ratio of the report being true in reality by the report being false in reality. This likelihood ratio (LR) is independent of the presumed prior. At the same time, the LR is computed without taking into account biases.

We find in the MCC-corrected Fig. 4b that most statistically significant results are clustered below a likelihood ratio of $LR = 25$. The sample has a

Pre-Study Odds (Prior Probability)

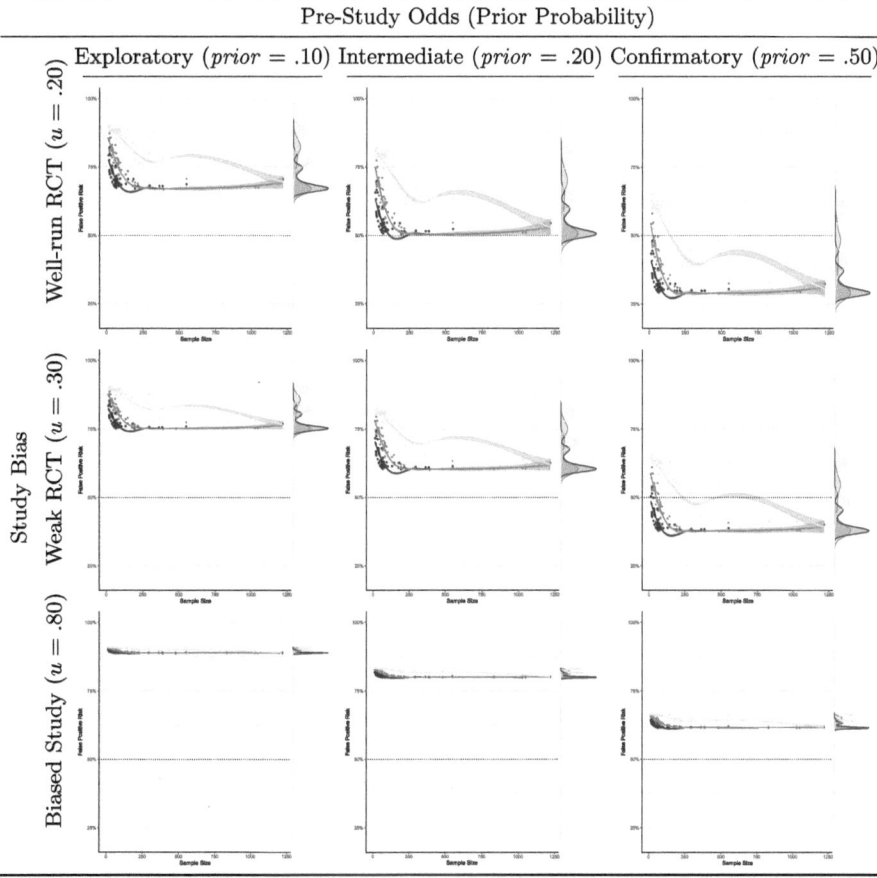

Fig. 1. False Positive Risk (FPR) versus bias and prior. *Note:* Statistics are based on family-wise multiple comparison corrections. Effect size thresholds are $(d = 0.2)$, medium $(d = 0.5)$, and large $(d = 0.8)$.

median likelihood ratio of 5.21. That is, for half the positive reports, the *a posteriori* odds are less than five times the pre-study odds.

Reverse Bayesian Prior. In this section, we evaluate the Reverse Bayesian Prior, that is, prior that one would have needed *a priori* to reach a fixed *a posteriori* false positive risk of 5%. In general, one would consider a required prior of greater than 50% as unreasonable. For this evaluation, we fix the effect size threshold to medium $(d = 0.5)$ and the bias to $u = .30$. We choose these parameters because medium effect sizes are typically considered as benchmark in the field and because assuming the biases of weak random-controlled trials is a conservative assumption.

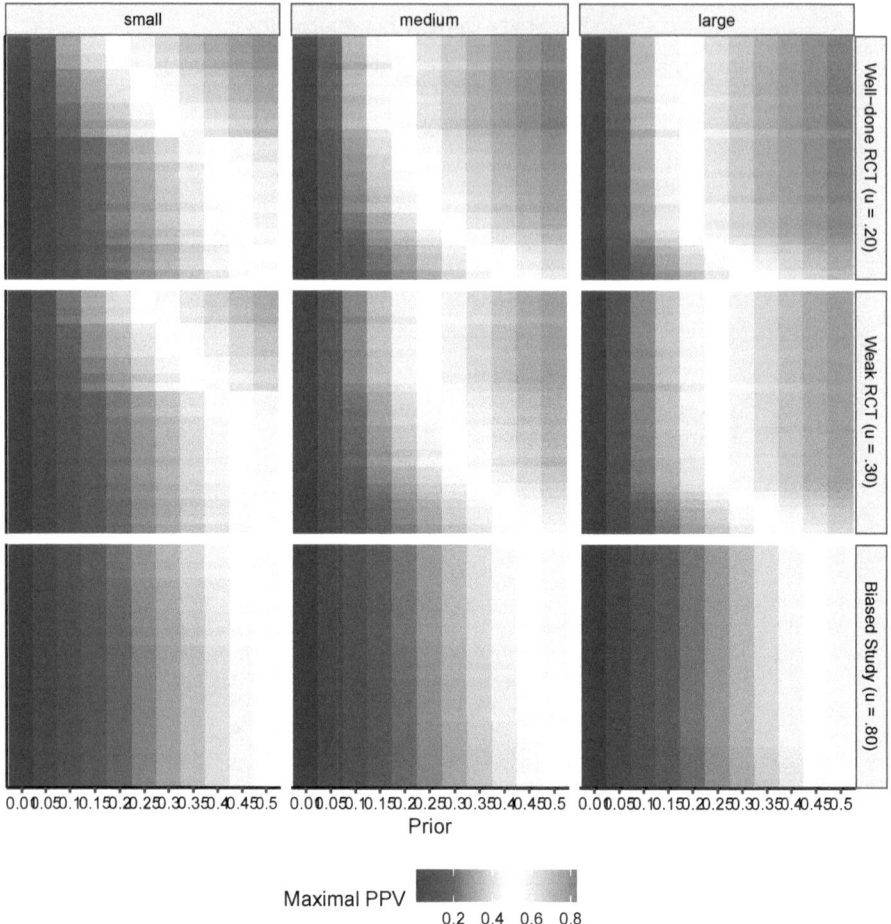

Fig. 2. Heatmap of Positive Predictive Value (PPV) by effect size threshold and bias.

Without multiple-comparison corrections, 10% of the 208 positive reports yield a reverse Bayesian prior greater than 50%. We observe that approximately half (48%) of the 145 positive reports after multiple-comparison corrections show a reverse Bayesian prior greater than or equal to 50%. The closer the RBP of a positive report is to zero, the stronger the evidence speaking for the report.

6.4   Relation to Citations

We conducted a hierarchical linear model with the paper ID as random-effect factor to investigate the correlation between the reverse Bayesian prior and a metric of the citations, the average citations per annum. The model is based on $n = 208$ statistically significant reports (after correction for multiple comparison corrections) from 25 papers. The model did not converge and could not confirm a correlation between these variables, failing to reject the null hypothesis $H_{C,0}$.

7   Discussion

7.1   Why Most Results of Socio-Technical User Studies Are False

Let us start with the eponymous question of this paper. While this is generally well understood for any field of empirical science [14] and extends naturally to other evidence-based studies in computer science, here, we quantified the understanding based on a systematically drawn empirical sample of cyber security user studies. Based on the sample at hand, we can estimate that for moderate biases ($u = .30$) of weak random controlled trials—arguably already an optimistic assumption—moderate priors (.20) and medium effect sizes in the population ($d = .05$), an expected *two thirds* (61%) of reported statistically significant results are likely false positives.

This should give us pause. Well-run random-controlled trials are rare in the field, we often see studies that incur a range of biases in their sampling, weakly randomized or unblinded experiment design, invalid or unreliable measurement and manipulation instruments, or failure to meet statistical assumptions. Exploratory studies seem to be relatively frequent, often investigating multiple relations, few of which are true in reality. Hence, in many cases we would expect false positives even more numerous. Overall the first response to the question "Why?" lies in the types and characteristics of studies conducted in the field.

7.2   The Impact of Biases

The simulation of false positive risk parametrized by bias and prior in Fig. 1 yields a number of important take-aways. Obviously, studies investigating a large number of relations, of which only a few are likely true in reality, incur a considerably greater false positive risk than highly confirmatory studies. The latter studies will typically be restricted to few relations in which we already have confidence.

The incurred bias, however, is a crucial factor to consider. As observed in Fig. 1, increasing bias depresses the capability of studies to yield new knowledge—irrespective of their confirmatoriness or statistical power. Hence, minimizing biases, for instance by conducting systematically sampled, well-run, double-blind random controlled trials, is crucial to reduce the false positive risk. The overall effect of this phenomenon is well visible in the upper-bound achievable positive predictive value in Fig. 2.

7.3   The Impact of Strength of Evidence

We observed in Fig. 4b that positive reports under appropriate multiple-comparison corrections were largely clustered around low likelihood ratios. Without accounting for biases, the a median $LR = 5.21$ against a medium effect size.

That means that—even without biases—the median post-study odds are only five times the pre-study odds.

7.4 Limitations

Generalizability. The study is founded on an existing sample of a systematic literature review (SLR) of the years 2006–2016. That sample has been obtained on Google Scholar and has been restricted to specific venues. In addition, there was a considerable drop-out rate in the refinement process. Hence, its generalizability to the entire field of socio-technical security user studies is limited. However, we believe that the distribution we observe in strength of evidence is not untypical of the field at large.

Probability Interpretation. The computations in this work are based on a particular interpretation of test probabilities, the p-less-than interpretation explained in Appendix A. That is, the likelihood ratio, for instance, is computed as the ratio of statistical power $(1 - \beta)$ by p-value itself. Colquhoun [2] made a convincing case that the p-equals interpretation is more appropriate for evaluating the strength of evidence of a single test. The p-equals interpretation puts into relation the ordinate of the probability distributions of the null and alternate hypotheses. However, as the p-less-than interpretation is typically underestimating the false positive risk, our choice is conservative.

8 Recommendations

How to improve the strength of evidence in the field?

Effect Sizes and Statistical Power. Our recommendations must inadvertently be founded on the considerations from the "new statistics" to establish on effect sizes and their confidence intervals [6,7], to take into account minimal effect size of interest and to plan for sufficient power for falsification [11,16]. While the need of adequate statistical power—and, thereby, sufficient sample size—is a timelessly valid point, statistical power only takes us that far: Increases in sample size to gain statistical power suffer from diminishing returns and are severely undermined by incurred biases.
   Is the study based on an a-priori power calculation with respect to the minimal effect size of interest?

Investigating Multiple Relations with the Pre-study Odds in Mind. Studies that investigate a wide range of relations, some of which likely true, many of which likely false, typically bear lower average pre-study odds. Such studies often also test many statistical inferences and require multiple-comparison corrections diminishing their statistical power. Hence, such studies suffer from greater the post-study false positive risk. Thereby, even a "highly significant" result requires further confirmation. This is *not* a case against exploratory studies, per se; those studies are important in early stages of a line of research to scope future routes of investigation. It simply cautions us against accepting results as fact, which were obtained in face of a low pre-study odds. It also asks the community to conduct further confirmatory studies with tightened pre-study odds. Our results support this process by raising awareness to the false positive risk present in the field, given an assessment a reader makes on the average pre-study odds.

What are the estimated pre-study odds R and what is their likely impact on the false positive risk after the results are in?

Curbing Biases. We intentionally considered "explorative" studies as defined by the number of relations investigated and the corresponding pre-study odds. Explorative study do not need to be biased. They can be designed and executed with great care—as a well-done random-controlled trial would be. Similarly, confirmatory studies can be designed and executed in a biased way. Hence, explorativeness and bias are orthogonal issues for us.

The biases actually incurred by a study are challenging to estimate after the fact. Still, there are overt research design and execution methods that are meant to curb the systematic impact of biases. They can, thereby, hint at the adequate consideration of biases by the researchers.

1. *Was the study pre-defined and pre-registered?* (bias from researcher degrees of freedom)
2. *Was the sample chosen randomly, with an appropriate sampling method, and taken from a well-defined population?* (sampling bias)
3. *Was the random assignment well-defined and appropriate?* (selection bias)
4. *Was the blinding well-defined and appropriate?* (experimenter bias)
5. *Were all participants in the sample accounted for?* (survivorship bias)
6. *Were the measurement and manipulation instruments independently confirmed as valid and reliable?* (instrument bias)
7. *Were the statistical inference methods well-defined and adequate?* (statistical inference bias)

Though checking such outward properties cannot guarantee the absence of biases, their presence in the report gives confidence that the study design sought to address them. To that end, there exist a number of checklists in the field to assess these overt properties, especially for random-controlled trials. Our results help to evaluate the consequences of biases typically present in studies of the field, visualizing the consequences of their presence.

Planning with the End in Mind. While the results of this work can help to sensitize to the effects of pre-study odds, biases and strength of evidence on the ultimate false positive risks of studies, we can also use the same tools to anticipate the outcome and plan ahead. While this argument holds for individual studies, we would also consider progressions of studies, whose research synthesis aims at establishing ever tighter interval estimates on effect sizes and at yielding an increasing compound strength of evidence.

9   Conclusions

We showed, based on an systematically drawn empirical sample, that most published findings in socio-technical security user studies are false. While this concern has been stated generally for studies of any field [14], we are the first to quantify the strength of evidence and expected number of false positive reports based on an empirical foundation in socio-technical security user studies.

While our simulations depend on external parameters (i) bias, (ii) prior, and (iii) effect size threshold in the population, which are inherently difficult to estimate accurately, we offer the readers a multi-faceted view of parameter combinations and their consequences. For instance, for the false positive risk, we can estimate make our own assumption on bias and prior present and then consider the consequences of setup.

We also offer investigations of positive reports, that is, results stated as statistically significant, showing the distribution of likelihood ratios and reverse Bayesian prior. These simulations establish an appraisal of the strength of evidence while being independent from an unknown prior.

Our results raise caution about believing positive reports out of hand and sensitize towards appraising the strength of evidence found in studies under consideration. Our work makes the case to drive biases down as a factor of experiment design and execution too often neglected in this field. Finally, we believe that we can see that strength of evidence is receiving little attention as a factor in the decision to cite publications, raising the awareness of including the strength-of-evidence consideration into the reporting recommendations for authors and reviewing recommendations for gatekeepers.

Acknowledgement. We would like to thank the anonymous reviewers of STAST'2022 for their helpful comments and the program chairs of the workshop for honoring this paper with the best-paper award. Early aspects of this study were in parts funded by the UK Research Institute in the Science of Cyber Security (RISCS) under a National Cyber Security Centre (NCSC) grant on "Pathways to Enhancing Evidence-Based Research Methods for Cyber Security." Thomas Groß was funded by the ERC Starting Grant CASCAde (GA n°716980).

A   Probability Interpretations

We distinguish two interpretations for probabilities around the p-value to establish the likelihood ratios, which were discussed by Colquhoun [2]. First, we have the so called *p-less-than interpretation*, which considers observations as extreme or more extreme as the ones obtained. Under this interpretation, the likelihood ratio considered above is computed by the statistical power divided by the p-value itself. Second, in the *p-equals interpretation*, which constitutes the likelihoods exactly at the probability of the observations made. Under this interpretation, the probability considered is exactly at the test statistic obtained under the alternative hypothesis divided by the probability at the test statistic under the null hypothesis. These two interpretations yield different results for the likelihood ratio and related evaluations, where typically the p-equals interpretation will yield a greater false positive risk than the p-less-than interpretation.

A.1   Anatomy of a False Positive Risk Plot

Figure 3 depicts simulation for a weak random-controlled trial (bias $u = .30$) on a intermediate pre-study odds ($R = 1 : 4$, *prior* = .20).

The three colors in the scatter plot represent assumed effect size thresholds in the population—small $\circ$: $d = 0.2$, medium $\bullet$: $d = 0.5$, and large $\bullet$: $d = 0.8$. Each dot represents one study in the sample at that parameters. We observe that—assuming a setting of a weak random-controlled trials and priors of .20— the false positive risk is at least 55%, irrespective of the size of the effect sizes thresholds assumed in the population or the additionally exerted power. On the right-hand margin of the graph, we included the density of the false positive risks for the SLR sample in the studz.

Considering the expectation on number of false positive results, we obtain that of the 145 MCC-corrected positive reports out of 444 tests under investigation only an expected 57 statistically significant results are true in reality, 39%. Conversely, 88 of the positive reports are likely false positives (61%).

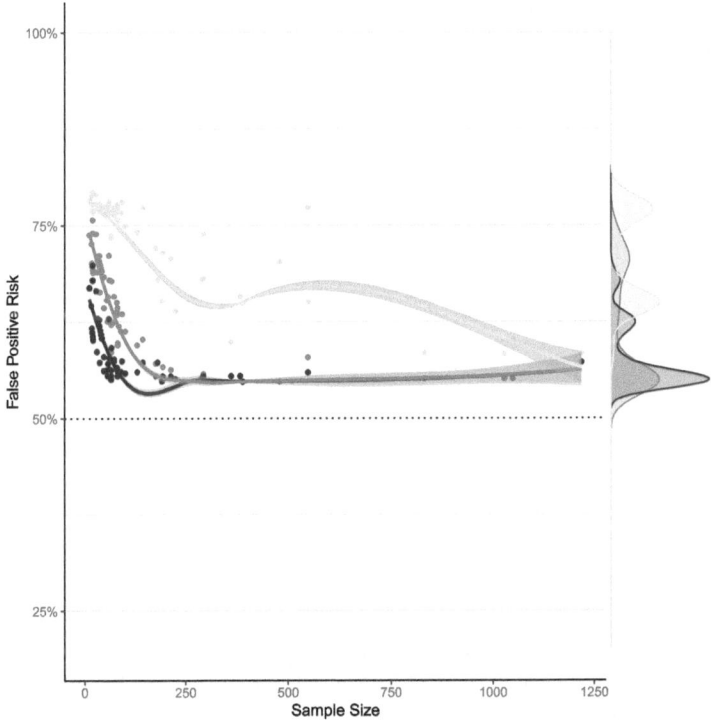

Fig. 3. False Positive Risk for a weak Random Controlled Trial. *Note:* Parameters are fixed to bias $u = .30$, *prior* = .20. The statistics are multiple-comparison corrected. Effect size thresholds are small ($d = 0.2$), medium ($d = 0.5$), and large ($d = 0.8$).

B   Strength Evidence of Positive Reports

In the scatterplots in Fig. 4 and 5, we display the distribution of likelihood ratios and reverse-Bayesian priors by sample size of studies. The figures only include positive reports, that is, effects that papers reported as statistically significant. The effect sizes are fixed to medium ($d = 0.5$). The figures distinguish between statistics with and without appropriate test-family-wise multiple-comparison corrections. Positive reports with a reverse-Bayesian prior greater than 50% are not gaining us additional information, in fact, they are muddling the water.

C   Planning for Strength of Evidence

The tools used in this study can be used to plan studies with strength of evidence in mind. The methods to achieve this are not new and essentially based on Ioannidis' estimation of positive predictive value (PPV) including an estimate of biases [14]. To complete the Shiny app[5] prepared with this study, we have not only included a visualization of the SLR sample properties, but also a planning tool shown in Fig. 6 to estimate the PPV from *a priori* power, biases and pre-study odds.

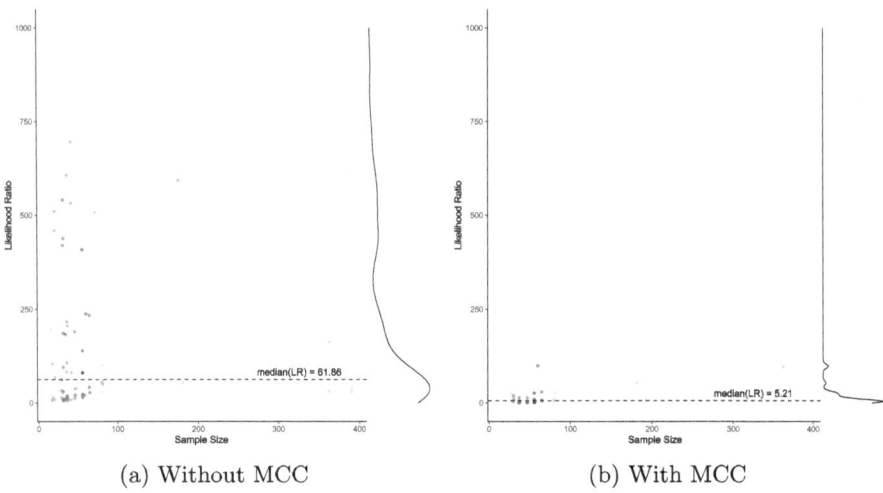

(a) Without MCC   (b) With MCC

Fig. 4. Distribution of the likelihood ratio by sample size. *Note:* The effect size threshold is fixed at medium ($d = 0.5$). We limited the displayed Likelihood Ratio to $LR < 1000$ for visual clarity.

---

[5] https://mybinder.org/v2/gh/tgrncl/StrengthOfEvidenceReproducable.git/master? urlpath=rstudio.

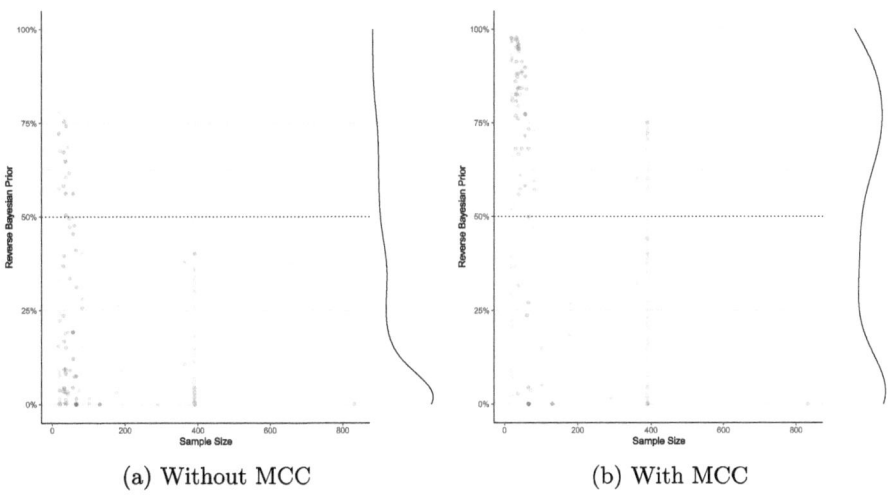

(a) Without MCC   (b) With MCC

Fig. 5. Reverse Bayesian prior without and with multiple-comparison corrections. *Note:* The effect size is fixed to medium ($d = 0.5$), the bias to $u = .30$ and the target post-hoc FPR to .05.

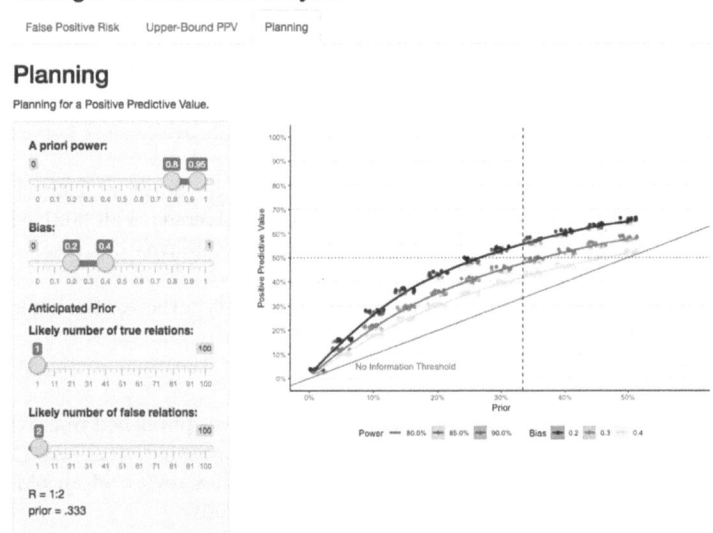

Fig. 6. Strength of evidence planning

References

1. Colquhoun, D.: An investigation of the false discovery rate and the misinterpretation of p-values. R. Soc. Open Sci. **1**(3), 140216 (2014)
2. Colquhoun, D.: The reproducibility of research and the misinterpretation of p-values. R. Soc. Open Sci. **4**(12), 171085 (2017)

3. Coopamootoo, K., Groß, T.: Systematic evaluation for evidence-based methods in cyber security. Technical report TR-1528, Newcastle University (2017)

4. Coopamootoo, K.P., Groß, T.: A codebook for experimental research: the nifty nine indicators v1.0. Technical report. TR-1514, Newcastle University (2017)

5. Coopamootoo, K.P., Groß, T.: Cyber security and privacy experiments: a design and reporting toolkit. In: IFIP International Summer School on Privacy and Identity Management, pp. 243–262. Springer, Cham (2017)

6. Coopamootoo, K.P., Groß, T.: Evidence-based methods for privacy and identity management. In: 11th International IFIP Summer School on Privacy and Identity Management. Springer, Cham (2017)

7. Cumming, G.: Understanding the New Statistics: Effect Sizes, Confidence Intervals, and Meta-analysis. Routledge (2013)

8. Fisher, R.A.: Statistical Methods for Research Workers. Genesis Publishing Pvt. Ltd. (1925)

9. Groß, T.: Fidelity of statistical reporting in 10 years of cyber security user studies. In: Proceedings of the 9th International Workshop on Socio-Technical Aspects in Security (STAST 2019). LNCS, vol. 11739, pp. 1–24. Springer, Cham (2019)

10. Groß, T.: Fidelity of statistical reporting in 10 years of cyber security user studies [extended version]. arXiv Report arXiv:2004.06672, Newcastle University (2020)

11. Groß, T.: Statistical reliability of 10 years of cybersecurity user studies. In: Proceedings of the 10th International Workshop on Socio-Technical Aspects in Security (STAST'2020). LNCS, vol. 12812, pp. 157–176. Springer, Cham (2020)

12. Groß, T.: Statistical reliability of 10 years of cybersecurity user studies [extended version]. arXiv Report arXiv:2010.02117, Newcastle University (2020)

13. Howson, C., Urbach, P.: Scientific Reasoning: The Bayesian Approach. Open Court Publishing (2006)

14. Ioannidis, J.P.: Why most published research findings are false. PLoS Med. **2**(8), e124 (2005)

15. Joyce, J.: Bayes' theorem. In: Zalta, E.N. (ed.) The Stanford Encyclopedia of Philosophy. Metaphysics Research Lab, Stanford University, Fall 2021 edn. (2021)

16. Kennedy, J.E., Watt, C.A.: How to plan falsifiable confirmatory research (2018). http://jeksite.org/psi/falsifiable_research.pdf

17. Lehmann, E.L., Romano, J.P.: Testing Statistical Hypotheses. Springer Texts in Statistics (2005)

18. Matthews, R.A.: Why should clinicians care about Bayesian methods? J. Stat. Plan. Inference **94**(1), 43–58 (2001)

19. Moonesinghe, R., Khoury, M.J., Janssens, A.C.J.: Most published research findings are false–but a little replication goes a long way. PLoS Med. **4**(2), e28 (2007)

20. Nickerson, R.S.: Null hypothesis significance testing: a review of an old and continuing controversy. Psychol. Methods **5**(2), 241 (2000)

21. Nuijten, M.B., van Assen, M.A., Hartgerink, C.H., Epskamp, S., Wicherts, J.: The validity of the tool "statcheck" in discovering statistical reporting inconsistencies (2017). https://psyarxiv.com/tcxaj/

22. Wacholder, S., Chanock, S., Garcia-Closas, M., Rothman, N., et al.: Assessing the probability that a positive report is false: an approach for molecular epidemiology studies. J. Natl Cancer Inst. **96**(6), 434–442 (2004)

Verification of the Socio-Technical Aspects of Voting: The Case of the Polish Postal Vote 2020

Yan Kim[1], Wojciech Jamroga[1,2]([✉]), and Peter Y. A. Ryan[1]

[1] Interdisciplinary Centre for Security, Reliability, and Trust, SnT,
University of Luxembourg, Esch-sur-Alzette, Luxembourg
{yan.kim,wojciech.jamroga,peter.ryan}@uni.lu
[2] Institute of Computer Science, Polish Academy of Sciences, Warsaw, Poland

Abstract. Voting procedures are designed and implemented by people, for people, and with significant human involvement. Thus, one should take into account the human factors in order to comprehensively analyze properties of an election and detect threats. In particular, it is essential to assess how actions and strategies of the involved agents (voters, municipal office employees, mail clerks) can influence the outcome of other agents' actions as well as the overall outcome of the election. In this paper, we present our first attempt to capture those aspects in a formal multi-agent model of the Polish presidential election 2020. The election marked the first time when postal vote was universally available in Poland. Unfortunately, the voting scheme was prepared under time pressure and political pressure, and without the involvement of experts. This might have opened up possibilities for various kinds of ballot fraud, in-house coercion, etc. We propose a preliminary scalable model of the procedure in the form of a Multi-Agent Graph, and formalize selected integrity and security properties by formulas of agent logics. Then, we transform the models and formulas so that they can be input to the state-of-art model checker Uppaal. The first series of experiments demonstrates that verification scales rather badly due to the state-space explosion. However, we show that a recently developed technique of user-friendly model reduction by variable abstraction allows us to verify more complex scenarios.

1 Introduction

In the last 30 years, the world has become densely connected. This results in a considerable space of potential threats, risks, and conflicting interests, that call for systematic (and preferably machine-assisted) analysis. What is more, IT services are implemented by people, with people, and for people. The intensive human involvement makes them hard to analyse beyond the usual computational complexity obstacles.

© The Author(s), under exclusive license to Springer Nature Switzerland AG 2025
M. Mehrnezhad and S. Parkin (Eds.): STAST 2022, LNCS 13855, pp. 52–72, 2025.
https://doi.org/10.1007/978-3-031-83072-3_4

Voting Procedures. Voting and elections are prime examples of services that are difficult to specify, hard to verify, and extremely important to the society [27]. If democracy is to be effective, it is essential to assess and mitigate the threats of fraud, manipulation, and coercion [44,53]. However, formal analysis of voting procedures must consider both the technological side of elections (i.e., protocols, architectures, and implementations) and the human and social context in which it is embedded [5]. The impact of the social factor has become especially evident during the US presidential elections of 2016 and 2020. In 2016, individual voters were targeted before the election by a combination of technology and social engineering to induce emotional reactions that would change their decisions, and possibly swing the outcome of the vote (the Cambridge Analytica scandal). In 2020, a large group of voters was targeted after the election by unfounded claims that severely undermined the public trust in the outcome. In both cases, it is impossible to understand the nature of what happened, and devise mitigation strategies, without the focus on human incentives and capabilities.

Specification and Verification of Multi-agent Systems. *Multi-agent systems (MAS)* provide models and methodologies for the analysis of systems that feature interaction of multiple autonomous components, be it humans, robots, and/or software agents. The theoretical foundations of MAS are based on mathematical logic and game theory [50]. In particular, logic-based methods can be useful to formally specify and verify the outcomes of multi-agent interaction [22].

Formal analysis with multi-agent logics is typically based on model checking [4]. The system is formalized through a network of graphs (or automata) that define its components, their available actions, and the information flow between them. The properties are usually given as *temporal properties*, expressing that a given temporal pattern must (or may) occur, or *strategic properties* capturing the *strategic abilities* of agents and their groups. Especially the latter kind of properties are relevant for MAS; e.g., one may try to capture voter-verifiability as the ability of the voter to verify her vote, and coercion-resistance as the inability of the coercer to influence the behavior of the voter [53]. There are many available model checking tools, though none of them is perfect. Some admit only temporal properties [8], some focus on the less practical case of perfect information strategies [38], and the others have limited verification capabilities [37]. Moreover, it is often unclear how to formalize an actual real-life scenario, including the "right" model of the system [32] and the formal "transcription" of its desirable properties [34].

Socio-Technical Aspects of Voting. In this paper, we use agent-based methodology to propose and analyze a simple multi-agent model of an actual election, that combines the technological backbone of the voting infrastructure with a model of possible human behaviors. The work is preliminary, in the sense that we do not explore the real breadth of participants' activities that might occur during the vote. Moreover, we mostly look at requirements that can be expressed as trace properties. This is because the computational complexity of the formal analysis turned out prohibitive even for such simple models and properties. We managed to mitigate the complexity by an innovative abstraction technique, but seeing if it scales well enough for realistic models of human interaction remains a subject for future work.

Case Study: Polish Postal Vote of 2020. To focus on a concrete scenario, we consider the Polish presidential election of 2020. That was the first time when postal voting was universally available in Poland. Unfortunately, the voting scheme was prepared under pressure, and without the involvement of experts. This might have opened up possibilities for various kinds of ballot fraud, in-house coercion, etc. We propose a preliminary scalable model of the procedure in the form of a Multi-Agent Graph [8,31], and formalize selected integrity and security properties by formulas of agent logics. Then, we transform the models and formulas so that they can be input to the state-of-art model checker Uppaal [8], chosen because of its flexible model specification language and user-friendly GUI. As expected, the verification of unoptimized models scales rather badly due to the state-space explosion. To improve the performance, we employ a recently developed technique of user-friendly abstraction [31], with more promising results.

Related Research. Formal verification of voting protocols has been the subject of research for over a decade. Prominent approaches include theorem proving in first-order, linear or higher order logic [14,20,21,25,26,46], and model checking of temporal, strategic and temporal-epistemic logics [29,32,33]. Most if not all results show that the task is very hard due to the prohibitive computational complexity of the underlying problems. For example, [20,21] conducted a formal analysis of voting protocols using ProVerif, and reported that they had to come up with workarounds for the model in order to the limitations of the tool.

Modelling and analysis of socio-technical systems is even more difficult because of the vast space of possible human behaviors, and problematic nature of the assumptions usually made about how users choose their actions. The theory of socio-technical systems dates back to the work of Trist and Bamforth in 1940s. In security, perhaps the best studied methodology is based on ceremonies [17], in particular the Concertina ceremony [9,10,40]. Some research has been also based on choreographies [15]. Moreover, game-theoretic models and analysis have been used in [5,16,30]. Here, follow up on the strand based on modeling and verification in multi-agent logics [29,32,33], while trying to put more emphasis on the social part of the system outside of the voting infrastructure.

When analyzing systems that involve human agents, it is important to take into account that they behave differently from the machines, and can make *errors*, or more generally, deviate from the prescribed protocol. This can happen due to a variety of reasons: misunderstanding, inattentiveness, malicious intention, or strategic self-interested action. Possible deviations from protocol in user behavior have been studied in [6,7], and we follow up on those ideas. To this end, we use the *skilled-human approach* to capture a variety of users' behaviors in our model of postal voting. That is, we extend the protocol specification of an "honest" behaviour through a hierarchy of *deviation sets*, i.e., sets of actions that deviate from the protocol and expand the repertoire of the participants. As pointed out in [6], there is a trade-off between the breadth of the deviation model and the computational feasibility of the formal analysis. In fact, our experiments in Sect. 4 show that even for the skilled human approach only, the explicit state model checking becomes hard enough, and dedicated techniques must be used to mitigate the complexity.

Related Verification Tools. We use the Uppaal model checker [8] in our case study, mainly because of its GUI and a flexible system specification language. Other verification tools that we considered when preparing the study are:

- *MCMAS* [39]: a state-of-art OBDD-based symbolic model checker for agent-based systems. The system is described using ISPL (Interpreted Systems Programming Language), and the requirements are specified as formulae of strategic or temporal-epistemic properties;
- *Tamarin-prover* [43]: a tool for security protocol verification and not a model checker per se. The system specification language is based on multiset rewriting theories, and the requirements are specified as first-order temporal properties;
- *STV* [36,37]: an experimental toolbox for explicit-state model checking of strategic properties; at the moment, custom input models are not fully supported;
- *ProVerif* [13]: an automated cryptographic protocol verifier, in the symbolic (Dolev-Yao) model. The protocol representation is based on Horn clauses; it can be used for proving secrecy, authentication and equivalence properties.

Among the above tools, only STV, Uppaal, and (to lesser extent) Tamarin provide a graphical view of the system structure. Of those, only Uppaal allows for *interactive graphical system specification*, which we claim to be crucial in modelling and analysis of voting protocols. Real-life voting procedures include the interaction of numerous participants, each of them with a possibly different agenda and capabilities. Furthermore, the behaviour of most participants is characterized with a mixture of controllable and uncontrollable nondeterminism. In consequence, interactive GUI is crucial if we want to ensure that the model we verify and the one we want to verify are the same thing, cf. [32] for discussion.

Moreover, Uppaal (and, to a smaller extent, STV) allow for parameterized specification of the system, without forcing the designer to program a dedicated model-generator (e.g., as in the verification of SELENE protocol with MCMAS in [29]).

2   Postal Voting Procedure

Postal voting is one of the oldest forms for voting. In its simplest version, it is easy to setup for the authorities and easy to follow for the voters. On the other hand, it can be susceptible to ballot fraud, lacks verifiability, and opens up potential for vote buying and coercion. What is more, only basic mechanisms of recovery are possible (e.g., cancelling the whole elections in case of irregularities). This sometimes leads to controversial ad hoc decisions when dealing with the irregularities [28].

The postal voting procedure employed for the Polish Presidential Election in 2020 is no exception. There was an overall impression that the procedure had been prepared in haste [2,51] and with no proper research on the existing postal voting schemes that were proposed and used during the last two decades, such as [12,35]. For example, voter authentication is based on the assumption that a voter's national identification number (PESEL) is secret, which is hardly the case in real life. Moreover, there are various ways how authorities can delete votes, e.g., by sending invalid ballots to districts with anti-government majority [24, 51,52]. In this paper, we make the first step towards systematic modeling and analysis of this kind of threats.

2.1   Postal Voting Procedure for the 2020 Presidential Election

The rules for organizing the election of the President of Poland, with the possibility of postal vote, were published on June 2 and June 3, 2020; the date of the election was set to June 28, 2020. A complete list of legal acts defining the election procedure can be found in [45,48]. For the postal vote, the regulations (mostly concerning the time limits) vary based on the voter's location and her current quarantine status. We focus on the non-expat and non-quarantined voters, but the protocol for the other types of voters is nearly the same.

The protocol consists of several, partly overlapping phases: the setup which involves expression of intention to vote by post, preparation and distribution of election packages (EPs), casting of the vote, validation of votes, and tallying, see Fig. 1.

Setup. A voter expresses her intention to vote by post to its local municipal office (MO) at the latest 12 days before the day of election (EDay). This can be done in either oral, written, or electronic form. The intent expression must contain the voter's personal information, such as full name, DOB, id number (PESEL), phone number, email, and residential and postal addresses. If the voter prefers to collect the EP in person, this must be specified instead of a postal address. Additionally, the voter can request to change municipality assigned to her in the voters' register once before the start of the election.

EP Preparation. Upon receipt of the intention, a municipal office employee checks the voters' register, and prepares and distributes the EP, provided that

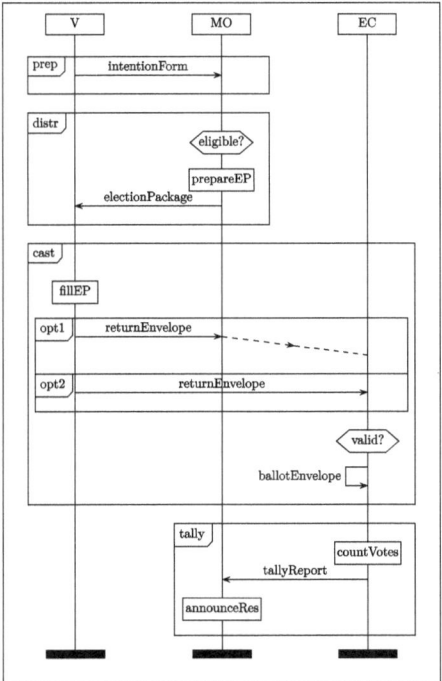

Fig. 1. A simplified diagram of the voting process

Fig. 2. EP content: return envelope, instruction card, voting card, ballot envelope, stamped ballot

the applicant is an eligible voter and no required information is missing. A complete EP (Fig. 2) must contain an instruction, a ballot stamped by both the National Electoral Commission (PKW) and the local electoral commission, a voting card, and two envelopes: one for the ballot and one to be returned. The EPs must be delivered or made available for collection to voters no later than five days before the EDay.

Casting. When a complete EP is collected, the voter should put a single 'X' mark against preferred candidate, put the ballot into a ballot envelope, sign a voting card and place it together with ballot envelope into a return envelope. Both ballot and return envelope must be sealed. If there is a deviation in any of the above steps (e.g., the ballot envelope is not sealed), this would invalidate the casting of the vote. Then, the voter must either send the filled REnv to MO,

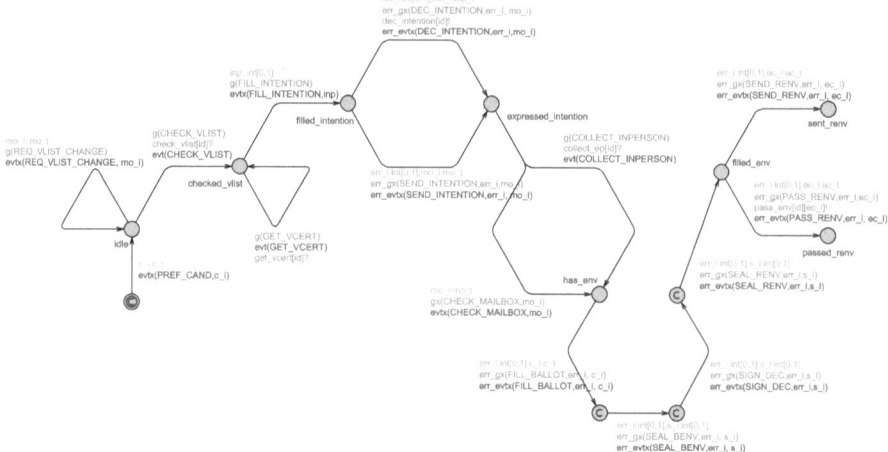

Fig. 3. Voter template (Color figure online)

where it will be stored until it is passed to the electoral commission (EC) on the EDay, or turn it in to the assigned electoral commission.

Validation. The EC has to print the voters' list (partitioned according to their municipality) one day before the election at the latest. This will be used to check the validity of the vote and make sure that no person can vote multiple times. If the voter is eligible and the REnv is complete, the BEnv is put into the ballot box.

Tallying. At the end of the EDay, when all REnvs are collected, the commission opens the BEnvs and prepares a voting protocol with information on the number of received REnvs, invalid votes, and the local tally. The protocol is sent to MO which checks it using a proprietary software. If the errors are within the margins allowed by legislation, the MO accepts the protocol. Otherwise, the protocol is rejected and the electoral commission must prepare a new one. When all protocols are accepted and merged, the final tally and the winner are publicly announced.

3   Formal Model of the Procedure

We can now present our preliminary model of the postal voting protocol. The code of the model is available at https://github.com/polishpostalvote2020/model.

3.1   Automata Networks, MAS Graphs, and Uppaal Model Checker

We chose the Uppaal model checker as the modeling environment because its user-friendly GUI and a flexible system specification language. The GUI is especially important, as it allows for a preliminary validation of a system specification even at the early stages of modeling.[1] A system in Uppaal is represented as a (parameterized) network of (parameterized) finite automata [8]. The parametrization can be used to define a set of almost identical processes in an easy way. In order to represent occurrence of events, as well as define the available strategies of participants, we use the extension of automata networks to *MAS graphs*, proposed in [31].

A MAS graph allows for the specification of a finite number of agents, possibly interacting via synchronized transitions and/or shared (i.e., global) variables. Formally, it consists of a set of *shared variables* and a number of *agent templates*, each of the templates being a graph with its own set of *locations*, *edges*, and *local variables*. An example agent graph is presented in Fig. 3. The locations are depicted by circles; the initial location (one per agent template) is marked by a double circle. Committed locations are marked by a circled 'C'. Whenever an agent is in such a location, the next transition must involve an edge from the committed location. Those are used to create atomic sequences of events, or to encode synchronization, so that there is no interleaving. The edges are annotated by selections (yellow), guards (green), synchronizations (teal) and updates (blue). A selection is a statement of the form `var:type`, which binds the identifier to a value from the given range in a non-deterministic way. These can be used to define a set of parameterized edges in an easy way (both for reading and writing the model). Uppaal allows having function calls for the updates and for the guards if it does not lead to side effects (i.e., without modifying value of any variable).

3.2   MAS Graph for the Postal Voting Procedure

The MAS graph for the procedure consists of the following agent templates: Voter (V, depicted in Fig. 3), Electoral Commission (EC, Fig. 4), Municipal Office (MO^2), and Time counter (whose graphs are omitted here due to lack of space). The numbers of agent instances are denoted by NV, NMO, and NEC. Their values, together with the number of candidates NC are specified as part of the model configuration. The sole Time agent is used to impose discrete time constraints on the actions of other agents.

We extend the base model (having infallible agents only) by specifying following mistakes for Voter - may initiate communication and send the forms to

---

[1] In Uppaal, system components are defined together with their graph-like (local) representation, which could greatly facilitate in reducing the number of bugs/errors, improve understanding and presentation of the model, and provide more confidence that *we know what we are modelling and if it is actually what wanted to model.*

[2] Its template consists of a single location with multiple self-loop edges; the figure was omitted due to space constraints.

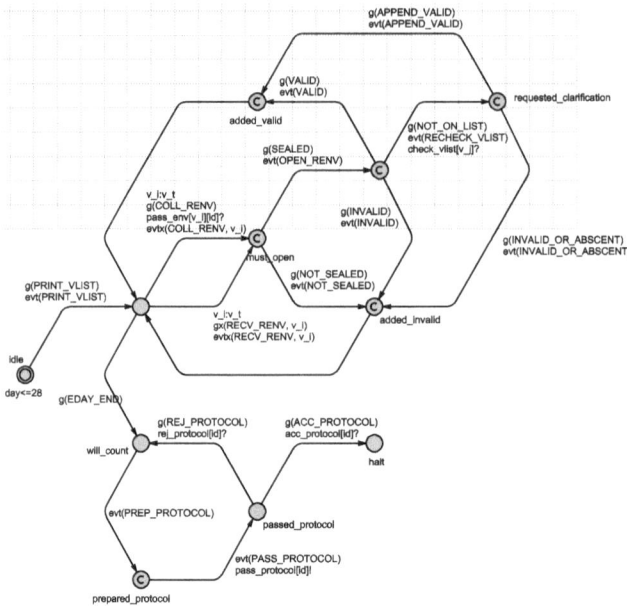

Fig. 4. Electoral Commission template

a wrong MO or EC, may leave ballot or return envelopes unsealed, misplace the cross mark on the ballot, forget to fill or sign the voting card, attempt to vote by post after obtaining voter's certificate, for Municipal Office (only in some explicitly specified experiments) - may prepare and then distribute ballots without a proper stamp, invalidating those. This yields a hierarchy of the (partially ordered) models, allowing us to study the satisfiability of properties on a finer-grained level, and furthermore get a better understanding of the potential impact of human errors on the system.

The agent templates include a variety of behaviours that can result from human errors as well as purposeful misbehavior. For example, a Voter may not fill the forms properly, or attempting to communicate with the wrong municipal office or electoral commission. Furthermore, a Municipal Office can send out an invalid ballot by using a photocopied rather than genuine stamp (which actually happened during the election). In this version, we do not explicitly model the postal services, and thus omit the possible malicious or erroneous actions of postal clerks, or an adversary.[3] Instead, we focus on analysis of human interactions and possible effects of their mistakes (as deviation from the expected behaviour). Similarly, we omit rare events, e.g., those that involve the power of attorney for in-person hand-in of the REnv.

The following data structures are used within the templates:

---

[3] It is worth noting that having a modular representation allows extending the model with other types of agents, including adversary, if needed.

```
typedef int[1,NC] c_t;              // candidate id
typedef int[1,NV] v_t;              // voter id
typedef int[-NMO,-1] mo_t;          // municipal office id
typedef int[-NMO-NEC,-NMO-1] ec_t;  // election commission id
typedef int[-NMO-NEC,NV] addr_t;    // domain of all agents ids
typedef struct{
    addr_t src;       // sender id
    addr_t dst;       // receiver id
    addr_t addr;      // address for EP delivery
    bool inperson;    // in-person collection preference
    v_tx pesel_of;    // PESEL number
}IntentionForm;
typedef struct{
    bool sealed;       // envelope sealed
    bool pkw_stamp;    // National Electoral Commission stamp
    bool dec_stamp;    // district electoral commission stamp
    int[0,2] cell[c_t]; // number of Xs near candidate cell
                       // (2 for any number greater than 1)
}Benv;                 // ballot envelope
typedef struct{
    addr_t src;        // sender id
    addr_t dst;        // recipient id
    Benv benv;
    mo_tx stamp;       // envelope stamp
    bool sealed;       // envelope was sealed
    bool dec_signature; // voter's card signed
    v_tx dec_pesel;    // voter's card PESEL
}Renv;                 // return envelope
typedef struct{
    addr_t src;    // sender id
    addr_t dst;    // recipient id
    Renv renv;
}ElectionPackage; // election package
typedef struct{
    addr_t mo_addr;  // assigned municipality
    addr_t ec_addr;  // assigned commission
    cmt_t comment;   // nominal field for
    bool changed;    // recently changed
}v_record           // an entry in the voters registry
```

Notice that the space of active agent names (or rather their unique identifiers) is partitioned with respect to the agent type. This allows to model intended parties for a given communication instance in an easy way. All the variables in Uppaal are assigned with either explicit initial or implicit default values. Thus, sometimes aliases which extend the existing data types will be used (e.g., c_tx for int[0,NC]).

Additionally, to improve readability and keep the graphical view 'clean' we use the following convention for the edge labels:

- all updates are of the form evt(EVT_CODE) or evtx(EVT_CODE,EVT_PARAMS);
- all guards are of the form g(EVT_CODE) or gx(EVT_CODE,EVT_PARAMS).

Where EVT_CODE is a string of characters (i.e., named value from the pre-defined enum of events), representing action name by means of a natural language. The sets of available/specified actions are disjoint among agents of a distinct type. On the level of the model code, functions evt/evtx and g/gx are declared using switch statement matching passed argument of EVT_CODE to its case clause, which should facilitate towards the modularity of a model and higher integrity of its graphical presentation.

4   Verification

As the next step, we specify some relevant properties of the voting system by formulas of multi-agent logics, in particular the branching-time temporal logic **CTL** and the strategic logic **ATL**. Then, we transform them to a form that can be interpreted by Uppaal, and run the model checking. To mitigate the impact of state-space explosion, we use abstraction on variables, proposed in [31].

4.1   Specification of Properties

Following [29, 32, 33, 53], we use the formulas of multi-agent logics to specify some interesting requirements on the election system. In particular, we use the branching-time temporal logic **CTL** [23] and strategic logic **ATL** [1]. We focus on the following requirements[4]:

(**P1**) The number of correctly received ballots cannot exceed the number of sent ballots (a weak variant of resistance against ballot stuffing);
(**P2**) For every voter, cast vote must be properly recorded and reflected by the tally (tally integrity);
(**P3**) The authorities should have no strategy to invalidate certain votes, even when the voters' preferences are known (no strategic ballot removal).

We formalize (*P1*) and (*P2*) by the following **CTL** formulas:

$$\varphi_{P1} \equiv \mathsf{A}\Box(\textstyle\sum_{i=1}^{NB} b\_received_i \leq \sum_{j=1}^{NV}(ep\_sent_j))$$
$$\varphi_{P2} \equiv \mathsf{A}\Box(elec\_end \wedge voted_{i,j} \Rightarrow tallied_{i,j})$$

where NB and NV stand for the maximum number of ballots and voters accordingly, $i \in NV$ is an arbitrary fixed voter, and $j \in NC$ a candidate. The (*P1*) says that, for all possible execution paths (A) and all future time points ($\Box$), the sum of received ballots must not exceed the number of sent election packets. Similarly, (*P2*) says that if election is closed and voter has cast her vote for candidate j, then it must be tallied for j.

Furthermore, we formalize (*P3*) by the following formula of **ATL** (in fact, we formalize the negation of (*P3*) and focus on ballot removal by a Municipal Office, thus expressing that the MO can strategically remove ballots):

$$\varphi_{\neg P3} \equiv \langle\!\langle MO_k \rangle\!\rangle\Box \bigwedge_{i \in NV} (vreg_{i,k} \wedge pref_{i,j} \wedge elec\_end \Rightarrow \neg tallied_{i,j})$$

where $i \in NV$, $j \in NC$ and $k \in MO$ is a municipal office. The reading of $\varphi_{\neg P3}$ is: "Municipal office k has a strategy ($\langle\!\langle MO_k \rangle\!\rangle$) such that, no matter what the other agents do, at all future time points ($\Box$) for any voter i if registered in this municipality ($vreg_{i,k}$), prefers candidate j ($pref_{i,j}$) and election is already closed ($elec\_end$), then her vote will not be tallied correctly ($\neg tallied_{i,j}$).

---

[4] Authors would want to stress out that the given properties are just an example, merely for illustration purpose, and they should not be viewed as complete list of requirements.

4.2   From Agent Logics to Uppaal Specifications

Our formalization of resistance to ballot stuffing and tally integrity has a straightforward transcription in Uppaal specification language:

(φ_{P1}) A[] (b_recv<=ep_sent),
(φ_{P2}) A[] (Time.end and (Voter(i).sent_renv or Voter(i).passed_renv) imply recorded_link[i]==Voter(i).pref_cand),

where b_recv, ep_sent and recorded_link are auxiliary variables added only for the verification of related property, and representing the number of received ballots, the number of sent election packages, and the mapping from voters to the way their votes have been tallied. Moreover, pref_cand is the voter's local variable storing her preferred candidate, sent_renv and passed_renv are labels of the corresponding locations in the voter's agent graph (see Fig. 3).

Unfortunately, Uppaal does not offer the verification of strategic abilities thus does not admit **ATL** operators. To deal with that, we propose to approximate formula $\varphi_{\neg P3}$ by its *under-approximation* $\varphi_{\neg P3}^{-}$ and *over-approximation* $\varphi_{\neg P3}^{+}$, both of which are **CTL** formulas that satisfy the following conditions:

$$M \models_{\textbf{CTL}} \varphi_{\neg P3}^{-} \qquad \Rightarrow \qquad M \models_{\textbf{ATL}} \varphi_{\neg P3}$$
$$M \models_{\textbf{ATL}} \varphi_{\neg P3} \qquad \Rightarrow \qquad M \models_{\textbf{CTL}} \varphi_{\neg P3}^{+}$$

That is, whenever $\varphi_{\neg P3}^{-}$ is true in a model, $\varphi_{\neg P3}$ must also be true there. Moreover, if $\varphi_{\neg P3}^{+}$ is false in a model, $\varphi_{\neg P3}$ must also be false. We use the following approximations:

$$\varphi_{\neg P3}^{-} \equiv \textsf{A}\square \bigwedge_{i \in NV} (vreg_{i,k} \wedge pref_{i,j} \wedge elec\_end \Rightarrow \neg tallied_{i,j})$$

$$\varphi_{\neg P3}^{+} \equiv \textsf{E}\square \bigwedge_{i \in NV} (vreg_{i,k} \wedge pref_{i,j} \wedge elec\_end \Rightarrow \neg tallied_{i,j})$$

This follows the intuition that, if ψ is guaranteed to always hold on all execution paths ($\textsf{A}\square\psi$), then it must also hold when MO plays strategically ($\langle\!\langle MO\rangle\!\rangle\square\psi$). Moreover, if MO has a strategy to maintain ψ ($\langle\!\langle MO\rangle\!\rangle\square\psi$), then ψ must always hold on at least one path ($\textsf{E}\square\psi$).

Now, formula $\varphi_{\neg P3}^{-}$ can be fed directly to Uppaal. Unfortunately, this is not the case for the upper approximation $\varphi_{\neg P3}^{+}$, as Uppaal does not interpret the $\textsf{E}\square$ combination of **CTL** operators correctly.[5] On the other hand, Uppaal's E[] combination is an over-approximation of the **CTL*** $\textsf{E}\square$ combination. Thus, we can use it to provide "over-over-approximation" of the original specification, which finally obtains the following list of Uppaal inputs:

---

[5] The satisfaction of **CTL** operators in a transition system is interpreted over *maximal runs*, i.e., ones that are either infinite or end in a state with no outgoing transitions. In contrast, Uppaal looks at *all finite runs*. While this does not change the semantics of $\textsf{A}\square$ and $\textsf{E}\Diamond$, the interpretation of both $\textsf{A}\Diamond$ and $\textsf{E}\square$ becomes nonstandard.

```
————————— Concrete model —————————          ————————— Abstact model —————————
typedef struct{                             typedef struct{
    bool sealed;                                bool invalid;
    bool pkw_stamp;                             c_tx cell;
    bool dec_stamp;                         }Benv;
    int[0,2] cell[c_t];                     typedef struct{
}Benv;                                          addr_t dst;
typedef struct{                                 bool invalid;
    addr_t src;                                 Benv benv;
    addr_t dst;                             }Renv;
    Benv benv;                              typedef struct{
    mo_tx stamp;                                bool sent;
    bool sealed;                                Renv renv;
    bool dec_signature;                     }ElectionPackage;
    v_tx dec_pesel;
}Renv;
typedef struct{
    addr_t src;
    addr_t dst;
    Renv renv;
}ElectionPackage;
```

Fig. 5. Fragment of code resulting from the abstraction, where all evaluations invalidating a vote are merged into a single variable (for REnv and BEnv)

$(\varphi^-_{\neg P3})$ A[] forall(i:v_t)(Time.end and vlist[i].mo_addr==k and
vpref
[i]==j imply recorded_link[i]!=j),
$(\varphi^{++}_{\neg P3})$ E[] forall(i:v_t)(Time.end and vlist[i].mo_addr==k and
vpref
[i]==j imply recorded_link[i]!=j),

where vlist refers to the voters' registry.

4.3   Mitigating State Space Explosion by Abstraction of Variables

One of the biggest challenges in the practical application of model checkers is the so called *state-space explosion*. Typically, model checking involves the generation of a huge state/transition graph that includes all the possible states (i.e., configurations) of the system. Clearly, the number of such configurations is exponential in the number of processes and their components – in our case, the number of agent instances and their local variables [18]. This is easy to see in our experimental results for formula φ_{P1}, see Table 1(left), the part under "φ_{P1} (concrete)," with the clear exponential growth of the verification time t and memory use m. As a consequence, the verification of φ_{P1} on the model presented in Sect. 3 scales up to only 2 voters, 1 municipal office, and 3 electoral commissions for an election with 3 candidates.

Mitigating state-space explosion has been an important topic of research for over 30 years. The most important techniques include partial-order reduction [47], symbolic verification [41], bounded and unbounded model checking [42] and state/action abstraction [19]. In particular, abstraction is an intuitive model reduction method, based on the idea of clustering "similar" states of the system (so called *concrete states*) into *abstract states*, hopefully reducing the model to a manageable size. The actual clustering must be carefully crafted. On the one hand, it must only remove information that is irrelevant for the verification of a given property, otherwise the verification results for the abstract model will be inconclusive with respect to the original model (so called "concrete model"). On the other hand, it has to remove sufficiently much of the concrete model, so that the model checking becomes efficient.

In this work, we use an intuitive and easy to use abstraction scheme, based on the removal of variables from agent graphs [31]. The method allows to select a subset of local variables to be removed (possibly with a subset of locations to serve as the scope of the abstraction). For example, the name of the voter's preferred candidate is irrelevant for the verification of resistance to ballot stuffing, hence the corresponding variables can be omitted in the voters' agent graphs. The abstraction generates *two* abstract models. The first one *under-approximates* the concrete model, in the sense that if formula ψ returns `true` on the abstract model, it must be also be true in the concrete model. The second *over-approximates* the concrete model, i.e., if ψ returns `false` on the abstract model, it must be also be false in the concrete model.

Alternatively, the user can define a mapping from the variables to a fresh variable that merge some of the information that used to be stored in the removed variables. For example, we might map the complex representation of all potential ballot faults (unsealed ballot envelope, missing stamps, more than one 'X' on the ballot, for one or more candidates) to a single boolean variable `invalid`, see Fig. 5.

In general, these abstraction parameters should be picked firstly to reduce the number of induced states of global model, and secondly to match the property, so that verification is conclusive. Naturally, there are variety of ways to chose fitting parameters for a given property; it is also possible that two distinct properties are matched by the same ones, and therefore same abstract models. We refer to [31] for the formal definitions, correctness proofs, and extensive discussion of the method.

4.4   Verification Experiments

Based on the input prepared in the previous sections, we have conducted a number of model checking experiments. All the results presented here were obtained with Uppaal 4.1.24 (32 bit) on a laptop with Intel i7-8665U 2.11 GHz CPU, running Ubuntu 20.04 on WSL2 with 4 GB RAM. The outcome of the experiments is shown in Tables 1 and 2. The notation is as follows:

- *conf* denotes the configuration of the experiment, i.e., the number of voters, Municipal Offices, Electoral Commissions, and election candidates;
- *Sat* reports the verification output, i.e., whether the model checker returned `true` or `false`;
- t and m show the time and memory used in the verification, with `memout` indicating that the model checking process ran out of memory.

Table 1(left) presents the experimental results for our formalization of weak resistance to ballot stuffing. The formula has turned out to be true in all the completed verification runs. However, as already observed, the verification scales rather badly due to state-space explosion. To mitigate that, we reduced the models by abstracting away the identity of candidates, and simplified the data structures representing the intention form and the election package. Moreover, we mapped variables `b_recv` and `ep_sent` to a single fresh variable `ballot_diff` = `ep_sent-b_recv`, so that the requirement specification became `AG(ballot_diff>=0)`. The results for model checking the under-approximating abstract model are also presented in Table 1(left).

Since the output of under-approximation was **true**, we conclude that φ_{P1} is also true in the original (concrete) model. Note that, for some configurations, the abstraction allowed to run the verification faster by orders of magnitude. Moreover, it allowed for the model checking of scenarios with 3 voters, 1 MO, 1 EC, and 3 candidates, i.e., one more voter than in the concrete case. This might seem slight, but in some cases 3 voters are necessary to demonstrate non-trivial attacks on a voting system [3].

For tally integrity (φ_{P2}), we used formula φ_{P2} proposed in Sect. 4.2. In this case, we additionally generated the under-approximating abstract models obtained by (a) mapping all the candidate names except j to a fresh value j', (b) for all voters other than i, removing their memory of the choices associated with their intention forms and election packages after they send those. The results in Table 1(right) show that the verification output was not conclusive, i.e., they do not imply whether φ_{P2} is true or false in the original model. However, the verification becomes conclusive under the assumption that voter i makes no errors and strictly follows the protocol, see the rightmost part of the table. In that case, we get **true** as the output, thus concluding the original property holds as well.

Lastly, the experimental results for strategic ballot removal ($\varphi_{\neg P3}$) are presented in Table 2. The table first shows the (inconclusive) output of model checking for under-approximation w.r.t. the formula, under-approximation w.r.t. the formula and the model, and over-approximation w.r.t. the formula. Thus, the original property might (but does not have to) be satisfied. Then, we fix a strategy for MO in the model, so that the municipal office sends a ballot with invalid stamps whenever the voter intends to vote for the "unwelcome" candidate. The results in the rightmost part of Table 2 show now conclusive output: the under-approximation is true, so the original property must be true as well. Thus, the proposed strategy indeed achieves the goal specified by $\varphi_{\neg P3}$. Note that it is essential to couple matching formula- and model-related approximations, otherwise the procedure is not sound. In our case, this meant using the *under-approximating* formula $\varphi^{-}_{\neg P3}$ with the *under-approximating* abstract model of the procedure.

Despite the technical limitations on the number of voters, it was possible to discover and verify attacks violating φ_{P2} and φ_{P3} respectively. For the next step (which remains as a subject of future work), we would want to scale up

Table 1. Experimental results for model checking of φ_{P1} (left) and φ_{P2} (right)

conf	φ_{P1} (concrete)			φ_{P1} (abstract)		
	Sat	t (s)	m(MB)	Sat	t (s)	m(MB)
1,1,1,1	true	0.07	31	true	0.07	30
1,1,1,2	true	0.10	31	true	0.07	30
1,1,1,3	true	0.12	31	true	0.07	30
1,1,2,1	true	0.12	31	true	0.08	31
1,1,2,2	true	0.20	31	true	0.08	31
1,1,2,3	true	0.27	31	true	0.08	31
1,1,3,1	true	0.29	31	true	0.14	31
1,1,3,2	true	0.54	32	true	0.14	31
1,1,3,3	true	0.80	33	true	0.14	31
1,1,4,1	true	0.92	33	true	0.39	31
1,1,4,2	true	1.8	35	true	0.39	31
1,1,4,3	true	2.7	36	true	0.39	31
1,2,2,1	true	0.27	31	true	0.14	31
1,2,2,2	true	0.48	32	true	0.14	31
1,2,2,3	true	0.71	33	true	0.14	31
1,2,3,1	true	0.75	32	true	0.32	31
1,2,3,2	true	1.4	34	true	0.32	31
1,2,3,3	true	2.2	35	true	0.32	31
1,2,4,1	true	2.5	35	true	0.97	32
1,2,4,2	true	4.9	39	true	0.97	32
1,2,4,3	true	7.5	58	true	0.97	32
2,1,1,1	true	5.0	91	true	1.0	32
2,1,1,2	true	21	271	true	1.0	32
2,1,1,3	true	48	618	true	1.0	32
2,1,2,1	true	15	172	true	2.9	34
2,1,2,2	true	64	581	true	2.9	34
2,1,2,3	true	148	1332	true	2.9	34
2,1,3,1	true	52	330	true	9.5	57
2,1,3,2	true	213	1180	true	9.5	57
2,1,3,3	true	496	2796	true	9.5	57
2,1,4,1	true	190	638	true	35	83
2,1,4,2	true	789	2429	true	35	83
2,1,4,3	memout			true	35	83
2,2,2,1	true	135	990	true	18	76
2,2,2,2	true	558	3901	true	18	76
2,2,2,3	memout			true	18	76
2,2,3,1	true	445	2168	true	59	152
2,2,3,2	memout			true	59	152
2,2,3,3	memout			true	59	152
2,2,4,1	memout			true	203	350
2,2,4,2	memout			true	203	350
2,2,4,3	memout			true	203	350
3,1,1,1	memout			true	80	365
3,1,1,2	memout			true	80	365
3,1,1,3	memout			true	80	365
3,1,2,1	memout			true	241	818
3,1,2,2	memout			true	241	818
3,1,2,3	memout			true	241	818
3,1,3,1	memout			true	793	1882
3,1,3,2	memout			true	793	1882
3,1,3,3	memout			true	793	1882
3,1,4,1	memout			memout		

conf	φ_{P2} (concrete)			φ_{P2} (abstract)			φ_{P2} (honest abstract)		
	Sat	t (s)	m(MB)	Sat	t (s)	m(MB)	Sat	t (s)	m(MB)
1,1,1,1	false	0.07	31	false	0.06	30	true	0.05	30
1,1,1,2	false	0.09	31	false	0.06	31	true	0.06	30
1,1,1,3	false	0.11	31	false	0.07	31	true	0.06	30
1,1,2,1	false	0.12	31	false	0.08	31	true	0.05	31
1,1,2,2	false	0.23	31	false	0.10	31	true	0.07	31
1,1,2,3	false	0.25	31	false	0.13	31	true	0.08	31
1,1,3,1	false	0.31	31	false	0.15	31	true	0.12	31
1,1,3,2	false	0.52	32	false	0.25	31	true	0.13	31
1,1,3,3	false	0.75	33	false	0.35	31	true	0.17	31
1,1,4,1	false	0.90	33	false	0.40	32	true	0.19	31
1,1,4,2	false	1.7	35	false	0.76	32	true	0.33	31
1,1,4,3	false	2.6	36	false	1.1	33	true	0.69	31
1,2,2,1	false	0.26	32	false	0.14	31	true	0.09	31
1,2,2,2	false	0.45	32	false	0.22	31	true	0.13	31
1,2,2,3	false	0.66	33	false	0.31	31	true	0.16	31
1,2,3,1	false	0.70	32	false	0.33	31	true	0.16	31
1,2,3,2	false	1.4	34	false	0.61	32	true	0.26	31
1,2,3,3	false	2.0	35	false	1.3	32	true	0.36	31
1,2,4,1	false	2.3	35	false	1.0	32	true	0.40	31
1,2,4,2	false	4.7	39	false	2.0	33	true	0.97	32
1,2,4,3	false	7.1	42	false	3.0	34	true	1.1	32
2,1,1,1	false	1.8	36	false	0.95	31	true	0.28	31
2,1,1,2	false	6.9	99	false	3.0	34	true	0.72	31
2,1,1,3	false	16	220	false	6.2	54	true	1.3	32
2,1,2,1	false	7.2	79	false	2.8	34	true	0.71	31
2,1,2,2	false	30	235	false	9.2	57	true	2.3	32
2,1,2,3	false	68	535	false	20	100	true	3.4	34
2,1,3,1	false	26	137	false	9.5	41	true	2.0	33
2,1,3,2	false	104	516	false	32	114	true	5.3	36
2,1,3,3	false	239	1180	false	68	200	true	10	57
2,1,4,1	false	95	305	false	35	84	true	6.4	38
2,1,4,2	false	384	1199	false	119	233	true	18	65
2,1,4,3	false	885	2768	false	254	477	true	33	97
2,2,2,1	false	60	377	false	19	77	true	4.0	33
2,2,2,2	false	241	1439	false	61	189	true	10	53
2,2,2,3	false	549	3338	false	126	382	true	19	74
2,2,3,1	false	205	829	false	61	153	true	10	38
2,2,3,2	false	832	3318	false	199	428	true	29	81
2,2,3,3	memout			false	413	881	true	55	130
2,2,4,1	false	729	2026	false	211	338	true	33	70
2,2,4,2	memout			false	696	1075	true	92	174
2,2,4,3	memout			false	1444	2264	true	177	307
3,1,1,1	false	60	683	false	73	340	true	10	54
3,1,1,2	memout			false	384	1855	true	37	153
3,1,1,3	memout			memout			true	88	332
3,1,2,1	false	346	2387	false	224	769	true	28	99
3,1,2,2	memout			memout			true	99	293
3,1,2,3	memout			memout			true	230	667
3,1,3,1	memout			false	775	1827	true	81	201
3,1,3,2	memout			memout			true	283	639
3,1,3,3	memout			memout			true	661	1503
3,1,4,1	memout			memout			true	261	451
3,1,4,2	memout			memout			true	920	1518
3,1,4,3	memout			memout			true	2157	3626
3,2,2,1	memout			memout			true	317	667
3,2,2,2	memout			memout			true	1143	2303
3,2,2,3	memout			memout			memout		
3,2,3,1	memout			memout			true	895	1427
3,2,3,2	memout			memout			memout		
3,2,3,3	memout			memout			memout		
3,2,4,1	memout			memout			true	1065	2433
3,2,4,2	memout			memout			memout		
3,2,4,3	memout			memout			memout		
4,1,1,1	memout			memout			memout		

the model to larger or even unbounded number of voters (the latter is currently

Table 2. Experimental results for model checking of $\varphi^-_{\neg P3}$ and $\varphi^{++}_{\neg P3}$ in a model, where MO may prepare EP without a valid stamp

conf	$\varphi^-_{\neg P3}$ (concrete)			$\varphi^-_{\neg P3}$ (abstract)			$\varphi^{++}_{\neg P3}$ (concrete)			$\varphi^-_{\neg P3}$ (str. abstract)		
	Sat	t (s)	m(MB)	Sat	t (s)	m(MB)	Sat	t (s)	m(MB)	Sat	t (s)	m(MB)
1,1,1,1	false	0.13	31	false	0.058	30	true	0.054	31	true	0.052	30
1,1,1,2	false	0.22	31	false	0.096	31	true	0.049	31	true	0.10	30
1,1,1,3	false	0.40	32	false	0.15	31	true	0.049	31	true	0.17	31
1,1,2,1	false	0.19	31	false	0.13	31	true	0.051	31	true	0.088	31
1,1,2,2	false	0.57	32	false	0.20	31	true	0.064	31	true	0.16	31
1,1,2,3	false	1.1	34	false	0.38	31	true	0.067	31	true	0.35	31
1,1,3,1	false	0.56	32	false	0.20	31	true	0.055	32	true	0.16	31
1,1,3,2	false	1.7	35	false	0.82	31	true	0.060	32	true	0.46	31
1,1,3,3	false	3.8	39	false	1.1	32	true	0.063	32	true	0.98	32
1,1,4,1	false	1.7	34	false	0.85	32	true	0.062	32	true	0.30	31
1,1,4,2	false	6.2	42	false	1.9	34	true	0.066	32	true	1.4	33
1,1,4,3	false	14	71	false	4.0	36	true	0.067	32	true	3.3	35
1,2,2,1	false	0.48	32	false	0.22	31	true	0.061	32	true	0.15	31
1,2,2,2	false	1.6	34	false	0.54	31	true	0.077	32	true	0.40	31
1,2,2,3	false	3.3	54	false	1.0	32	true	0.064	32	true	1.2	31
1,2,3,1	false	1.4	34	false	0.46	31	true	0.087	32	true	0.26	31
1,2,3,2	false	5.1	39	false	1.5	32	true	0.076	32	true	1.1	32
1,2,3,3	false	11	81	false	3.0	34	true	0.082	32	true	2.5	33
1,2,4,1	false	4.9	37	false	1.5	33	true	0.075	32	true	0.74	32
1,2,4,2	false	18	85	false	4.9	36	true	0.075	32	true	3.5	34
1,2,4,3	false	39	142	false	10	41	true	0.075	32	true	8.4	39
2,1,1,1	false	8.3	115	false	2.0	33	true	0.065	31	true	0.62	31
2,1,1,2	false	78	833	false	23	120	true	0.076	31	true	13	77
2,1,1,3	false	323	3496	false	105	495	true	0.062	32	true	75	337
2,1,2,1	false	36	230	false	6.1	53	true	0.070	32	true	1.6	32
2,1,2,2	false	336	2145	false	71	265	true	0.088	32	true	39	152
2,1,2,3	memout			false	321	1140	true	0.079	32	true	224	748
2,1,3,1	false	105	486	false	20	84	true	0.074	32	true	4.8	36
2,1,3,2	memout			false	244	613	true	0.082	32	true	129	326
2,1,3,3	memout			false	1114	2752	true	0.10	32	true	741	1745
2,1,4,1	false	400	1160	false	75	152	true	0.083	32	true	17	48
2,1,4,2	memout			false	896	1502	true	0.094	32	true	457	761
2,1,4,3	memout			memout			true	0.11	32	memout		
2,2,2,1	false	273	1424	false	40	121	true	0.091	32	true	10	53
2,2,2,2	memout			false	443	1156	true	0.11	32	true	241	604
2,2,2,3	memout			memout			true	0.10	32	true	1332	3282
2,2,3,1	false	904	3352	memout			true	0.097	32	true	32	83
2,2,3,2	memout			memout			true	0.096	32	true	756	1388
2,2,3,3	memout			memout			true	0.094	33	memout		
2,2,4,1	memout			memout			true	0.097	33	true	107	163
2,2,4,2	memout			memout			true	0.099	33	true	2575	3482
2,2,4,3	memout			memout			true	0.14	33	memout		
3,1,1,1	memout			memout			true	0.073	32	true	92	289
3,1,1,2	memout			memout			true	0.070	32	memout		
3,1,1,3	memout			memout			true	0.083	32	memout		
3,1,2,1	memout			memout			true	0.11	32	true	167	622
3,1,2,2	memout			memout			true	0.081	32	memout		
3,1,2,3	memout			memout			true	0.089	32	memout		
3,1,3,1	memout			memout			true	0.093	32	true	296	1446
3,1,3,2	memout			memout			true	0.10	33	memout		
3,1,3,3	memout			memout			true	0.093	33	memout		
3,1,4,1	memout			memout			true	0.11	33	true	811	3828
3,1,4,2	memout			memout			true	0.14	33	memout		
3,1,4,3	memout			memout			true	0.11	33	memout		
3,2,2,1	memout			memout			true	0.14	33	true	1056	6175
3,2,2,2	memout			memout			true	0.12	33	memout		
3,2,2,3	memout			memout			true	0.11	33	memout		
3,2,3,1	memout			memout			true	0.12	33	memout		
3,2,3,2	memout			memout			true	0.15	33	memout		

beyond technical feasibility of the tool), or to come up with rigorous arguments that certain number of voters is sufficient for certain cases.

5   Conclusions

In this paper, we demonstrate how multi-agent methodology can be used to specify and analyze the impact of human aspects on security and integrity of voting protocols. We also argue that postal voting protocols provide good material for case studies, that will hopefully increase our understanding of the subject, and help to design better protocols.

Speaking in more concrete terms, we propose a preliminary analysis of the Polish postal vote used in the presidential election of 2020. We use Multi-Agent Graphs to represent the participants and their interaction, and formulas of multi-agent logics **CTL** and **ATL** to encode interesting properties. Then, we transform those to match the input of the state-of-art model checker Uppaal. This way, the obtained models are given an intuitive visual representation and a modular structure that allows for easier modifications and detection of errors. We also use a recently proposed method of state abstraction by variable removal to reduce the models and mitigate state-space explosion. The method is guaranteed to preserve the truth of universal **CTL** specifications and thus generates correct-by-design abstract models. No less importantly, it is easy to use, requires almost no technical knowledge from the user, and provides significant savings in terms of the verification performance.

Despite the limitations of Uppaal in the expressive power of its property specification language, we have managed to conclusively verify the selected properties for nontrivial configurations of voters, electoral commissions, and candidates. To this end, we used approximation over formulas (by providing weaker or stronger versions of the original requirements) and approximation w.r.t. models (by generating appropriate abstract models). Choosing the right approximations was by no means obvious and required some skill. We believe, however, that this is inevitable: successful formal analysis of real-life scenarios requires both science and art. With more than a little bit of understanding and domain knowledge.

For the future work we plan to employ alternative verification tool to conduct analysis of a broader scope of interesting properties, and adapt our abstraction methods for that. One of the interesting directions is to adopt a methodology defining a families of possible human mistakes as in [49], where human agent deviates from the protocol through a combination of skipping, modifying, or adding action(s), or in [11], which also advocates using the epistemic modal logic distinguishing between knowledge and possession.

Acknowledgements. The work was supported by NCBR Poland and FNR Luxembourg under the PolLux/FNR-CORE project STV (POLLUX-VII/1/2019).

References

1. Alur, R., Henzinger, T.A., Kupferman, O.: Alternating-time temporal logic. J. ACM **49**, 672–713 (2002). https://doi.org/10.1145/585265.585270
2. Andrzej Rzepliński, M.S.: Statement on election irregularities [polish: Oświadczenia w sprawie nieprawidłowości dotyczących wyborów]. https://ow.org.pl/2020/08/05/oswiadczenia-w-sprawie-nieprawidlowosci-dotyczacych-wyborow/

3. Arapinis, M., Cortier, V., Kremer, S.: When are three voters enough for privacy properties? In: Askoxylakis, I., Ioannidis, S., Katsikas, S., Meadows, C. (eds.) ESORICS 2016. LNCS, vol. 9879, pp. 241–260. Springer, Cham (2016). https://doi.org/10.1007/978-3-319-45741-3_13

4. Baier, C., Katoen, J.P.: Principles of Model Checking. MIT Press, Cambridge (2008)

5. Basin, D., Gersbach, H., Mamageishvili, A., Schmid, L., Tejada, O.: Election security and economics: it's all about eve. In: Krimmer, R., Volkamer, M., Braun Binder, N., Kersting, N., Pereira, O., Schürmann, C. (eds.) E-Vote-ID 2017. LNCS, vol. 10615, pp. 1–20. Springer, Cham (2017). https://doi.org/10.1007/978-3-319-68687-5_1

6. Basin, D.A., Radomirovic, S., Schmid, L.: Modeling human errors in security protocols. In: Computer Security Foundations Symposium, CSF, pp. 325–340. IEEE Computer Society (2016). https://doi.org/10.1109/CSF.2016.30

7. Beckert, B., Beuster, G.: A method for formalizing, analyzing, and verifying secure user interfaces. In: International Conference on Formal Engineering Methods, pp. 55–73. Springer, Cham (2006)

8. Behrmann, G., David, A., Larsen, K.: A tutorial on UPPAAL. In: Formal Methods for the Design of Real-Time Systems: SFM-RT. LNCS, pp. 200–236, vol. 3185. Springer, Cham (2004)

9. Bella, G., Curzon, P., Giustolisi, R., Lenzini, G.: A socio-technical methodology for the security and privacy analysis of services. In: COMPSAC Workshops, pp. 401–406. IEEE Computer Society (2014). https://doi.org/10.1109/COMPSACW.2014.69

10. Bella, G., Curzon, P., Lenzini, G.: Service security and privacy as a socio-technical problem. J. Comput. Secur. **23**(5), 563–585 (2015). https://doi.org/10.3233/JCS-150536

11. Bella, G., Giustolisi, R., Schürmann, C.: Modelling human threats in security ceremonies. J. Comput. Secur. (Preprint) 1–23 (2022)

12. Benaloh, J., Ryan, P.Y., Teague, V.: Verifiable postal voting. In: Cambridge International Workshop on Security Protocols, pp. 54–65. Springer, Cham (2013)

13. Blanchet, B., et al.: Modeling and verifying security protocols with the applied pi calculus and proverif. Found. Trends® Privacy Secur. **1**(1-2), 1–135 (2016)

14. Bruni, A., Drewsen, E., Schürmann, C.: Towards a mechanized proof of Selene receipt-freeness and vote-privacy. In: Krimmer, R., Volkamer, M., Braun Binder, N., Kersting, N., Pereira, O., Schürmann, C. (eds.) E-Vote-ID 2017. LNCS, vol. 10615, pp. 110–126. Springer, Cham (2017). https://doi.org/10.1007/978-3-319-68687-5_7

15. Bruni, A., Carbone, M., Giustolisi, R., Mödersheim, S., Schürmann, C.: Security protocols as choreographies. In: Dougherty, D., Meseguer, J., Mödersheim, S.A., Rowe, P. (eds.) Protocols, Strands, and Logic. LNCS, vol. 13066, pp. 98–111. Springer, Cham (2021). https://doi.org/10.1007/978-3-030-91631-2_5

16. Buldas, A., Mägi, T.: Practical security analysis of e-voting systems. In: Proceedings of IWSEC. LNCS, vol. 4752, pp. 320–335. Springer, Cham (2007)

17. Carlos, M.C., Martina, J.E., Price, G., Custódio, R.F.: A proposed framework for analysing security ceremonies. In: SECRYPT, pp. 440–445. SciTePress (2012)

18. Clarke, E.M., Henzinger, T.A., Veith, H., Bloem, R., et al.: Handbook of model checking, vol. 10. Springer, Cham (2018)

19. Clarke, E., Grumberg, O., Long, D.: Model checking and abstraction. ACM Trans. Program. Lang. Syst. **16**(5), 1512–1542 (1994)

20. Cortier, V., Filipiak, A., Lallemand, J.: Beleniosvs: secrecy and verifiability against a corrupted voting device. In: 2019 IEEE 32nd Computer Security Foundations Symposium (CSF), pp. 367–36714. IEEE (2019)
21. Cortier, V., Galindo, D., Turuani, M.: A formal analysis of the neuchâtel e-voting protocol. In: 2018 IEEE European Symposium on Security and Privacy (EuroS&P), pp. 430–442. IEEE (2018)
22. Dastani, M., Hindriks, K., Meyer, J. (eds.): Specification and Verification of Multi-Agent Systems. Springer, Cham (2010)
23. Emerson, E.: Temporal and modal logic. In: van Leeuwen, J. (ed.) Handbook of Theoretical Computer Science, vol. B, pp. 995–1072. Elsevier (1990)
24. Fakt.pl: Ballot papers without stamp were delivered. Will the votes be invalid? [Polish: Dostali karty do głosowania bez pieczęci. Czy głosy będą nieważne?]. https://www.fakt.pl/wydarzenia/polityka/dostali-karty-do-glosowania-bez-pieczeci-czy-glosy-beda-niewazne/6cwhzg4
25. Haines, T., Goré, R., Tiwari, M.: Verified verifiers for verifying elections. In: Proceedings of CCS, pp. 685–702. ACM (2019). https://doi.org/10.1145/3319535.3354247
26. Haines, T., Goré, R., Sharma, B.: Did you mix me? Formally verifying verifiable mix nets in electronic voting. In: 42nd IEEE Symposium on Security and Privacy, SP 2021, San Francisco, CA, USA, 24–27 May 2021, pp. 1748–1765. IEEE (2021). https://doi.org/10.1109/SP40001.2021.00033
27. Hao, F., Ryan, P.: Real-World Electronic Voting: Design, Analysis and Deployment. Auerbach Publications (2016)
28. Holroyd, M.: Dutch election: rule change to accept wrongly sealed mail-in ballots. Euronews (2021). https://www.euronews.com/2021/03/17/dutch-election-rule-change-to-accept-wrongly-sealed-mail-in-ballots
29. Jamroga, W., Knapik, M., Kurpiewski, D.: Model checking the SELENE e-voting protocol in multi-agent logics. In: Proceedings of the 3rd International Joint Conference on Electronic Voting (E-VOTE-ID). LNCS, vol. 11143, pp. 100–116. Springer, Cham (2018)
30. Jamroga, W., Tabatabaei, M.: Preventing coercion in e-voting: be open and commit. In: Krimmer, R., et al. (eds.) E-Vote-ID 2016. LNCS, vol. 10141, pp. 1–17. Springer, Cham (2017). https://doi.org/10.1007/978-3-319-52240-1_1
31. Jamroga, W., Kim, Y.: Practical abstraction for model checking of multi-agent systems (2022). https://doi.org/10.48550/ARXIV.2202.12016
32. Jamroga, W., Kim, Y., Kurpiewski, D., Ryan, P.Y.A.: Towards model checking of voting protocols in UPPAAL. In: Krimmer, R., et al. (eds.) E-Vote-ID 2020. LNCS, vol. 12455, pp. 129–146. Springer, Cham (2020). https://doi.org/10.1007/978-3-030-60347-2_9
33. Jamroga, W., Kurpiewski, D., Malvone, V.: Natural strategic abilities in voting protocols. In: Proceedings of STAST 2020 (2021, to appear)
34. Jamroga, W., Mestel, D., Roenne, P.B., Ryan, P.Y.A., Skrobot, M.: A survey of requirements for COVID-19 mitigation strategies. Bull. Polish Acad. Sci. Tech. Sci. **69**(4), e137724 (2021). https://doi.org/10.24425/bpasts.2021.137724
35. Killer, C., Stiller, B.: The swiss postal voting process and its system and security analysis. In: International Joint Conference on Electronic Voting, pp. 134–149. Springer, Cham (2019)
36. Kurpiewski, D., Jamroga, W., Knapik, M.L.: STV: model checking for strategies under imperfect information. In: Proceedings of the 18th International Conference on Autonomous Agents and Multiagent Systems, AAMAS 2019, pp. 2372–2374. IFAAMAS (2019)

37. Kurpiewski, D., Pazderski, W., Jamroga, W., Kim, Y.: STV+Reductions: towards practical verification of strategic ability using model reductions. In: Proceedings of AAMAS, pp. 1770–1772. ACM (2021)
38. Lomuscio, A., Qu, H., Raimondi, F.: MCMAS: an open-source model checker for the verification of multi-agent systems. Int. J. Softw. Tools Technol. Transfer **19**(1), 9–30 (2017). https://doi.org/10.1007/s10009-015-0378-x
39. Lomuscio, A., Qu, H., Raimondi, F.: MCMAS: an open-source model checker for the verification of multi-agent systems. Int. J. Softw. Tools Technol. Transfer **19**(1), 9–30 (2017)
40. Martimiano, T., Santos, E.D., Olembo, M., Martina, J.: Ceremony analysis meets verifiable voting: individual verifiability in Helios. In: SECURWARE (2015)
41. McMillan, K.: Symbolic Model Checking: An Approach to the State Explosion Problem. Kluwer Academic Publishers (1993)
42. McMillan, K.: Applying SAT methods in unbounded symbolic model checking. In: Proceedings of Computer Aided Verification (CAV). LNCS, vol. 2404, pp. 250–264 (2002)
43. Meier, S., Schmidt, B., Cremers, C., Basin, D.: The tamarin prover for the symbolic analysis of security protocols. In: International Conference on Computer Aided Verification, pp. 696–701. Springer, Cham (2013)
44. Meng, B.: A critical review of receipt-freeness and coercion-resistance. Inf. Technol. J. **8**(7), 934–964 (2009)
45. National Electoral Commission [Polish: Państwowa Komisja Wyborcza]: Presidential election 2020. [Polish: Wybory Prezydenta Rzeczypospolitej Polskiej 2020 r] (2020). https://prezydent20200628.pkw.gov.pl/prezydent20200628/pl
46. Pattinson, D., Schürmann, C.: Vote counting as mathematical proof. In: Pfahringer, B., Renz, J. (eds.) AI 2015. LNCS (LNAI), vol. 9457, pp. 464–475. Springer, Cham (2015). https://doi.org/10.1007/978-3-319-26350-2_41
47. Peled, D.: All from one, one for all: on model checking using representatives. In: Courcoubetis, C. (ed.) CAV 1993. LNCS, vol. 697, pp. 409–423. Springer, Heidelberg (1993). https://doi.org/10.1007/3-540-56922-7_34
48. of the Republic of Poland, S.: Internet Legal Acts System [Polish: Internetowy System Aktów Prawnych] (2022). https://isap.sejm.gov.pl/isap.nsf/search.xsp?status=O&kw=wybory
49. Sempreboni, D., Vigano, L.: X-men: a mutation-based approach for the formal analysis of security ceremonies. In: 2020 IEEE European Symposium on Security and Privacy (EuroS&P), pp. 87–104. IEEE (2020)
50. Shoham, Y., Leyton-Brown, K.: Multiagent Systems - Algorithmic, Game-Theoretic, and Logical Foundations. Cambridge University Press (2009)
51. Skubiszewski, M.: Electoral Observatory to the President of the NEC: Incorrectly printed ballots abroad - need to address the problem [Polish: Obserwatorium Wyborcze do Przewodniczącego PKW: Nieprawidłowo wydrukowane karty do głosowania za granicą - konieczność rozwiązania problemu]. https://monitorkonstytucyjny.eu/archiwa/14355
52. Spotted-Lublin: Election 2020 ballot papers without red DEC seal [Polish: Wybory 2020. Karty do głosowania bez czerwonej pieczęci obwodowej komisji wyborczej]. https://spottedlublin.pl/wybory-2020-karty-do-glosowania-bez-czerwonej-pieczeci-obwodowej-komisji-wyborczej/
53. Tabatabaei, M., Jamroga, W., Ryan, P.Y.A.: Expressing receipt-freeness and coercion-resistance in logics of strategic ability: Preliminary attempt. In: Proceedings of the 1st International Workshop on AI for Privacy and Security, PrAISe@ECAI 2016, pp. 1:1–1:8. ACM (2016). https://doi.org/10.1145/2970030.2970039

"I Feel Spied on and I Don't Have Any Control over My Data": User Privacy Perception, Preferences and Trade-Offs in University Smart Buildings

Rawan Taher[1]([⊠]), Maryam Mehrnezhad[2], and Charles Morisset[1]

[1] School of Computing, Newcastle University, Newcastle upon Tyne, UK
{r.a.a.taher1,charles.morisset}@newcastle.ac.uk
[2] Information Security Group, Royal Holloway, University of London, Egham, UK
maryam.merhnezhad@rhul.ac.uk

Abstract. Smart buildings operate based on the widespread adoption of sensors and devices to monitor the environment and provide services. This monitoring reveals data related to the occupants' activities and behaviours. Privacy perception and preferences have been previously studied in smart homes, where users tend to partly own and control the infrastructure, but less so in the context of large smart buildings (e.g., in universities), where visitors and occupants might have limited choices on the deployment and usage of the sensors. In this study, we interview 20 participants to investigate their privacy perceptions, preferences and trade-offs they are willing to make in university smart buildings as their work or study place. We found some similarities between the users' views on their privacy in university smart buildings and smart homes. We discovered that the users of smart buildings are in doubt about data practices in these buildings, and their privacy concerns are broadly shaped by their experiences and knowledge in other computing contexts. We also identified several desired services and recommendations for the future of smart buildings that contribute to the user's sense of trust in such buildings. These findings are important and shed light on potential practices by the industry for the next generation of the infrastructures, systems and privacy and security features of such smart buildings.

Keywords: Smart University buildings · Privacy at work · Data protection regulations · Smart work environments · Cybersecurity

1 Introduction

A smart building can be defined as a network of interconnected devices, sensors and systems observing the presence of occupants and automatically managing building functions, such as heating, ventilation and air conditioning (HVAC), access control, and lighting [11], thus optimising performance and ensuring

M. Mehrnezhad and S. Parkin (Eds.): STAST 2022, LNCS 13855, pp. 73–92, 2025.
https://doi.org/10.1007/978-3-031-83072-3_5

Indoor Environmental Quality (IEQ) for the well-being and comfort of the occupants [6,18].

In this paper, we consider a smart building to be different from a smart home in the sense that academic and commercial activities can take place, possibly containing one or more of many types of businesses, including retailers, university campuses, offices, or manufacturing [2,24,27,41,44,46,55]. A key difference in our paper between a smart home and a smart building is that smart building occupants have limited to no control of their captured data. In addition, their awareness is limited [19,20,25], and there is a lack of disclosure from those who manage these buildings [47]. Moreover, its unknown if users privacy preferences in smart buildings is similar to smart homes.

The focus of our study is university smart buildings, which in the rest of the paper, will be referred to as smart buildings. While smart buildings aim to improve productivity, health and/or safety, the amount of occupant data collected and processed on such a large scale may present various forms of risks to user privacy and security [1,10,19,29,57]. Privacy can be described as the ability of an individual to control who can access what, when and how their personal information is processed and disclosed to others. Ziegeldorf [58] defines information privacy, in the context of the Internet of Things (IoT), as a guarantee to the data subjects, the awareness of the privacy risks associated with the smart things and services, user control over their data, and the awareness and control of the subsequent use of personal data. In [50], Wang et al., considered data privacy to cover transparency, consent, control, portability and guarantee against re-identification. Moreover, in [12] the study revealed that poor disclosure about data sharing raises significant concerns about the security and privacy of users.

Smart buildings raise a range of possible violations of occupant privacy through surveillance, monitoring, tracking, profiling and identification [22,28,38, 48,49]. Smart buildings can develop by using integration features and adding new devices to the environment [16], introducing new security and privacy threats to the systems and users of such buildings. Moreover, data aggregation through different IoT devices such as carbon dioxide (CO_2) sensors can be used to track and monitor occupants' activities [15]. Part of the data is considered public [19,35] and may be openly and unintentionally accessed via IoT search engines (e.g., shodan.io). Studies on user perceptions of privacy in smart homes [3,7,56] show that users value the convenience and connectivity of these buildings and that influences their vision over privacy. These users believe that allowing their data to be accessed by external entities depends on the perceived benefits. They also expect their privacy to be protected based on their trust in the manufacturers of IoT devices. Smart home users are generally unaware of the different analytical techniques that can be used to reveal sensitive information. However, to the best of our knowledge it is unknown if the user perception of privacy in smart buildings is different from smart homes. Both smart buildings and smart homes have several features in common, including climate control, lighting automation, and security and fire safety. However, in smart homes, occupants have more control over the environment. They have a certain level of awareness over the installed technologies as it is considered their choice for their homes. Moreover, the number of inhabitants is limited, and they can be easily identified in terms of privacy. In smart buildings, the occupants are subject to unexpected and continuous monitoring. They visit these buildings regularly, and their data, and activities could be accessed by the building management, and even external parties. Moreover, these buildings are used by different groups with different preferences, and the data-ownership model is distinct yet not defined well in the relevant data protection regulations such as the GDPR [19].

We aim to address this research gap by conducting a user study of occupants' perceptions, privacy concerns and preferences within smart university buildings. Previous studies have focused either on the impacts of the shared control environments on users' behaviour and levels of user interaction or threats to users' privacy while using these environments [19,33,45,47]. Our literature review (Sect. 2) confirms that users' perceptions of privacy in smart buildings have not been extensively investigated. Therefore, the main focus of our study is to investigate the user perception of privacy in two smart-university buildings with similar capabilities (i.e., new energy systems, novel materials, and smart engineering) to highlight the threats, concerns, perceptions, and preferences from the user perspective. These two buildings were managed by the universities and selected as an instance of smart buildings in universities. Privacy investigation in these buildings is crucial, where staff privacy is a matter and thousands of students. We adopt a qualitative approach [21,37] to conduct semi-structured interviews with 20 participants. In this research, we examine users' perceptions and experiences of smart buildings, threats, and concerns associated with these buildings, acceptable trade-offs, and recommendations for the future of smart buildings.

Our results demonstrate that the participants' general perception is defined by their level of involvement with these buildings (e.g., researchers in the field of smart building technologies) and their technical and cultural backgrounds. Moreover, the participants' experiences reveal that they don't perceive any significant personal advantages in these environments, where limited types of services and user control are obstacles to user adoption. In addition, the lack of transparency, and awareness activities arranged by the building management raises various issues about user trust. Last but not least, our participants recognise the benefits of data collection and processing, yet they feel these buildings can be spying on them, leading to significant privacy concerns unattended by the relevant regulations.

2   Background and Related Work

2.1   Smart Buildings

Smart buildings use a wide range of sensors and systems to collect data and improve functionality [19]. Although the number is increasing, a limited number of smart buildings are available for study. Therefore, our study focus on smart buildings in universities with over 1500 occupants, incorporates over 4000

Table 1. Smart University Building Data Collectors and Sources

Environmental Data Collectors	Environmental Data Sources
Water meters	Water management systems
Door releases	Electronic door locks
Contact sensors	Doors and Windows
Elevator controls	Elevators
Smart card readers	Electronic locks, Elevators, Attendance
Surveillance cameras	CCTV systems
Card payment terminals	Cafe, Vending machines
Energy meters, Occupancy sensors	HVAC and lighting systems
Light level sensors, Lighting controls	Lighting systems
Smoke detectors, Heat detectors, Manual fire call points	Fire detection system
Thermostats, Temperature, CO_2, and Humidity sensors	HVAC systems

embedded sensors collecting a million data points a day on average and has around 16,000 data networks. These buildings are usually used by mixed population staff, visitors and students. Installed sensors collect data related to temperature, sound, presence, and to the building systems' performance to monitor operations and detect faults. Lists of the common sensors allocated in the two smart university buildings understudy, which collect environmental data, can be found in Table 1. Sensor data is stored in a central Building Management System (BMS) server. The data can be accessed through a web-based user interface. Building managers can use this visualization to view information related to the current state of the building's systems and environment. Building data is stored temporarily in the controllers of building systems and BMS networks. Captured data is shared with multiple parties to manage and monitor building performance. These include management staff, estate services, IT support, etc. Finally, building data can be shared for research purposes.

2.2 User Experience and Concerns

With an increased number of smart buildings in diverse sectors, limited research focuses on users' perceptions of these buildings. In terms of the experience, Martin studied users' experience of a smart university building in [33], identifying conflicts in shared control systems. This study measure the effect of the control interface and the conflict type among the users. The results illustrate the limited impacts of shared control systems in conflict with management decisions to manage the set value for temperature and noise levels. The results reveal complaints concerning temperature and noise controls. Overall, this paper suggests that the technology evolution should provide a pleasant user experience.

In terms of the concerns, a user study was conducted by Vasileva et al. [47], focusing on smart campuses as a smaller scale of smart cities. The results indicated that using data and making this data available in public is beneficial, as open data could improve users' experience and provide an example of a smart city. However, this data needs to be explained to the user, and sufficient protection measures must be in place. Via an online survey, Harper et al. [19,20] studied 81 participants who were the occupants of a university smart building for their privacy concerns and preferences. They found a lack of knowledge among the smart building occupants regarding the data collection. Additionally, they reported a shared concern regarding the privacy of the data collected. Finally, the participants expressed a desire for more transparency about the data practices.

2.3   Privacy in Shared Places and at Work

Several studies have been conducted to understand user privacy perception in shared smart buildings. For example, Mare et al. surveyed 82 hosts and 554 guests to explore their preferences for smart devices, data collection and sharing, and their privacy concerns about Airbnb accommodations [30]. They found some forms of tension, and disagreement between the guests and the hosts regarding data collection. Although the guests generally like the presence of some smart devices, they are concerned about the monitoring of the users by these devices. In [5], Bernd et al. studied bystanders' privacy concerns in the context of babysitting. This research conducted 26 interviews with nannies and 16 with parents to examine domestic workers' experiences, and privacy concerns in smart homes. The results show that, although most nannies expect the house that they work in may have cameras and acknowledge the benefits of cameras, they would like to be informed by their employers about these cameras and their purposes.

In [23], Introna studied workplace surveillance, privacy and distributive justice. Modern technologies are used in workplaces and open opportunities for employee surveillance, especially when these technologies are parts of the work infrastructure -the case of smart buildings. This paper argues that the private/public distinction is not effective in workplace surveillance since the fundamental claim for workplace privacy is not related to some personal space but rather protection against the inherently political interests in the 'gaze' of the employer. Furthermore, allocating privacy rights and transparency is heavily related to organizational justice. These findings suggest that monitoring at work should be avoided unless explicitly justified by the employer, and employees have control over using these data. While the previous research has studied the privacy concerns and preferences of the occupant of smart buildings in a limited set of contexts e.g., smart home, work monitoring via cameras, etc., there is a lack of an in-depth study to discover the user perception of their privacy in such buildings. In this paper, we contribute to closing this gap by conducting semi-structured interviews to understand the factors affecting user privacy perception about smart buildings in the university.

3   Methodology

In this section, we will present our methods for the interview design and data collection and analysis.

3.1   Interview Design

The benefits of conducting qualitative research lie in presenting a holistic understanding of the phenomenon under enquiry using predominantly subjective qualitative data, where the results are concluded based on observational and other quantitative data [13,40]. We adopted a semi-structured interview methodology to conduct this study because it allows us to explore in-depth participants' thoughts, feelings and beliefs about smart buildings and their privacy [4,26]. Our study design consists of three phases; the pre-interview forms and questions, the actual interview to collect data, and post-interview procedure to analyse collected data. **General Perception:** We asked the participants to define smart buildings based on their perceptions and experience. Participants' understanding differs according to their technical and cultural background and level of involvement with these buildings. The benefits of using smart technologies in these buildings were discussed with participants to identify the main advantages from the users' perspective. The key questions were: (1) What is a smart commercial[1] building from your perspective? (2) How would you describe your experience with smart buildings? (3) What are the benefits of using smart buildings?

User Concerns: We asked participants to identify various concerns and drawbacks regarding employing these buildings based on their experiences. Moreover, we discussed the mitigation strategies adopted by the participants when they visit a smart building. Finally, we asked the participants about their opinion about data practices in a smart building. The key questions were: (4) What are your concerns regarding utilising these buildings? (5) Would you act differently if you were in a smart building instead of a regular building? (6) What do you think of data practices in smart buildings?

Trade-Offs: To understand what the users regard as an acceptable trade-off between the data collection and the offered services by these buildings, we asked them to identify the type of ideal services they wish to receive while using these buildings. During the interviews, several service scenarios were presented to participants to understand their perception of data collection trade-offs. These scenarios include building services, public health, safety, research purposes, commercial usage, energy efficiencies, indoor environmental quality and sustainable building, attractive to user needs. The key questions were: (7) If you were in an ideal world, what type of services would you like to receive from these buildings? (8) What do you think about data collection to receive better services?

User Preferences: To highlight the participants' vision regarding the future of smart buildings, we asked them to portray an ideal smart building and provide recommendations according to their preferences. The key questions were: (9) What do you think is the future of smart buildings? (10) How can these buildings be improved to meet users' preferences? Finally, we provided a brief conclusion

---

[1] We used "smart commercial buildings" at the start of the interview to distinguish them from smart homes. When such a distinction was established, we continued with "smart building".

to participants, and we allowed time to ask any clarification questions about the study.

Ethics: At Newcastle University, the Faculty Ethics Committee reviewed and approved our research project. Before each interview, we asked the participants to read the information sheet and sign the consent form, which describes the purpose of this study and highlights confidentiality concerning participants' data.

3.2   Participants

A single trained researcher followed a previously designed procedure (i.e., starting the conversation off with the similar set of questions) to conduct a series of semi-structured interviews. Before interviewing the participants, two pilot interviews were conducted to confirm that the questions could be understood and to determine any potential problems in the script in advance so that the methodology could be adjusted before commencing with the main study. We conducted 20 interview sessions online via Zoom and in English. Each interview lasted for approximately 45–60 min. Each participant received a voucher worth £20 as compensation for their time. The interviewer allowed the participants to elaborate, share their perceptions and thoughts, and clarify any questions during the interview.

We recruited our participants by emailing the university staff who reside in a smart building in two universities, one in the UK and the other one in Saudi Arabia[2]. We asked the interested participants to complete an online questionnaire, to capture demographic information and assess participants' technical knowledge in terms of the level of familiarity with smart building technologies, security and privacy via simple questions. Therefore, 20 participants completed the online questionnaire. 16 were from a university in the UK, and 4 were from Saudi Arabia. These participants (8 male, 11 female, and 1 non-binary) were aged between (20 to 50) and had different roles (student, post-doc, teaching and research staff, and support). Most of them visited a smart building for more than half of the week.

3.3   Data Analysis

To develop insight into our research, after conducting each interview, we analysed and summarised conclusion. 20 semi-structured interviews were transcribed and then analysed individually. We noted that data saturation appeared after the fifteenth interview[3], where no new themes arose, so we stopped recruiting. All interviews were audio-recorded, transcribed and subsequently independently coded, using thematic analysis [36]. This method helps identify, analyse, and report patterns within data. It aims to identify themes embedded throughout qualitative data. After coding all the interviews and creating the final code-book,

---

[2] We used university in Saudi Arabia as the main author of the paper is partially based their.

[3] Participants from Saudi Arabia were interviewed in the middle of this saturation.

we conducted a second round of analysis to make sure all significant themes, were captured through manual coding. This process was independently completed by two of the authors of the paper in case of an inconsistency, it was discussed and resolved before reporting.

Table 2. Summary of Recurring Themes

Theme 1: User General Perception	Theme 2: User Concerns
Cultural background	Unpleasant user experience
Technical background	Limited variety of services
Level of involvement	Data management, control and consent
Modern technologies usage	Causes of drawbacks and mitigation strategies
Awareness of existing sensors	
Theme 3: Trade-Offs	Theme 4: User Preferences & Recomm
Services, Public health, Safety, Research	Increase users' awareness and disclosure
Efficiencies, Sustainable building	Improve the quality of services
Indoor environmental quality, Commercial	Understand users perception of privacy

4   Results

This section presents the extracted themes from the interviews as presented in Table 2. We conveyed participants' statements by labelling them from P1 to P20. In addition, we report how many participants mentioned each theme to produce an idea of the density and distribution of different themes.

4.1   User General Perception

We asked our participants to define a smart building and how it works based on their perception and to identify the type of sensors used in the building during the interview. We also asked about the benefits of using smart technologies in these buildings. Their responses helped us identify to what extent the participants understood the smart building concept. We found that awareness of technology and the context influencing user perceptions of smart buildings.

We observed that the user **technical background**, i.e., the level of awareness regarding technology, is the primary factor in the participants' perception of a smart building. Participants with technical background (e.g., computer researchers) have an adequate understanding of the operations, data collection and potential threats associated with using these buildings. Of the 20 participants, eight explicitly described themselves as technology experts. These participants described these buildings as a combination of different Internet of Things (IoT) devices, where any smart device can connect to these buildings. P9 a research assistant, mentioned *"whoever is in charge of the IDs can tell when* *somebody is in and out and who has been in the space at that time"*. Moreover, they were able to identify most of the existing obvious sensors.

On the other hand, participants with limited technical knowledge are less aware of these buildings. They state that there is no noticeable impact of smart buildings on the environment and the users. As stated by P6, a general worker with limited technology knowledge *"I know people sold it as a smart building. But I'm not sure what features we have in the building"*.

Another factor contributing to the user perception of a smart building was **user involvement** in the building, i.e., whether they are general workers or technical researchers. For instance, the participants who researched IoT technologies described it as more accurate than those who did not. However, in general, their perception is that it consists of a vast number of IoT devices with a central system that collects a considerable amount of data to track occupants, and monitor the environment.

Similarly, if someone is **technically involved** in a smart building, e.g., IT professional support, they would naturally express more accurate knowledge about smart buildings. However, participants with a lower level of involvement with these buildings are less familiar with the building technologies concept. These participants defined it as a regular building with some automation functionality, but they could not identify most of the installed sensors. For example, one of the participants from Saudi Arabia believe that there are a limited number of these buildings in the country. P20 stated *"I can not call it a smart building as a whole. If it only has a few smart features"*. As a result, their understanding of smart buildings' concept is narrow.

Five of our participants believed that a smart building is a **modern concept** which, aside from its general benefits, provides a boost to the name of an organisation. For instance, P13 described these buildings as *"that seems like a luxury"*. We also found out that our participants generally consider a smart building equipped with multiple **sensors**, though they are not confident about the variety of these sensors. In terms of the awareness of existing sensors, the most mentioned sensors are CCTV, temperature, lights and smart cards, while carbon dioxide is the least mentioned. Participants referred to their lack of awareness of the sensors as the absence of signs and their installed location. All the users understand that the smart card mechanism creates a log to record identification numbers and user accessibility dates/times. All 20 participants recognised CCTV and smart card sensors. The building uses CCTV to ensure safety and security within the building. 2 out of 20 of our participants prefer to use an environment with CCTV installed, as they feel safer. P2 mentioned that *"I like the idea of having cameras, it makes me feel safe"*. Only 8 of our participants acknowledged the existence of the carbon dioxide sensors and their benefits, including using the data to measure occupancy levels within a specific area.

4.2   User Concerns

Our participants highlighted a few concerns around smart buildings, including unpleasant user experience, limited variety of services, data management, control and consent, security and privacy, and they recognised multiple reasons behind these drawbacks and concerns. In Fig. 1, we can see those concerns in the form of a word count bar chart, which represents the number of participants who mentioned particular privacy concerns. All our 20 participants stated that smart buildings are attempting to be advanced technologically, though they provide a **poor user experience** due to several factors. These factors were around the building's reliability and availability, e.g., the systems failing occasionally. Participants complained the most about the temperature and light sensors in their area. For example, motion and light sensors sometimes fail to sense the presence of occupants where lights turn off suddenly when users are still working on their desks. In addition, temperature sensors do not work correctly, resulting in an uncomfortable environment because of the fixed value set. P1 stated that it is like *"living inside a prototype"*. In addition, although these systems are advertised as 'smart' systems, they are highly automated and inflexible, which allows limited occupant interaction. This high level of automation leads to user disempowerment for specific tasks. As P5 stated, *"they are not configured based on what the user wants"*. 8 participants expressed that working in a regular building is better because users have more control over their environment. However, 7 participants described these buildings as a public places where data is collected to manage building operations. Moreover, using a smart card to manage access is occasionally regarded as an obstacle because if the card is forgotten, stolen or lost, participants complain that their basic activities will be restricted. For example, P6 stated *"if you lose your card, you can not do simple things like going to the bathroom"*. The concept of smart technology in buildings is to provide occupants with smart services from participants' perspectives. All of the participants assess the adoption of smart buildings based on the services offered by these buildings. Participants complained that there are **limited types of services** provided to the occupants, compared to the services provided to the management. In addition, 9 participants mentioned that although parts of the collected data are related to the occupants, there are no perceived personalised advantages concerning them. This lack of personalised experiences conflicted with participants' feelings about why these systems should collect such data at all. P6 expressed that *"I have never seen any kind of output from data collection, what it is monitoring and how it benefits anyone?"*.

All of our participants were aware of the data collection in a smart building and that such data comes from the environment and the occupants. Our participants understood that they were in a public place (as described by some of them) where they had to give up part of their privacy. Our participants valued their privacy and demanded notifications that provided more details about what was being disclosed about them and what type of threat was associated with these data. All the participants stated that although the data collection is essential for managing building operations, they are concerned about the **data management, control and user consent**. All participants highlighted that there is a **lack of transparency and disclosure** regarding the data practices in smart buildings. Participants complained that users could not view these data,

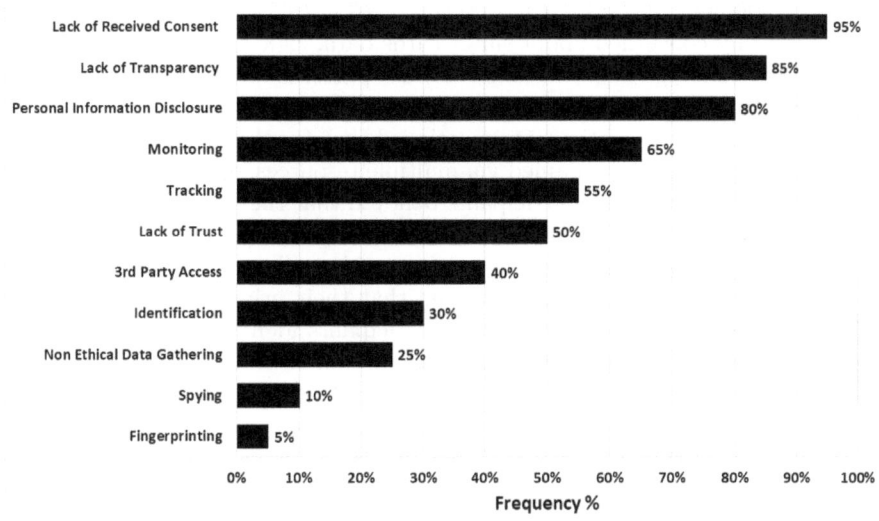

Fig. 1. Word Counts Representing Participants Privacy Concerns

and there is no proper user notification about the data collected or control to opt-in or out. P10 mentioned *"people will appreciate being notified about what are the consequences of those things"*. Moreover, all the participants discussed that it is essential to obtain **user consent**, which is not the case right now. Finally, our participants mentioned no clear regulations and laws regarding smart buildings. Conversely, some participants are aware of Data Protection Laws and General Data Protection Regulation (GDPR), but they are unclear if these regulations are applicable in smart buildings. Our participants also discussed that such consent must be clear and understandable. All the participants agreed that **security** is a significant threat in smart buildings. Our participants provided different scenarios concerning the danger of the potential hacking of such buildings. To support this argument, P10 alleged that: *"there are resources that are available and affordable (e.g., Raspberry Pi), which, via a simple intrusion, can conduct malicious activities, such as spying"*. Moreover, the IoT environment enables other build-on systems, sensors, and gadgets where security compatibility could open new doors to novel attacks. For instance, P3 stated that: *"there was a cyber-attack on infrastructure. This concern raised a question about the amount of data leaked"*. The majority of our participants (17) were concerned with their **privacy** in smart buildings. These individuals defined individual privacy as any information related to personal identity, activities, and behaviour and the right to choose to opt-in or out of data collection and to view collected data. The participants stated that the building managers and IT departments might have the greatest accessibility to these data. Moreover, our participants worried that the gathered data could be profitable and shared with some third parties. P17 stated, *"I do not want to be under surveillance all the time"*. Various smart technologies are the source of user concern in this context. We found that users are mainly concerned about smart cards data, as it is associated with personal information, e.g., ID, location, office use patterns and activities related to date/time. Hence, participants believed that smart card data is **fingerprinting and profiling** users. 8 participants mentioned that **tracking and monitoring** are possible through data obtained via multiple resources, e.g., smart cards, and carbon dioxide sensors. Our participants believed that they might act differently if they know they are being monitored and that such tracking and monitoring might be used for *"malicious purposes"* (e.g., using office hours for promotion) and is *"not ethical"*. Participants believed that their privacy could be invaded due to the power relationship at work. Participants identified common threats across computing contexts, such as breaches and financial threats that influence their privacy perception. Despite these concerns, they didn't view these concerns as high risks and adopted a few mitigation practices, e.g., not using the building Wi-Fi. Our participants declared that allowing tracking and monitoring depends on the building type and the organisation managing the building. For instance, university and airport buildings conduct monitoring for security purposes, and these types of buildings are permitted to gain users' trust. P1 said that *"what I see is that people assume that just because safety is important, people don't worry about privacy, that's not the case"*.

4.3   Trade-Offs

Most participants (18 out of 20) understand the benefits of data collection within smart buildings, and at the same time, they value their privacy. We found that, participants are willing to trade-off some of their data for services they perceive to be valuable, given that there is notice and consent and non-personalized tracking. During the interviews, several scenarios were presented to the participants to understand their perception of data collection trade-offs. These services scenarios were developed based on the perceived benefits from data collection in smart buildings which include; public health, safety, research purpose, commercial use, energy efficiencies, indoor environmental quality and sustainable building. The data collected to provide valuable **services** e.g., navigating the users to the available meeting rooms is considered a favourable service offered by these buildings. Nineteen of our participants asked for some form of data consent, confidentiality, and transparency to agree to share their data for service purposes. 5 participants believe that people are currently willing to share their data for the desired services. This idea is similar to Facebook and Google, which allow tracking of personal information in return for using their services. Thus, a smart building could be an extension of internet websites. Nineteen Participants mentioned that data collected to provide **environmental quality** of indoor spaces is essential for public health and considered a fair trade-off. However, building management should be transparent and give details on the type of data collected, who accessed the data and for what purpose. P19, who described herself as *"a security expert and a conservative person"*, stated that she dislikes the current state of data gathering and refuses to share hers.

All 20 participants stated that collecting data for **public health** purposes is highly recommended, especially with Covid-19, as management can use the data to manage crowded areas and social distancing effectively. Participants are willing to share their data for this reason as long as the tracking is not personal. Furthermore, almost all our participants agreed that they care about their **safety** and understand how the infrastructures in smart buildings would bring such protection via continuous monitoring. For instance, P13 stated: *"individuals who notice the existence of these devices are less likely to commit crimes"*.

The data collected in some smart buildings (e.g., smart university) are used for **research purposes** too. All 20 participants agreed that smart building data is beneficial to academic research, but at the same time, it should be anonymised and cannot be linked to individuals. The smart building concept aims to provide occupants with a sustainable building which uses resources **efficiently** and saves energy, and provides an environmentally friendly building. 7 out of 20 participants stated that working in a **sustainable building** is essential and provides a comfortable environment. Similarly, 9 out of 20 participants agreed that a smart building collects data to achieve energy efficiencies and that the data are related to building utilisation of resources. Moreover, 18 out of 20 participants believe that collecting data for **commercial use** is not preferable because third parties are using such data for advertisement purposes or selling the data as P13 stated *"there could be a more malicious side to like maybe selling the data"*.

4.4   User Preferences and Recommendations

We asked our participants about their opinions of the future of smart buildings and their recommendations to improve their experience within these buildings. Participants discussed this topic and suggested the following examples regarding **ideal services**; P18 and P20 suggested multiple approaches for user-building interaction platforms, such as "voice sensor communication" or visually through "dashboards" or "remotely without having to use hands", especially with the current Covid-19 pandemic and other diseases that may appear in the future. Our participants also advised that users should control the surrounding environment through a "control board" with buttons in their room. Ideal services could relate to controlling the noise level in dedicated quiet areas in libraries, as mentioned by P1: *"for example, a sensor that could measure the noise level and notify users that these are quiet areas"*. However, at the same time, users will need to be assured about their privacy.

Our participants suggested several recommendations to improve these buildings, where smart buildings should provide occupants with security and safety, but at the same time, buildings should **respect user's privacy**. For intense, using trusted third party concept to act as a decision maker on behalf of users for managing data request. In addition, three participants mentioned that with the expansion of the IoT, many devices and things would be interconnected universally. Considering that users' privacy should be handled with a high degree of urgency, these technologies will collect more data.

Five participants emphasised that the data should be handled ethically, anonymised, encrypted and deleted within the specified time frame to protect the user's confidentiality. Moreover, **dedicated laws, regulations and legislation** should be set and enforced in these buildings. Three of our participants mentioned the GDPR law, their right to delete their data, and the obligation of the smart building owner to provide disclosure about collected data.

5   Comparison to Previous Work

Our results identified several recurring themes related to user privacy in smart buildings. First, users value the convenience and connectivity of these buildings impacting their vision regarding privacy. Users believe that allowing their data to be accessed by external entities depends on the benefits provided to the users. These conclusions are similar to previously conducted research in the context of smart homes [31,53]. These conclusions demonstrate that user privacy perception for smart buildings is partially similar to the users of smart homes. Users expect their privacy to be protected based on their trust in the purpose of the building and the organization managing the building. Related studies, e.g., [3,53] likewise found that smart home users' trust to protect their privacy is dependent on the IoT device manufacturers. Our study demonstrates that there are areas where user perception in smart buildings is different from smart homes. For instance, the data in smart buildings is collected in a public place with broader access. In addition, as we discussed earlier, users of such buildings are unaware if they are in a smart building, as opposed to a smart home. Therefore the level of awareness about the two smart buildings is different. Furthermore, these awareness variations may have impacted our participants, who believed that smart buildings are fingerprinting users. Moreover, in smart homes, the number of users is limited, and individuals are easier to identify than in smart buildings. The number of users in these buildings is much higher, and data aggregation techniques could identify individuals' behaviours. The power relationships in smart buildings could be a factor that influences people's privacy perceptions; this means the ability of individuals or groups with higher authority to control others. This feature exists in smart environments such as workplaces, unlike smart home environments. Users of these buildings believe that their privacy could be invaded due to the power relationship at work. For example, their managers could monitor employees' activities by observing smart card captured data. This idea is similar to a recent study [8], where they investigated the rebalancing of the power relationships between governments and citizens in smart cities. Privacy issues can be even more serious when cenrtain elements such as gender and ethnicity are taken into account [14,34].

In terms of recommendations to ease these concerns, several studies [19, 42,43] recommend modification to the privacy law and in smart buildings. In addition, these studies suggest that the level of awareness and control over data collection practices and protection measures need to be improved, similar to our studies [19,51,52,54]. We emphasise that there are several blind areas related to this sector and need further dedicated study. For instance, is the user's privacy perception in a smart building the same or different from a smart home. Note that the main purpose of this study was to understand user privacy perception preferences and trade-offs in smart buildings, and for an in-depth comparison between smart buildings, dedicated research should be conducted in the future.

6   Discussion

In this section, we further discuss some of our findings related to the current status of users' experience, awareness of smart buildings, and privacy.

6.1   User Experience

We noted that the users' experience within these buildings reveals that they do not work effectively and efficiently. Smart building users have a **high expectation** of these buildings, and expect them to adapt to personal needs. These high expectations could apply to smart homes, where occupants have control of these systems. However, compared to smart homes, smart buildings are a much broader environment comprising many occupants sharing these systems and meeting personal preferences in a shared area is an obstacle.

6.2   User Awareness

According to our findings and previous research [19], the occupants are unaware of the benefits of data collection, which is similar to smart home users [42]. Several studies focused on visitors' privacy awareness in smart homes; in [32], the paper describes privacy for visitors as their ability to control and view the captured data in a smart environment. Privacy awareness can be performed through **privacy labels and visualisations**; in [52], the paper suggested distributing physical signs with QR (Quick Response) codes to provide information for visitors. This type of awareness is considered applicable to smart buildings like smart homes. Moreover, Smart building management should utilise more **transparent practices** to increase users' awareness. For example, by placing signs alongside sensors that enable monitoring to inform users of their existence. Nonetheless, allowing users to be able to view captured data would help them understand the overall benefits of data collection. Such knowledge will help users to understand the trade-offs for their privacy in return for received services [32].

6.3   Privacy in Smart Buildings

The fact that streams of data need to be collected to operate smart buildings was clearly understood by our participants. This perception is similar to smart home user perception [42]. Notwithstanding, several concerns arise related to tracking and fingerprinting users through data collection.

Moreover, some of the collected data is deemed semi-public and accessible to everyone, including their managers. The **power relationship** in these environments is a considerable concern as it could introduce disputes among users. Furthermore, third parties' accessibility to these data is another concern as it could target users with advertisements. Moreover, systems running these buildings are under the threat of possible cyber-attacks, given that a data breach could occur. Our participants complained that there is no particular and precise **laws or regulations** related to data collection in these buildings. There is a lack of transparency regarding the type and aim of data collection as well as the data retention period, which is similar to smart home users' perception [42].

Data needs to be handled ethically and lawfully; otherwise, the risks are considerable. To earn users' trust, two-way communication, where users can view data, receive privacy notifications, and consent to data collection, is necessary, as stated by our participants.

7   Limitations

Despite the sample size for a qualitative study, we did not cover a broad cultural background or users of different smart buildings. Interviews were completed during lockdown, which may have impacted number of responses, concerns or preferences. We have selected these two university buildings as they have similar capabilities. Nonetheless, the followed protocol steps are documented and can be used by researchers to conduct similar studies. Like all qualitative studies, the quality of a piece of research relies on the researcher's skills and might introduce personal bias. We observed that the interview length meant that the participants generally felt tired after 30 min, as they tended to provide shorter answers from this point. However, the interviewer prompted participants to elaborate and give more details.

8   Conclusion

This paper is based on 20 semi-structured interviews to explore user privacy perception, practice, and preference when working or studying in university smart buildings. The extracted themes show that there are some similarities in user views about these commercial smart buildings compared to smart homes [42]. Our participants expressed a desire for the convenience and connectivity in such buildings, influencing their vision over privacy. Similar to smart homes, users in smart buildings understand that there is a wide range of data being collected while interacting with these buildings. Since the data is more public in commercial smart buildings, our participants believed that the threat of privacy invasions in such buildings could pose higher risks compared to smart homes. Our participants also believed that these smart buildings are considered public. However, although they may accept such a data collection about them, it needs to be approached and managed ethically with transparency. In view of these results, we believe that there is a clear need to improve the way personal privacy is handled in smart buildings, especially in the presence of modern data protection regulations such as the GDPR. This could be enabled by, e.g., taking user-centred and privacy-by-design approaches as suggested by other studies [9,17,39].

Acknowledgments. This work has been partially supported by the PETRAS National Centre of Excellence for IoT Systems Cybersecurity, which has been funded by the UK EPSRC under grant number EP/S035362/1.

References

1. Akkaya, K., Guvenc, I., Aygun, R., Pala, N., Kadri, A.: IoT-based occupancy monitoring techniques for energy-efficient smart buildings. In: 2015 IEEE Wireless Communications and Networking Conference Workshops (WCNCW), pp. 58–63. IEEE (2015)
2. Alansari, Z., Soomro, S., Belgaum, M.R.: Smart airports: review and open research issues. In: International Conference for Emerging Technologies in Computing, pp. 136–148. Springer (2019)
3. Barbosa, N.M., Park, J.S., Yao, Y., Wang, Y.: "what if?" Predicting individual users' smart home privacy preferences and their changes. Proc. Priv. Enhancing Technol. **2019**(4), 211–231 (2019)
4. Barriball, K.L., While, A.: Collecting data using a semi-structured interview: a discussion paper. J. Adv. Nurs.-Inst. Subscription **19**(2), 328–335 (1994)
5. Bernd, J., Abu-Salma, R., Frik, A.: Bystanders' privacy: the perspectives of nannies on smart home surveillance. In: 10th USENIX Workshop on Free and Open Communications on the Internet (FOCI 20) (2020)
6. Buckman, A.H., Mayfield, M., Beck, S.B.: What is a smart building? Smart Sustain. Built Environ. (2014)
7. Bugeja, J., Jacobsson, A., Davidsson, P.: On privacy and security challenges in smart connected homes. In: 2016 European Intelligence and Security Informatics Conference (EISIC), pp. 172–175. IEEE (2016)
8. Castelnovo, W., Romanelli, M.: Power relationships in the co-production of smart city initiatives. In: Digital Transformation and Human Behavior, pp. 329–342. Springer (2021)
9. Cavoukian, A.: Privacy by design [leading edge]. IEEE Technol. Soc. Mag. **31**(4), 18–19 (2012). https://doi.org/10.1109/MTS.2012.2225459
10. Chen, H., Chou, P., Duri, S., Lei, H., Reason, J.: The design and implementation of a smart building control system. In: 2009 IEEE International Conference on e-Business Engineering, pp. 255–262. IEEE (2009)
11. Ciholas, P., Lennie, A., Sadigova, P., Such, J.M.: The security of smart buildings: a systematic literature review (2019)
12. Colnago, J., et al.: Informing the design of a personalized privacy assistant for the Internet of Things. In: Proceedings of the 2020 CHI Conference on Human Factors in Computing Systems, pp. 1–13 (2020)
13. Coopamootoo, K.P.: Usage patterns of privacy-enhancing technologies. In: Proceedings of the 2020 ACM SIGSAC Conference on Computer and Communications Security, pp. 1371–1390 (2020)
14. Coopamootoo, K.P., Mehrnezhad, M., Toreini, E.: "i feel invaded, annoyed, anxious and i may protect myself": individuals' feelings about online tracking and their protective behaviour across gender and country. In: 31st USENIX Security Symposium (USENIX Security 22), pp. 287–304 (2022)

15. Díaz, J., Jiménez, M.: Experimental assessment of room occupancy patterns in an office building. Comparison of different approaches based on CO2 concentrations and computer power consumption. Appl. Energy **199**, 121–141 (2017)
16. Froufe, M.M., Chinelli, C.K., Guedes, A.L.A., Haddad, A.N., Hammad, A.W., Soares, C.A.P.: Smart buildings: systems and drivers. Buildings **10**(9), 153 (2020)
17. Grace, P., Surridge, M.: Towards a model of user-centered privacy preservation. In: Proceedings of the 12th International Conference on Availability, Reliability and Security, pp. 1–8 (2017)
18. Han, Z., Gao, R.X., Fan, Z.: Occupancy and indoor environment quality sensing for smart buildings. In: 2012 IEEE International Instrumentation and Measurement Technology Conference Proceedings, pp. 882–887. IEEE (2012)
19. Harper, S., Mehrnezhad, M., Mace, J.: User privacy concerns in commercial smart buildings. J. Comput. Secur. **30**(Preprint), 1–33 (2022)
20. Harper, S., Mehrnezhad, M., Mace, J.C.: User privacy concerns and preferences in smart buildings. In: Socio-Technical Aspects in Security and Trust: 10th International Workshop, STAST 2020, Virtual Event, 14 September 2020, Revised Selected Papers, pp. 85–106. Springer (2021)
21. Harry, B., Sturges, K.M., Klingner, J.K.: Mapping the process: an exemplar of process and challenge in grounded theory analysis. Educ. Res. **34**(2), 3–13 (2005)
22. Huang, Q., Mao, C., Chen, Y.: A compact and versatile wireless sensor prototype for affordable intelligent sensing and monitoring in smart buildings. In: ASCE International Workshop on Computing in Civil Engineering, pp. 155–161. Computing in Civil Engineering 2017 (2017)
23. Introna, L.D.: Workplace surveillance, privacy and distributive justice. ACM SIG-CAS Comput. Soc. **30**(4), 33–39 (2000)
24. Jaremen, D., Jedrasiak, M., Rapacz, A.: The concept of smart hotels as an innovation on the hospitality industry market-case study of puro hotel in wrocław. Zeszyty Naukowe Uniwersytetu Szczecińskiego Ekonomiczne Problemy Turystyki **36**(4) (2016)
25. Jin, M., Bekiaris-Liberis, N., Weekly, K., Spanos, C.J., Bayen, A.M.: Occupancy detection via environmental sensing. IEEE Trans. Autom. Sci. Eng. **15**(2), 443–455 (2016)
26. Kallio, H., Pietilä, A.M., Johnson, M., Kangasniemi, M.: Systematic methodological review: developing a framework for a qualitative semi-structured interview guide. J. Adv. Nurs. **72**(12), 2954–2965 (2016)
27. Le Gal, C., Martin, J., Lux, A., Crowley, J.L.: Smart office: design of an intelligent environment. IEEE Intell. Syst. **16**(04), 60–66 (2001)
28. López, G., Marín, G., Calderón, M.: Human aspects of ubiquitous computing: a study addressing willingness to use it and privacy issues. J. Ambient. Intell. Humaniz. Comput. **8**(4), 497–511 (2017)
29. Mace, J.C., Morisset, C., Smith, L.: A socio-technical ethical process for managing access to smart building data. In: Living in the Internet of Things (IoT 2019), pp. 1–6. IET (2019)
30. Mare, S., Roesner, F., Kohno, T.: Smart devices in airbnbs: considering privacy and security for both guests and hosts. Proc. Priv. Enhancing Technol. **2020**(2), 436–458 (2020)
31. Marikyan, D., Papagiannidis, S., Alamanos, E.: A systematic review of the smart home literature: a user perspective. Technol. Forecast. Soc. Chang. **138**, 139–154 (2019)

32. Marky, K., Voit, A., Stöver, A., Kunze, K., Schröder, S., Mühlhäuser, M.: "i don't know how to protect myself": understanding privacy perceptions resulting from the presence of bystanders in smart environments. In: Proceedings of the 11th Nordic Conference on Human-Computer Interaction: Shaping Experiences, Shaping Society, pp. 1–11 (2020)

33. Martin, D.: Behaviour in conflict scenarios in a smart office environment. Master thesis, Eindhoven University of Technology (2019)

34. Mehrnezhad, M., Coopamootoo, K., Toreini, E.: How can and would people protect from online tracking? Proc. Priv. Enhancing Technol. **1**, 105–125 (2022)

35. Morgner, P., et al.: Privacy implications of room climate data. In: European Symposium on Research in Computer Security, pp. 324–343. Springer (2017)

36. Neuendorf, K.A.: Content analysis and thematic analysis. In: Advanced Research Methods for Applied Psychology, pp. 211–223. Routledge (2018)

37. Onwuegbuzie, A.J., Leech, N.L.: Validity and qualitative research: an oxymoron? Qual. Quant. **41**(2), 233–249 (2007)

38. Pappachan, P., et al.: Towards privacy-aware smart buildings: capturing, communicating, and enforcing privacy policies and preferences. In: 2017 IEEE 37th International Conference on Distributed Computing Systems Workshops (ICDCSW), pp. 193–198. IEEE (2017)

39. Perera, C., McCormick, C., Bandara, A.K., Price, B.A., Nuseibeh, B.: Privacy-by-design framework for assessing Internet of Things applications and platforms. In: Proceedings of the 6th International Conference on the Internet of Things, pp. 83–92 (2016)

40. Rogers, Y., Sharp, H., Preece, J.: Interaction Design: Beyond Human-Computer Interaction. Wiley (2011)

41. Sutagundar, A., Ettinamani, M., Attar, A.: IoT based smart shopping mall. In: 2018 Second International Conference on Green Computing and Internet of Things (ICGCIoT), pp. 355–360. IEEE (2018)

42. Tabassum, M., Kosinski, T., Lipford, H.R.: "i don't own the data": end user perceptions of smart home device data practices and risks. In: Fifteenth Symposium on Usable Privacy and Security (SOUPS 2019), pp. 435–450 (2019)

43. Tabassum, M., Kosinski, T., Lipford, H.R.: "i don't own the data": end user perceptions of smart home device data practices and risks. In: Fifteenth Symposium on Usable Privacy and Security (SOUPS 2019), pp. 435–450. USENIX Association, Santa Clara (2019), https://www.usenix.org/conference/soups2019/presentation/tabassum

44. Torcelini, P., et al.: Doe commercial building benchmark models. Technical report, National Renewable Energy Lab.(NREL), Golden, CO, United States (2008)

45. Tuzcuoglu, D., Yang, D., de Vries, B., Sungur, A.: Social interaction in an office environment: A qualitative study after relocation to a smart office. In: Transdisciplinary Workplace Research Conference 2020 (2020)

46. Uskov, V.L., Bakken, J.P., Pandey, A., Singh, U., Yalamanchili, M., Penumatsa, A.: Smart university taxonomy: features, components, systems. In: Smart Education and E-Learning 2016, pp. 3–14. Springer (2016)

47. Vasileva, R., Rodrigues, L., Hughes, N., Greenhalgh, C., Goulden, M., Tennison, J.: What smart campuses can teach us about smart cities: user experiences and open data. Information **9**(10), 251 (2018)

48. Vattapparamban, E., Çiftler, B.S., Güvenç, I., Akkaya, K., Kadri, A.: Indoor occupancy tracking in smart buildings using passive sniffing of probe requests. In: 2016 IEEE International Conference on Communications Workshops (ICC), pp. 38–44 (2016)

49. Wachter, S.: Normative challenges of identification in the Internet of Things: privacy, profiling, discrimination, and the GDPR. Comput. Law Secur. Rev. **34**(3), 436–449 (2018)
50. Wang, L., et al.: Data capsule: a new paradigm for automatic compliance with data privacy regulations. In: Heterogeneous Data Management, Polystores, and Analytics for Healthcare, pp. 3–23. Springer (2019)
51. Yao, Y., Basdeo, J.R., Kaushik, S., Wang, Y.: Defending my castle: a co-design study of privacy mechanisms for smart homes. In: Proceedings of the 2019 CHI Conference on Human Factors in Computing Systems, pp. 1–12 (2019)
52. Yao, Y., Basdeo, J.R., Mcdonough, O.R., Wang, Y.: Privacy perceptions and designs of bystanders in smart homes. Proc. ACM Hum.-Comput. Interact. **3**(CSCW), 1–24 (2019)
53. Zeng, E., Mare, S., Roesner, F.: End user security and privacy concerns with smart homes. In: Thirteenth Symposium on Usable Privacy and Security (SOUPS 2017), pp. 65–80 (2017)
54. Zeng, E., Roesner, F.: Understanding and improving security and privacy in multi-user smart homes: a design exploration and in-home user study. In: 28th USENIX Security Symposium (USENIX Security 19), pp. 159–176 (2019)
55. Zhang, H., Li, J., Wen, B., Xun, Y., Liu, J.: Connecting intelligent things in smart hospitals using NB-IoT. IEEE Internet Things J. **5**(3), 1550–1560 (2018)
56. Zheng, S., Apthorpe, N., Chetty, M., Feamster, N.: User perceptions of smart home IoT privacy. Proc. ACM Hum.-Comput. Interact. **2**(CSCW), 1–20 (2018)
57. Zheng, X., Cai, Z., Li, Y.: Data linkage in smart Internet of Things systems: a consideration from a privacy perspective. IEEE Commun. Mag. **56**(9), 55–61 (2018)
58. Ziegeldorf, J.H., Morchon, O.G., Wehrle, K.: Privacy in the Internet of Things: threats and challenges. Secur. Commun. Netw. **7**(12), 2728–2742 (2014)

Situation Critical: Intensive Cybersecurity Care Needed

Lynne Coventry[1]([✉]) [ID], Elizabeth Sillence[2] [ID], Richard Brown[2] [ID],
Dawn Branley-Bell[2] [ID], Pasquale Mari[3] [ID], Caruso Saverio[3], Alessandra Casaroli[3],
Fabio Rizzoni[3] [ID], and Sabina Magalini[3] [ID]

[1] University of Abertay, Dundee, UK
l.coventry@abertay.ac.uk
[2] Northumbria University, Newcastle upon Tyne, UK
[3] Catholic University of the Sacred Heart, Milan, Italy

Abstract. Healthcare organisations are increasingly targeted by cybercriminals. Such attacks are not just an attack on data but on this critical infrastructure – putting lives at risk. They face multiple challenges in maintaining their cybersecurity, including the technology infrastructure in use, the heterogeneity of healthcare and admin staff and the IT and cybersecurity skills within the organization.

This paper focuses on healthcare and admin staff within a single hospital in Italy. The study sought to understand the differences in perceptions of culture between different staff groups and the overall relationship between these perceptions and behaviours.

The methodology consisted of a cultural, behavioural and data use questionnaire, translated into Italian and distributed to doctors, nurses and administrators.

Linear regression models suggest that security culture significantly predicts how important and achievable staff perceive cybersecurity behaviours to be. Further analyses found significant differences between the doctors and other staff groups. Doctors reported a significantly more negative perception of cybersecurity culture. They also perceived cybersecurity behaviours to be significantly less important and less achievable than the other two groups. Doctors were also most likely to copy and access patient data outside of the institution, albeit for benign or patient centered reasons.

Overall, in terms of cybersecurity, doctors were the least compliant staff group – albeit with the best of intentions (i.e., focus upon patient care). These data, alongside other research, suggest that healthcare staff focus on delivering patient care and see cybersecurity as interfering with, rather than facilitating, their clinical practice. There is a need for change to ensure that cybersecurity measures are appropriate, work within the clinical workflow and staff accept cybersecurity as crucial to protecting patients.

Keywords: cybersecurity · culture · perception · behaviours

© The Author(s) 2025
M. Mehrnezhad and S. Parkin (Eds.): STAST 2022, LNCS 13855, pp. 93–112, 2025.
https://doi.org/10.1007/978-3-031-83072-3_6

1 Introduction

The rapid global proliferation of Health Information Technology (HIT) alongside emerging networked medical devices has introduced significant risk to healthcare organisations (HCOs), who are charged with protecting the privacy and integrity of large databases of protected health information as well as a critical infrastructure. Unfortunately, this proliferation has not been matched with investment in cybersecurity, resulting in an ongoing increase in cybersecurity breaches in HCOs which has put patients' privacy, health and ultimately their lives at risk. Despite these risks, and the operational and financial consequences for HCOs, very few studies have systematically examined the cybersecurity threats in healthcare; and specifically the role of staff behaviour in those risks.

Cybersecurity in HCOs is an ongoing challenge and is still underdeveloped compared to other sectors such as finance [1]. The sector faces many problems ranging from technical issues such as legacy systems and a lack of security designed into equipment, to personnel issues such as a workforce that is overworked and fatigued, and an inability to attract high calibre cybersecurity staff as a result of low pay in comparison to other sectors.

Despite the growing threat of cyberattacks in healthcare, the research on this topic is nascent and there are major gaps in existing knowledge [2]. The literature tends to focus on technological solutions. Safeguards such as encryption, shredding documents, locking doors, and using passwords, should be implemented to limit both inadvertent information disclosures and cyberattacks. However, these safeguards rely on staff to act securely and there are few user studies focusing on cybersecurity culture and how this is manifest in staffs' cybersecurity behaviours. ENISA defines cybersecurity culture as the knowledge, beliefs, perceptions, attitudes, assumptions, norms and values of people relating to cybersecurity [4]. Organisational culture researchers point to the idea that organisations, rather than having a single culture may have a number of coexisting subcultures linked to different management teams [5]. In addition there may be other aspects of the overall organizational culture that are in conflict with the cybersecurity culture, for example medical ethics [6].

This study investigates the attitudes of different staff groups across a large Italian hospital It is important to note that the purpose of this study is not to highlight a lack of cybersecurity behaviours by particular staff or attribute blame, rather it is to understand more about the culture and the impact this has on behaviours. Secondly, restricting this study to a single hospital avoided issues around potential differences in culture and ICT policies between hospitals but, it is not our intention to single out this hospital but present it as representative of the sector.

In this study, we sought to answer the following: (1) Do different staff groups have different perceptions of cybersecurity? (2) Do these staff groups differ in their perceptions of the importance and difficulty of carrying out cybersecurity behaviours mandated in the IT policy? (3) Do perceptions of cybersecurity predict importance and implementation difficulty? To answer these questions, we conducted a survey which first measured staff attitudes and then asked about their perceived importance and difficulty of enacting each of the behaviours required by the hospital's IT policy.

In this paper we first summarise the background literature, then detail our method and findings. We finish with a discussion of the issues and make recommendations for hospitals and other HCOs to improve their cybersecurity culture.

2   Background Literature

HCOs have utilised advances in information and communication technologies to achieve theirs goals of boosting the quality and efficiency of patient services. However, the healthcare sector is consistently the number one target for cybercriminals [7]. Attacks on HCOs have increased exponentially in recent years driven by several key factors including the simple fact that they are an easy and lucrative target. A health data record is worth more than a bank record in some countries [8]. Attacks may use ransomware to extort money. Other target the equipment and services, for example by leaking their protected health information or hacking medical devices on which they rely, such as insulin pumps. There are several gangs operating in this space including Vice Society [9], Mespinoza [10] and the Conti group [11].

Attacks on HCOs have made headlines around the world. WannaCry in 2017 targeted Microsoft Windows XP systems. While not specifically aimed at HCOs, HCOs were particularly affected with Britain's National Health Service (NHS) reporting different equipment impacted and an inability to provide care for a period of time [12].More recently the attack on HSE in Ireland [13] was the biggest attack against any health service in history. The attack impacted the HSE's 54 public hospitals, and other private hospitals which rely on its IT infrastructure. This resulted in over 700GB of unencrypted data being exfiltrated; 75% of the IT environment encrypted by the attackers, resulting in restricted access to medical records and staff being forced to revert to using pen and paper methods and test results being delivered by Deliveroo.

Over the last decade, the vast majority of HCOs have experienced a cyberattack [14]. This has resulted in many critical data breaches exposing the sensitive medical records of millions of patients [15]. Cyberattacks continued to increase during the COVID-19 pandemic. The CyberPeace Institute [16] analysed data from 313 incidents in the healthcare sector across 35 countries during the period 19 August 2020 to 7 January 2022, finding 55 attacks on hospitals across 17 countries. These attacks resulted in a breach of 15 million records, including social security numbers, patient medical, financial data, HIV test results and private details of medical donors. These also impacted operations, with an incident's impact averaging 12 days for hospitals with a reported maximum of 42 days. Cyberbreaches add to the financial burden of the healthcare industry because of subsequently imposed penalties and fines. However, the problem of cybersecurity goes beyond financial consequences and patients' privacy; it also poses a threat to patient safety [17]. The impact on operations can lead to patients being redirected to other locations, systems going offline, appointment cancellations etc. These cause delays, which no matter how short, can lead to significant negative impacts on patient wellbeing, and ultimately patient deaths. It's not just delays that can lead to patient harm.

The use of technology supports doctors and employees in their duties through remote work for health treatment and administrative purposes [18]. However, networked medical devices and other mobile health technologies are a double-edged sword: The benefits of medical device technology advances are transformative for healthcare, but they also carry hidden dangers that expose patients and HCOs to safety and security risks [19]. Among the unintended consequences of healthcare's increased digitisation and networked connectivity are the risks of being hacked, being infected with malware, and being vulnerable to unauthorised data access [20]. These attacks even extend to the World Health Organisation (WHO) [21].

Given the high-risk nature of the sensitive data handled through HCOs, the critical services they deliver 24/7 and the impact of delays on service users it is important for the healthcare sector to be fully aware of their vulnerabilities. It is then important to investigate the root cause of these to enable them to be addressed. Unfortunately, the Healthcare industry lags behind other industries in terms of their cybersecurity practices [18, 22] and preventing data breaches and other cyberattacks will involve major changes in the Heathcare sector – from development and procurement to organisational culture and staff behaviours [23].

Attackers exploit technical vulnerabilities and staff behaviour [24]. This is not a new problem, security has been a major concern for those adopting electronic health record systems (EHRs) for over 25 years [25] and continues to be a concern [26] as records and medical devices can increasingly be accessed remotely. The portable and accessible nature of EHRs and devices make them susceptible to unauthorised access and modifications [27]. Hackers can fraudulently use remote access to obtain information in HCO databases [27]. Hackers can also take advantage of staff loopholes and poor cyberhygiene to steal data [28].

Recently, the COVID-19 pandemic has placed further pressures on the global health care system with increasing number of attacks targeting HCOs [29], not just hospitals, and cybercriminals even impersonating the WHO [21]. The pandemic has created new challenges such as increased reliance on remote working including: Healthcare staff may have limited experience in working remotely, leaving them more vulnerable [30]; Remote consultations and sharing of information may have opened up new attack vectors [31].; and some scams aimed specifically at the health care sector, for example the sale of Personal Protective Equipment which may have phished sensitive information or money through luring emails [32].

Phishing is a particular problem for HCOs, with hospitals receiving a significant volume of potentially malicious emails [24]. While staff may be aware of phishing, and completion of mandatory training may increase awareness of the risk, staff can be more vulnerable to spear phishing and must be aware of leaking information on social media which can be used as part of the bait.

A number of review articles point to numerous issues contributing to poor cybersecurity in the healthcare sector. For example, a narrative review of this area concludes that areas of human behaviour, technology, internal processes and governance all contribute [33]. Dykstra et al. [34] found that lack of expertise, time, and money were reported as the primary barriers to improved cybersecurity for private practices. Despite the variety of contributors, a bibliometric analysis [2] of 472 journal articles revealed that the majority of research focusses on technology. Therefore, the non-technical aspects such as human and organisational aspects, strategies and management are less well understood. Clearly in such a complicated environment, a holistic sociotechnical understanding is required [35–37].

A scoping review identified 9 main challenges: Remote working security assurance; endpoint device management; staff behaviour; security awareness; board-level risk assessment communication; business continuity plans; lack of coordinated incident response; limited budget and vulnerable medical devices. The review highlighted that while some solutions had been put in place more effort was needed in terms of human behaviours [38].

2.1 Device Security

Researchers have demonstrated cybersecurity vulnerabilities in medical devices including automated internal cardioverter defibrillators, bedside infusion pumps, and implantable insulin delivery systems [17, 39]. Such flaws, if abused, could lead to a number of consequences ranging from exposure of personal and private health information to the malfunction of devices resulting in physical harm. Though there are not yet any reports of patients directly affected by the exploitation of a medical device's cybersecurity vulnerability, the potential for such events has led to concerted efforts from manufacturers, regulators, and security professionals to advocate for and improve medical cybersecurity practices.

In 2019 the U.S. Food and Drug Administration (FDA) historically announced the first recall of a connected diabetes device. Other companies have also had warning letters issued relative to insulin pumps where the communication between the pump and its remote control can be hijacked, settings modified and data extracted [19, 40].

A recommendation within the literature is to improve technical cybersecurity measures for medical devices using the "secure-by-design" approach, i.e., building security into the design of the device rather than as an afterthought. For medical device manufacturers it is often very costly and ineffective to secure devices after the healthcare facilities have purchased them.

Legaspi [41] report on an exploratory qualitative study which aimed to explore the cybersecurity measures healthcare managers use to reduce patient endangerment resulting from backdoor intrusions into medical devices. They interviewed 8 participants in managerial positions who were knowledgeable about the logistics of how information is uploaded from medical devices and encryption. The managers agreed that risky cyberhygiene behaviours when using medical devices pose a significant threat to patient information privacy and patient safety. Therefore it is essential that security system designers understand and accommodate user behaviour to reach an optimal level of security assurance [36].

2.2 Haphazard Security Behaviours

A major challenge for organisations is ensuring that employees adhere to information security policies and the behaviours listed within these [42]. Existing research suggests that many security incidents are a result of human behaviour [43]. Many employees routinely make a conscious decision to violate cybersecurity mandates because they want to expedite their work or increase their own productivity [44] or fulfil a goal they perceive as in conflict with such policies.

Behaviour can also be driven by staff beliefs. For example medical practice owners consider patient data to be well protected and an unlikely target for cyber-attacks and breaches and therefore may not see the need to change their security behaviours [34]. There are additional, unique pressures within healthcare as care providers must balance patient safety/care with patient confidentiality and security. Hence, there is a conflict in healthcare professionals' values and cybersecurity [6]. While they may understand the importance of security, they may choose to circumvent it when it is perceived to interfere with delivery of efficient patient care. Frequently, staff may feel forced to make a decision whether to adhere to a security measure or live with a level of insecurity to deliver patient care quickly. Qualitative studies in hospitals have observed a number of security workarounds to facilitate patient care. For example computers left unlocked to save time logging on and off the system, and sharing user credentials with new staff due to delays in IT issuing new staff credentials [36, 37].

Albarrak [15] studied password behaviours of 352 randomly selected nurses. 92% of the nurses agreed that password management was important, but this did not mean that they followed best practice. 81% had never changed from the default password, 54% would not change their password if it might be compromised, 33% shared their password with colleagues, 32% allowed others to use their credentials and 16% did not log off applications at the end of a work session. 33% thought it was the joint responsibility of the system administrator and the user to protect user passwords. Studies such as this call for raised awareness among staff to reduce user "misbehaviour". Such calls may be misguided if staff are aware of the importance of password management in this instance but place more emphasis on a conflicting value such as efficacy of patient treatment. It is therefore vital that we understand the factors driving insecure staff behaviour, when awareness is not the issue.

There are many different factors which could potentially influence staff cybersecurity behaviour. Hospital staff are widely known to be overworked, with a high prevalence of burnout and fatigue experienced [45] this can result in mistakes with regards cybersecurity [46] which they do not prioritise over duty of care [37].

Jalali et al. [47] investigated employee phishing threat perceptions in a healthcare setting. Their findings suggest that the intentions of staff to follow security protocols do not significantly influence an employee's rate of clicking on simulated phishing emails – however, there was a significant positive correlation between employee workload and phishing vulnerability. In other words, while staff may fully intend to detect phishing attacks, they are not able to do so, and the higher their workload and fatigue, the less likely they were to detect such attacks.

Another example is Stobert et al. [48] who surveyed 347 Canadian nurses and doctors working in Emergency Departments. They found that many different security behaviours were required of staff. The difficulty of implementing some of these behaviours led to circumvention of these behaviours, for instance over half used another staff member's login.

2.3 Cybersecurity Culture

Research is starting to explore organisational culture as a key influencer of security behaviours. There are various definitions of organisational culture, but an overarching theme is that it is represented by a system of shared values and beliefs among employees [49]. As such, culture can be viewed as a tool to shape the behaviour of employees [50]. Although various subcultures exist within a single organisation (e.g. distinguished on the basis of occupation, work group or hierarchical level), a "strong" or integrated organisational culture is reflected in key values and beliefs being shared relatively consistently organisation-wide [49]. Similarly cybersecurity culture reflects the values and beliefs relating to security shared by all members at all levels of the organisation [51] but there is disagreement in terms of how to operationalise the concept [52]. Security advocates contend that only a significant change in security culture can reduce the number of security breaches experienced and that user behavior can be cultivated through a security culture that promotes security-conscious decision-making and adherence to security policy [53].

There are numerous constructs related to security culture as well as disagreement in terms of how to operationalize the concept. Despite this, there have been several attempts to measure cybersecurity culture in HCOs. For example surveys in Poland [54] and Finland [55] reported that medical professionals lack sufficient cybersecurity training. Similarly, Gioulekas et al. [56] found a lack of security training and competence in their large scale survey of the cybersecurity culture within 3 European HCOs (in Greece, Portugal & Romania). Their findings revealed that only 22% of non-technical staff felt sufficiently trained in cybersecurity, 38% were confident they could recognise a cybersecurity issue, 30% understood the consequences of sharing their login credentials. Although not feeling competent, 76% of staff did feel that following security policy would enable them to do their job better.

Kessler et al. [28] developed the Information Security Climate Index (ISCI), which aimed to measure shared perceptions of IT security policies within an organisation. The index included what is practiced in the organisation; the importance placed on cybersecurity, and laxness surrounding cybersecurity activities. A strong cybersecurity culture (or information security climate) would mean that clear rules and procedures were in place for handling confidential data, and importance is placed on keeping data secure even if it means taking extra time to do so. They surveyed 261 employees across four occupational groups (Certified nursing assistants, dentists, pharmacists and physician assistants). There was a significant relationship between the ISCI and employee motivation to behave securely and their actual behaviour. In addition to differences reported in the culture and behaviours of the different occupational groups; pharmacists reported a better IS culture and behaviours than physician assistants. Other research has also investigated if there are differences between the different professional staff groups regarding their cybersecurity behaviours but this area is still sparse and what evidence exists is mixed. For example, in a comparison of 453 healthcare professionals in Kuwait, nurses were found to exhibit higher cybersecurity aptitude than other disciplines [57].

In the remainder of this paper, we will discuss our method for comparing three groups of staff within a large hospital in Italy, comparing doctors, nurses and administrators in terms of their individual attitudes towards cybersecurity culture and their perceptions of the importance and difficulty to follow those behaviours described in the hospital's IT policy.

3   Method

3.1   Data Protection and Ethics Considerations

Our study was approved by Northumbria Psychology Department and by the Ethics Committee of the hospital. As requested by the Ethics Committee and in line with GDPR, specific informed consents to the processing of personal data submitted to the participants were completed before completing the questionnaire. An online platform was used to distribute the questionnaire to ensure that it was pseudonymised. This was necessary as the researchers collecting the data were based in the same institution and their identity was not to be known by the researchers.

3.2   Participants

Participants were all from the same large hospital in Italy. The hospital has around 6000 staff. However not all staff fall into the three categories of staff for this study. 247 hospital staff completed the questionnaire (96 administrative staff, 85 nurses, 64 doctors, 2 missing occupational data). The mean participant age was 42.17 years (range = 23–64yrs, $SD = 11.67$yrs). A convenience sample was used of those willing to complete the survey after being contacted through their hospital email. The doctors were all residents from the Schools of Surgery and Internal Medicine and were recruited via the school's administration. The nurses were from across the hospital and were recruited via the Nurse Management System. Administrative staff were from across the hospital and were recruited via the Human Resource Office.

3.3   Measures

Participants provided their age, department and occupational group for their role at the hospital. Participants were asked a series of questions to explore staff engagement with cybersecurity behaviours within their HCO. This was developed as part of the EU Panacea research project (www.panacearesearch.eu). Three measurement instruments were used for this particular study:

Cybersecurity attitudes explored underlying attitudes towards cybersecurity in the workplace and was used to assess the current cybersecurity culture within the hospital. This measure was adapted for a health care setting from the Integrated Behaviour Model [37] Participants were asked to indicate their agreement with 34 statements relating to the following 9 dimensions: *responsibility, attitudes, descriptive norms, subjective norms, patient care, rewards and sanctions, perceived control, response efficacy, and self-efficacy*. Participants responded on a five-point Likert scale from '*strongly disagree*' to '*strongly agree*'. The chronbachs alpha was calculated at $\alpha = .7$ (an '*acceptable*' level of internal consistency).

Data Access consisted of a set of questions were created which explored technology use and staff access to patient data outside of the official work system. Participants were asked how frequently they access patient data outside of the workplace and the technology used to access this data. These included use of USBs, personal mobile, email etc. This data was only used for descriptive purposes to assess the frequency with which different groups were accessing data outside of the official system.

Lastly, we explored how **importance and achievability beliefs** of staff. 52 security behaviours were extracted from the HCO's IT security policy and participants were asked to rate each of these behaviours in terms of importance (on a five-point Likert scale from *'not at all important'* to *'very important'*) and achievability (on a five-point Likert scale from *'not at all possible'* to *'always stick to this behaviour'*). These behaviours ranged from not sharing passwords, logging out of workstations to unplugging devices at the end of the day.

3.4 Procedure

An informed consent and questionnaires were created in English and then translated into Italian and validated by the Italian researchers. The questionnaire was distributed to the three staff groups (nurses, doctors & administration staff) and responses gathered pseudo-anonymously via the online system by the Italian researchers. The data was then anonymised and sent to the UK researchers for statistical analysis.

3.5 Analysis

All statistical analyses were performed using SPSS software (v.26). The majority of analyses are descriptive in nature. The main inferential analysis was an analysis of covariance (ANCOVA). An a priori power analysis indicated that a sample size of 206 was required to detect a small to medium effect of .25 for an ANCOVA with power of .90 and an alpha of .05. This would allow us to investigate the difference in importance and achievability dimensions between occupational groups, whilst accounting for differences in security attitudes. To account for the possibility of missing data, our final recruited sample size was 247 participants. Individual responses for survey items were provided as ordinal variables. The sum of these responses were treated as continuous variables for the analysis of attitudinal and behavioural constructs, a practice common in the treatment of Likert-style data [58]. For this main inferential analysis, the dependent variables (importance and achievability dimensions) were found to violate the assumption of normality for analysis of covariance (ANCOVA). However, previous research has found that when sample size is high (as in this study) the parametric ANCOVA test is robust to such violations [59, 60]. All other assumptions were met.

4 Results

Data access results revealed that 70% of staff reported never accessing data outside of the workplace. However, this rate varied by occupational group (see Table 1). Table 2 presents technology that hospital staff reported using to access patient data.

Table 1. Percentage of staff accessing data externally

Access outside work	Frequently	Regularly	Occasionally	Infrequently	Never
Nurses *(N = 85)*	0.0%	0.0%	2.3%	1.2%	95.3%
Admin *(N = 96)*	2.2%	1.1%	3.3%	8.8%	67.0%
Doctors *(N = 64)*	4.7%	4.7%	31.2%	20.3%	39.1%
Overall *(N = 247)*	2.0%	1.6%	10.1%	8.9%	70.4%

Table 2. Use of technology to access patient data

Technology	Yes	No	N/A
Personal smartphone	26.32%	66.80%	6.88%
Work smartphone	7.69%	85.02%	7.29%
USB	17.81%	74.09%	8.10%
VPN	23.89%	68.02%	8.10%
CD/DVD	8.50%	83.00%	8.50%
Email	42.51%	49.39%	8.10%
Other	1.62%	90.28%	8.10%

A chi-square test examined the relationship between occupational group and the use of different technology types to access patient data. Each binary response (yes/no) for use of technology was treated as a separate observation for each participant, to determine the difference between groups for the overall technology use. The relationship between group and use of technology was significant, $\chi 2(2, n = 1579) = 148.15$, p $< .001$. Examining this group-based difference, over 70% of doctors reported having recorded/accessed/or copied patient data via email, compared to 29% nurses and 36% admin staff. Similarly, 61% of doctors reported accessing patient data via their personal smartphone, compared to 16% of nurses and 13% of administrators (see Fig. 1).

The cybersecurity attitudes results varied by dimension. The highest overall agreement score was for statements from the 'descriptive norms' dimension (statements about how other staff are perceived to behave securely). The lowest overall agreement score was for the 'sanctions' dimension (statements about how staff believe there will be sanctions for failing to behave securely; see Table 3 and Fig. 3).

There were occupational group differences in security attitude scores. A one-way analysis of variance found a significant difference in overall security attitude between groups (nurses, administrators, doctors) $F(2,242) = 22.25, p < .001$. Post-hoc analyses showed that overall security attitudes reported by doctors ($M = 3.2/5, SD = .37$) were significantly lower than that of nurses ($M = 3.56/5, SD = .30$) and administrators ($M = 3.51/5, SD = .38$). (See Fig. 3).

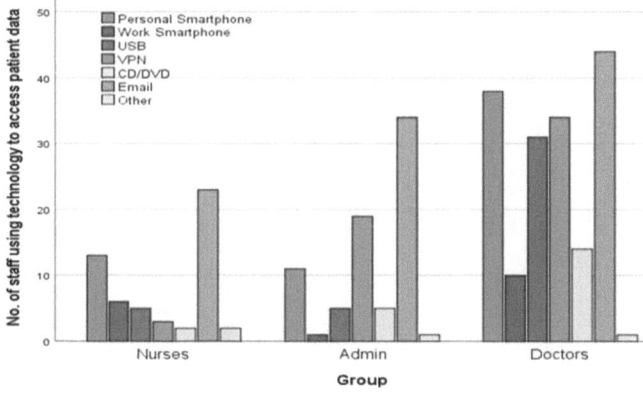

Fig. 1. Reported use of technology types to access patient data by occupational group

Table 3. Security culture attitude scores by dimension

Dimension	n	Min (1)	Max (5)	Mean	SD
Responsibility	247	1	5	3.20	0.71
Attitudes	247	1.67	4.67	3.44	0.44
Descriptive Norms	247	1.75	5	4.10	0.59
Subjective Norms	247	1	5	3.42	0.81
Patient Care	247	0	5	3.85	0.76
Rewards	247	0	5	3.60	0.73
Sanctions	247	1	5	2.70	0.83
Perceived Control	247	1	4.2	2.80	0.56
Response Efficacy	247	1	5	3.26	0.62
Self-efficacy	247	1.67	5	3.87	0.64
Total security attitude	247	83	149	117.2	12.94

4.1 Security Protective Behaviours

The overall ratings for the perceived importance and achievability of security behaviours were high. Over 67% of all staff gave all behaviours the highest rating and over 63% provided the highest rating for the perceived achievability of these behaviours (see Table 4). Of the individual security behaviours, the lowest rating was for 'Always switch off workstation, printers and scanners at the socket after use' with over 25% of participants indicating that this behaviour is neither important nor achievable.

Two linear regression models assessed the influence of security perceptions. Model 1 assessed the effect on perceived importance and the Model 2 on perceived achievability of cybersecurity behaviours. Age and occupational group were included as covariates. The results indicated that 25% of variance in perceived importance of protective behaviours was explained by Model 1 and that the model was significant, $F(4,237) = 19.28$, p < .001. Security attitudes significantly predicted the perceived importance of protective

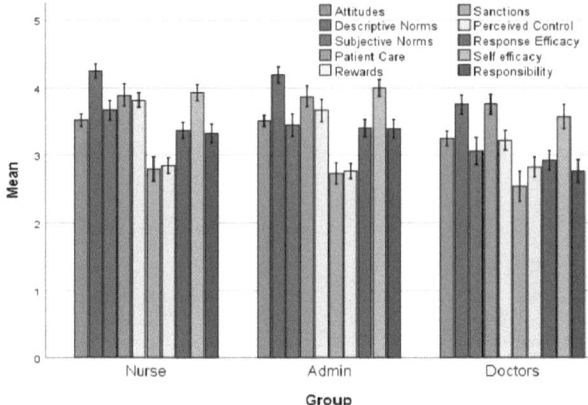

Fig. 2. Comparison of occupational group attitude scores by dimension Error bars represent 95% confidence intervals.

Table 4. Overall responses for importance and achievability of cybersecurity behaviours

Dimension	*1 (low)*	*2*	*3*	*4*	*5 (high)*	*N/A*	*Missing*
Importance	3.46%	2.55%	11.62%	10.64%	67.50%	2.62%	1.62%
Achievability	3.94%	3.58%	13.34%	11.30%	63.35%	2.87%	1.62%

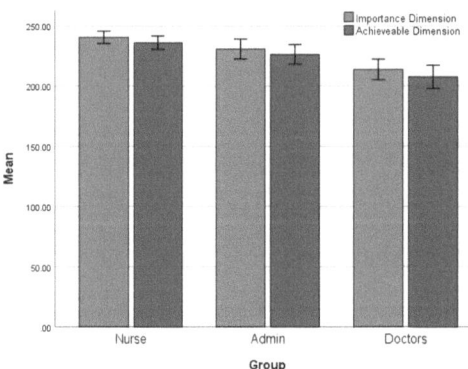

Fig. 3. Comparison of importance and achievability btw groups (min:52, max:260)

behaviours ($\beta = .41$, $p < .001$). Model 2 explained 27% of variance in perceived achievability and the model was significant, $F(4,237) = 22.00$, $p < .001$. Security attitudes significantly predicted perceived achievability ($\beta = .44$, $p < .001$).

Analyses of covariance found significant effects for occupational group on both importance ($F(2,237) = 3.196$, $p = .043$, $\eta2 = .026$) and achievability ($F(2,237) = 3.103$, $p = .047$, $\eta2 = .026$), whilst controlling for group differences in perceptions. Doctors reported lower perceived importance of behaviours ($M = 213.60$, $SD = 34.16$)

than nurses (M = 240.83, SD = 24.41) and administrators (M = 229.10, SD = 39.67). Doctors also reported lower perceived achievability scores for behaviours (M = 207.74, SD = 38.20) compared with nurses (M = 236.36, SD = 25.95) and administrators (M = 224.47, SD = 39.17; see Fig. 3).

5   Discussion

The results, in terms of the relationship between general security attitudes (or culture) and perceptions of different behaviours, are in line with the findings of Kessler [28] and AlKabani et al. [61] and have important practical implications. Fundamentally, the cybersecurity culture has the potential to positively impact employees' motivation and behaviour, which in turn could reduce the number of cybersecurity breaches, or at least reduce the likelihood of such breaches. While many cybersecurity breaches result from insider behaviours or lack thereof, it is essential to focus on organizational features that influence employee behaviours rather than simply the behaviour itself. Particularly when staff may be acting insecurely with good intent (e.g., aiming to prioritise patient care). Investigated the role of socio-organizational factors on the compliance with IT security policy. Of particular interest was the low rating for Perceived Control. Cultural factors such as training, management commitment, and accountability play a critical role in how policies are received and implemented.

Another interesting finding was that different professional groups had significantly different perceptions suggesting different subcultures. Kessler et al. [28] found differences between other professional groupings, finding pharmacists to have the best IS culture, motivation, and behaviours. Understanding the underlying reasons for these differences is fundamental to finding appropriate interventions. It may be that different interventions are needed for different groups. In this study, the doctors having significantly lower perceptions of the culture and the importance of behaviours may result from the relationship between junior and senior doctors that we found in our earlier qualitative studies [37]. Different levels of staff are required to share logins to maintain productivity and do not feel that it is something they can control. The role of senior staff in this instance is crucial. As Zohar [62] suggests, the training the supervisor is important given the central role they play in shaping the organizational culture [63]. It is therefore essential that we explore within each staff group, any potential mismatch between the cybersecurity policy, their relationship with other staff levels, and clinical workflow and how this is experienced in terms of actual behaviour. Understanding which cybersecurity behaviours are misaligned with the workflow allows the system to be redesigned to support the workflow rather than leaving the user trying to bridge the gap.

Hedström et al. [64] identify the control-based compliance model as problematic in healthcare situations, and instead propose value-based compliance as a solution. Identifying value conflicts can be used as a strategic tool and an opportunity to reflect on and improve healthcare practice and cybersecurity governance. This includes reviewing the nature and number of cybersecurity behaviours expected from staff. Indeed, Loi et al. [6] point to the conflict between the values of medical ethics and cybersecurity. One area for consideration in terms of alignment with values is whether cybersecurity behaviours should be seen as part of the Hippocratic oath that clinicians take as a symbolic decla-ration to provide care in the best interests of the patient and to maintain their privacy [65].

While many researchers would propose new technology to resolve cybersecurity issues, the idea that technology always solves the cybersecurity problem is a miscon-ception and may just create new problems. It may be the case that the Healthcare sector needs to learn to live with some insecurity and effectively manage the risks as they do in other contexts. Effectively managing a certain level of insecurity within the environ-mental constraints can be more effective than deploying expensive or invasive security mechanisms (which are simply worked around) which are in conflict with other medical values. However, this must be done with knowledge of what is actually going on to enable effective risk management and shared values.

5.1 Limitations

This work was carried out within a single hospital. The nature of the security behaviours required by different hospitals may vary, making it difficult to generalize results when using different sets of behaviours to calculate the outcome variable. Carrying out the work within a single hospital, also meant that we did not have the power to utilize the factors within the cybersecurity attitude measurement as individual items in the subsequent regression analyses and so attitude was treated as a single measurement. More refined work on each of the culture variables and the impact on behaviour is needed. As with much research on cybersecurity behaviours, a self report measure was used to indirectly infer the behaviours that may be enacted in the hospital. More work is required with objective measures of actual behaviours in the workplace.

5.2 Future Work

This work forms part of a small number of studies directly exploring cybersecurity culture and behaviours within the healthcare sector and there is clearly a lot more work needed to understand cybersecurity culture and how to create an effective cybersecurity culture which is not in conflict with other values such as medical ethics. Other factors relating to cybersecurity culture are also worthy for investigation including perceptions of fairness and trust in the organization. While we have seen variation in the attitudes of different professional groups, they are not the only users of some healthcare systems – the patient can also be a user and may have access to their healthcare records and be users of different connected medical devices. Very little has been researched from the patient perspective. As connected medical technology is increasingly prevalent offering a host of new therapeutic potentials, and medicine has shifted from a paternalistic approach where patients are informed and instructed by clinicians, to a collaborative effort of shared goal setting and decision making between parties, so too has the understanding of the ethics and acquisition of consent evolved. It may be necessary as we move forward to include discussions about cybersecurity related risks as part of the informed consent obtained by clinicians, though exactly what form this take requires further research [66].

In terms of medical device development, a grass roots movement started in 2016 suggested that there should be a Hippocratic Oath for medical devices containing 5 principles [67]. Its mission is to ensure technologies with the potential to impact public safety and human life are worthy of our trust" [68].

6   Conclusion

HCOs have made some efforts to address cybersecurity challenges but these mainly focus on technical measures, and raising security awareness, through mandatory training. This has led to an additive approach to security controls and expected behaviours –adding more – but expecting staff to remember and follow over 50 security behaviours (in this instance) is problematic. HCOs should review their policy and minimize the pressure on staff.

Broader research is required to explore how to deploy the necessary technical controls but ensure they are appropriate and fit the clinical workflow and medical professionals appreciate the value of these controls. It is also important to build more cyber resilience by ensuring a coordinated cybersecurity capacity to systematically assess vulnerabilities through the complex health care supply chain and respond to cyber threats; reduce human-related security incidents by exploring cybersecurity culture and the impact this has on security behaviours; and enhance strategic cybersecurity management by exploring crisis management planning, security risks reprioritization, and the optimization of cybersecurity budget and resource reallocation.

In conclusion, cyber-attacks on HC)s are likely to continue. Some of these will attempt to exploit poor cyberhygiene behaviours. A cybersecurity culture approach is required to fundamentally change behaviour. However, it is important that the technology is designed to fit with the clinical workflow, allow staff to maintain focus on the patient and ensure that systems are always immediately available so that the behaviours expected of staff are appropriate and not creating unnecessary burden and distraction from their goal of treating the patient or conflict with their medical values.

Acknowledgements. This work was completed as part of Panacea. Funded by the European Union's Horizon 2020 Research and Innovation Programme, under Grant Agreement no 826293.

Appendix 1

Responsibility: I believe everyone in the organisation should take responsibility in protecting the organisation from cybercrime/cyberattacks. It should be IT's responsibility to protect the organisation from cybercrime/cyberattacks. It is my responsibility to act securely to protect the organisation from cybercrime/cyberattacks.

Attitudes: It is inappropriate to act insecurely, even if a colleague asks me to. There are sometimes good reasons to ignore security rules. It is better to carry out my job securely, even if it is not as convenient and/or slows things down. I pride myself on acting securely and sticking to IT rules/policy.

Descriptive Norms: My colleagues behave securely at work. My colleagues will act less securely if they feel security slows them down. My colleagues regularly engage in at least one insecure behaviour at work.

Subjective Norms: My line manager believes that I should act securely at work. My colleagues believe I should act securely at work. My organisation believes that I should act securely at work. People at work expect me to support the team, even if this means insecure working.

Patient Care: Protecting patient data is just as important as providing good healthcare. I act less securely if I feel that it will enable me to provide better care for my patient. I act securely, even if it slows down patient care. Acting less securely puts patient care at risk.

Rewards and Sanctions: Secure behaviour at work is recognized. There is no incentive for secure behaviour at work. I am not aware of anyone ever being disciplined for behaving insecurely at work. I have previously been disciplined for behaving insecurely at work. I could suffer financial consequences for behaving insecurely at work. My organisation could incur substantial fines as a result of my insecure behaviour. The likelihood that I would be disciplined for insecure behaviour is very low.

Perceived Control: I have control over my security behaviours. The behaviour of other people in the organisation affects my security behaviours. It is not always possible to act securely.

Response Efficacy: My behaviour protects the organisation from cyberattacks and data breaches. It makes no difference if I act securely, if my colleagues do not do the same. Security behaviours are an unnecessary burden.

Self-efficacy: I do not have the right skills to be able to protect my organisation from a cyberattack or data breach. I am confident that I would be able to spot the signs of a cyberattack. I feel confident in my ability to act securely.

References

1. European Union Agency for Cybersecurity (ENISA): ENISA Threat Landscape 2021 (2021)
2. Jalali, M.S., Razak, S., Gordon, W., Perakslis, E., Madnick, S.: Health care and cybersecurity: bibliometric analysis of the literature. J. Med. Internet Res. **21**, e12644 (2019). https://doi.org/10.2196/12644
3. Office for Civil Rights (OCR): Summary of the HIPAA Privacy Rule. https://www.hhs.gov/hipaa/for-professionals/privacy/laws-regulations/index.html
4. ENISA: Cybersecurity Cultures in Organisations. European Union Agency for Network and Information Security (2017)
5. Deal, T.E., Kennedy, A.A.: Corporate Cultures: The Rites and Rituals of Corporate Life. Perseus Books (2000)
6. Loi, M., Christen, M., Kleine, N., Weber, K.: Cybersecurity in health – disentangling value tensions. J. Inf. Commun. Ethics Soc. **17** (2019). https://doi.org/10.1108/JICES-12-2018-0095
7. Zorabedian, J.: Why cybercriminals attack healthcare more than any other industry. https://nakedsecurity.sophos.com/2016/04/26/why-cybercriminals-attack-healthcare-more-than-any-other-industry/. Accessed 10 Feb 2022
8. Trustwave: 2019 Trustwave Global Security Report (2019)

9. Vice Society Ransomware Gang Attacks United Health Centers of San Joaquin Valley. https://www.hipaajournal.com/vice-society-ransomware-gang-attacks-united-health-centers-of-san-joaquin-valley/. Accessed 10 Feb 2022
10. HealthITSecurity: Mespinoza, Pysa Ransomware Pose Threat to Healthcare Cybersecurity. https://healthitsecurity.com/news/mespinoza-pysa-ransomware-pose-threat-to-healthcare-cybersecurity. Accessed 10 Feb 2022
11. HealthITSecurity: CISA, FBI, NSA Release Advisory Warning of Conti Ransomware Attacks. https://healthitsecurity.com/news/cisa-fbi-nsa-release-advisory-warning-of-conti-ransomware-attacks. Accessed 10 Feb 2022
12. Ehrenfeld, J.M.: WannaCry, cybersecurity and health information technology: a time to act. J. Med. Syst. **41**, 104 (2017). https://doi.org/10.1007/s10916-017-0752-1
13. HealthITSecurity: Ireland HSE Cyberattack is a Cautionary Tale for US Healthcare Orgs. https://healthitsecurity.com/news/ireland-hse-cyberattack-is-a-cautionary-tale-for-us-healthcare-orgs. Accessed 08 Feb 2022
14. Filkins, B.: Health care cyberthreat report: widespread compromises detected, compliance nighmare on horizon. https://www.qualityplusconsulting.com/res/infosec/2014-2_HealthCareCyberthreatReport.pdf. Accessed 10 Feb 2022
15. Albarrak, A.: Information security behavior among nurses in an academic hospital. HealthMED **6**, 2349–2354 (2012)
16. Cyber Incident Tracer #HEALTH. https://cit.cyberpeaceinstitute.org/. Accessed 10 Feb 2022
17. Perakslis, E.D.: Cybersecurity in health care. https://www.nejm.org/doi/10.1056/NEJMp1404358. https://doi.org/10.1056/NEJMp1404358. Accessed 08 Feb 2022
18. Kim, D., Choi, J., Han, K.: Risk management-based security evaluation model for telemedicine systems. BMC Med. Inform. Decis. Mak. **20**, 106 (2020). https://doi.org/10.1186/s12911-020-01145-7
19. Kintzlinger, M., Nissim, N.: Keep an eye on your personal belongings! The security of personal medical devices and their ecosystems. J. Biomed. Inform. **95**, 103233 (2019). https://doi.org/10.1016/j.jbi.2019.103233
20. Lecklider, T.: Mitigating medical device risk. EE-Eval. Eng. **56**, 28 (2017)
21. WHO: Cybersecurity. https://www.who.int/about/cyber-security. Accessed 15 Feb 2022
22. Sardi, A., Rizzi, A., Sorano, E., Guerrieri, A.: Cyber risk in health facilities: a systematic literature review. Sustainability **12** (2020). https://doi.org/10.3390/su12177002
23. Blumenthal, D., McGraw, D.: Keeping personal health information safe: the importance of good data hygiene. JAMA **313**, 1424 (2015). https://doi.org/10.1001/jama.2015.2746
24. Priestman, W., Anstis, T., Sebire, I.G., Sridharan, S., Sebire, N.J.: Phishing in healthcare organisations: threats, mitigation and approaches. BMJ Health Care Inform. **26**, e100031 (2019). https://doi.org/10.1136/bmjhci-2019-100031
25. Anderson, R.: Clinical system security: interim guidelines. BMJ **312**, 109–111 (1996)
26. Moura, P., Fazendeiro, P., Inácio, P.R.M., Vieira-Marques, P., Ferreira, A.: Assessing access control risk for mHealth: a delphi study to categorize security of health data and provide risk assessment for mobile apps. J. Healthc. Eng. **2020**, e5601068 (2020). https://doi.org/10.1155/2020/5601068
27. Almulhem, A.: Threat modeling for electronic health record systems. J. Med. Syst. **36**, 2921–2926 (2012). https://doi.org/10.1007/s10916-011-9770-6
28. Kessler, S.R., Pindek, S., Kleinman, G., Andel, S.A., Spector, P.E.: Information security climate and the assessment of information security risk among healthcare employees. Health Inform. J. **26**, 461–473 (2020). https://doi.org/10.1177/1460458219832048
29. NCSC: Cyber warning issued for key healthcare organisations in UK and USA. https://www.ncsc.gov.uk/news/warning-issued-uk-usa-healthcare-organisations

30. Offner, K.L., Sitnikova, E., Joiner, K., MacIntyre, C.R.: Towards understanding cybersecurity capability in Australian healthcare organisations: a systematic review of recent trends, threats and mitigation. Intell. Natl. Secur. **35**, 556–585 (2020). https://doi.org/10.1080/02684527.2020.1752459

31. Weil, T.R., Murugesan, S.: IT risk and resilience - cybersecurity response to COVID-19 (2020)

32. Schneck, P.A.: Cybersecurity during COVID-19. IEEE Secur. Priv. **18**, 4–5 (2020). https://doi.org/10.1109/MSEC.2020.3019678

33. Coventry, L., Branley, D.: Cybersecurity in healthcare: a narrative review of trends, threats and ways forward. Maturitas **113**, 48–52 (2018). https://doi.org/10.1016/j.maturitas.2018.04.008

34. Dykstra, J., Mathur, R., Spoor, A.: Cybersecurity in medical private practice: results of a survey in audiology. In: 2020 IEEE 6th International Conference on Collaboration and Internet Computing (CIC), pp. 169–176 (2020). https://doi.org/10.1109/CIC50333.2020.00029

35. Singh, H., Sittig, D.F.: A sociotechnical framework for safety-related electronic health record research reporting: the SAFER reporting framework. Ann. Intern. Med. **172**, S92–S100 (2020). https://doi.org/10.7326/M19-0879

36. Heckle, R.: Security dilemma: healthcare clinicians at work. IEEE Secur. Priv. **9**, 14–19 (2011). https://doi.org/10.1109/MSP.2011.74

37. Coventry, L., et al.: Cyber-risk in healthcare: exploring facilitators and barriers to secure behaviour. In: Moallem, A. (ed.) HCII 2020. LNCS, vol. 12210, pp. 105–122. Springer, Cham (2020). https://doi.org/10.1007/978-3-030-50309-3_8

38. He, Y., Aliyu, A., Evans, M., Luo, C.: Health care cybersecurity challenges and solutions under the climate of COVID-19: scoping review. J. Med. Internet Res. **23**, e21747 (2021). https://doi.org/10.2196/21747

39. Tabasum, A., Safi, Z., AlKhater, W., Shikfa, A.: Cybersecurity issues in implanted medical devices. In: 2018 International Conference on Computer and Applications (ICCA), pp. 1–9 (2018). https://doi.org/10.1109/COMAPP.2018.8460454

40. Cybersecurity and Infrastructure Security Agency: Fresenius Kabi Agilia Connect Infusion System (Update A). CISA. https://www.cisa.gov/uscert/ics/advisories/icsma-21-355-01

41. Legaspi, J.: Exploring the cybersecurity measures healthcare managers use to reduce patient endangerment resulting from backdoor intrusions into medical devices (2022). https://www.proquest.com/docview/2234288053/abstract/E9939BCAD63E4B96PQ/1

42. Arain, M.A., Tarraf, R., Ahmad, A.: Assessing staff awareness and effectiveness of educational training on IT security and privacy in a large healthcare organization. J. Multidiscip. Healthc. **12**, 73–81 (2019). https://doi.org/10.2147/JMDH.S183275

43. Evans, M., He, Y., Maglaras, L., Janicke, H.: HEART-IS: a novel technique for evaluating human error-related information security incidents. Comput. Secur. **80**, 74–89 (2019). https://doi.org/10.1016/j.cose.2018.09.002

44. Beautement, A., Sasse, A.: The economics of user effort in information security. Comput. Fraud Secur. **2009**, 8–12 (2009). https://doi.org/10.1016/S1361-3723(09)70127-7

45. Hall, L.H., Johnson, J., Watt, I., Tsipa, A., O'Connor, D.B.: Healthcare staff wellbeing, burnout, and patient safety: a systematic review. PLoS ONE **11**, e0159015 (2016). https://doi.org/10.1371/journal.pone.0159015

46. Branley-Bell, D., et al.: Your hospital needs you: eliciting positive cybersecurity behaviours from healthcare staff. Ann. Disaster Risk Sci. (ADRS) **3** (2020). https://doi.org/10.51381/adrs.v3i1.51

47. Jalali, M.S., Bruckes, M., Westmattelmann, D., Schewe, G.: Why employees (still) click on phishing links: an investigation in hospitals. J. Med. Internet Res. **22**, e16775 (2020). https://doi.org/10.2196/16775

48. Stobert, E., Barrera, D., Homier, V., Kollek, D.: Understanding cybersecurity practices in emergency departments. In: Proceedings of CHI, pp. 1–8. ACM, New York (2020)

49. Martin, J.D., Frost, P., O'Neill, O.A.: Organizational culture: beyond struggles for intellectual dominance (2004). https://doi.org/10.4135/9781848608030.n26

50. Alvesson, M.: Understanding organizational culture, London (2002). https://doi.org/10.4135/9781446280072

51. Chang, S.-E., Lin, C.: Exploring organizational culture for information security management. Ind. Manag. Data Syst. **107**, 438–458 (2007). https://doi.org/10.1108/02635570710734316

52. D'Arcy, J., Greene, G.: Security culture and the employment relationship as drivers of employees' security compliance. Inf. Manag. Comput. Secur. **22**, 474–489 (2014). https://doi.org/10.1108/IMCS-08-2013-0057

53. von Solms, R., von Solms, B.: From policies to culture. Comput. Secur. **23**, 275–279 (2004). https://doi.org/10.1016/j.cose.2004.01.013

54. Hyla, T., Fabisiak, L.: Measuring cyber security awareness within groups of medical professionals in Poland (2020). https://doi.org/10.24251/HICSS.2020.473

55. Haukilehto, T., Hautamäki, J.: Survey of cyber security awareness in health, social services and regional government in South Ostrobothnia, Finland. In: Galinina, O., Andreev, S., Balandin, S., Koucheryavy, Y. (eds.) NEW2AN ruSMART 2019. LNCS, vol. 11660, pp. 455–466. Springer, Cham (2019). https://doi.org/10.1007/978-3-030-30859-9_39

56. Gioulekas, F., et al.: A cybersecurity culture survey targeting healthcare critical infrastructures. Healthcare **10**, 327 (2022). https://doi.org/10.3390/healthcare10020327

57. Alhuwail, D., Al-Jafar, E., Abdulsalam, Y., AlDuaij, S.: Information security awareness and behaviors of health care professionals at public health care facilities. Appl. Clin. Inform. **12**, 924–932 (2021). https://doi.org/10.1055/s-0041-1735527

58. Sullivan, G.M., Artino, A.R.: Analyzing and interpreting data from likert-type scales. J. Grad. Med. Educ. **5**, 541–542 (2013). https://doi.org/10.4300/JGME-5-4-18

59. Olejnik, S.F., Algina, J.: Parametric ANCOVA and the rank transform ANCOVA when the data are conditionally non-normal and heteroscedastic. J. Educ. Stat. **9**, 129–149 (1984). https://doi.org/10.3102/10769986009002129

60. Rheinheimer, D.C., Penfield, D.A.: The effects of type I error rate and power of the ANCOVA F test and selected alternatives under nonnormality and variance heterogeneity. J. Exp. Educ. **69**, 373–391 (2001). https://doi.org/10.1080/00220970109599493

61. AlKalbani, A., Deng, H., Kam, B.: Investigating the role of socio-organizational factors in the information security compliance in organizations. In: Australasian Conference on Information Systems 2015, p. 11 (2015)

62. Zohar, D., Luria, G.: The use of supervisory practices as leverage to improve safety behavior: a cross-level intervention model. J. Saf. Res. **34**, 567–577 (2003). https://doi.org/10.1016/j.jsr.2003.05.006

63. Zohar, D., Luria, G.: A multilevel model of safety climate: cross-level relationships between organization and group-level climates. J. Appl. Psychol. **90**, 616–628 (2005). https://doi.org/10.1037/0021-9010.90.4.616

64. Hedström, K., Kolkowska, E., Karlsson, F., Allen, J.P.: Value conflicts for information security management. J. Strateg. Inf. Syst. **20**, 373–384 (2011). https://doi.org/10.1016/j.jsis.2011.06.001

65. Tyson, P.: The hippocratic oath today. https://www.pbs.org/wgbh/nova/article/hippocratic-oath-today/

66. Tully, J., Coravos, A., Doerr, M., Dameff, C.: Connected medical technology and cybersecurity informed consent: a new paradigm. J. Med. Internet Res. **22**, e17612 (2020). https://doi.org/10.2196/17612

67. Woods, B., Coravos, A., Corman, J.D.: The case for a hippocratic oath for connected medical devices: viewpoint. J. Med. Internet Res. **21**, e12568 (2019). https://doi.org/10.2196/12568

68. I Am The Cavalry. https://iamthecavalry.org/. Accessed 08 Feb 2022

Design and Evaluation
of an Anti-phishing Artifact Based
on Useful Transparency

Christopher Beckmann(✉) ⓘD, Benjamin BerensⓘD, Niklas KühlⓘD,
Peter MayerⓘD, Mattia MossanoⓘD, and Melanie VolkamerⓘD

Karlsruhe Institute of Technology, Kaiserstraße 12, 76131 Karlsruhe, Germany
{christopher.beckmann,benjamin.berens,niklas.kuhl,peter.mayer,
mattia.mossano,melanie.volkamer}@kit.edu

Abstract. Background: Many security interventions to support users
in detecting phishing emails exist including providing the URL in a
tooltip or the statusbar.
Aim: Designing and evaluating an anti-phishing artifact based on the
Useful Transparency theory.
Method: We used the design science research approach for the entire
process. As evaluation we ran a between-subjects study with 109 participants from the UK to determine the anti-phishing artifact effectiveness
to support users distinguishing between phishing and legitimate emails.
Results: Our results show that, when compared against the state of
the art security interventions (displaying the URL in the statusbar), our
anti-phishing artifact increase the detection significantly, i.e. phishing
detection increased from 50% to 72%.
Conclusion: Albeit further studies are required, the evaluation demonstrate that the Useful Transparency theory can result in promising security interventions. Thus, it might be worth considering it for other security interventions, too.

Keywords: Anti-phishing · Tool evaluation · Design Science Research

1 Introduction

The Federal Bureau of Investigation (FBI) ranked phishing as 2020's most common cybercrime (see [14]) and the International Business Machines Corporation (IBM) rated it as the second most expensive cause of breaches (see [22]).
Although phishing detection tools have improved over the years, users still find
phishing attempts in their inbox and they will continue to do so in future. The
main reasons are that (1) phishers keep developing their attack strategies and (2)
legitimate messages sometimes contain phishing indicators, e.g., call to urgency.

Supported by funding from topic 46.23.01 Methods for Engineering Secure Systems of
the Helmholtz Association and by KASTEL Security Research Labs.

M. Mehrnezhad and S. Parkin (Eds.): STAST 2022, LNCS 13855, pp. 113–133, 2025.
https://doi.org/10.1007/978-3-031-83072-3_7

Advanced phishing emails containing links can only be reliably detected with careful analysis of the URL behind the links. If the URL behind a link in an Amazon email is, e.g., https://www-amazon.com or https://www.arnazon.jp, the email is clearly a phishing email. However, Wash [60] showed that most people are not aware of this defense and Albakry et al. [1] showed that lay users have difficulties reading URLs correctly, being rarely aware that they should mainly consider the domain and top-level-domain (TLD) of a URL (e.g., for https://www.amazon.com.host-shop.com, "host-shop.com").

Security experts have released and discussed various approaches to support users, i.e., technical means to detect phishing (e.g., in [63]), phishing awareness and training (e.g., in [4, 42, 48]) and tooltips containing the URL behind a link and appearing when hovering the mouse over a link (e.g., in [40, 56]), as well as exploring the reasons for phishing attacks success (e.g., in [50, 59, 62]).

We focus on designing and evaluating a novel anti-phishing artifact, which underlying idea is based on the Useful Transparency theory from Hosseini et al. [21]: Enhancing the transparency of URLs behind links in emails. We integrate so called "transparent-strings" in all emails, in most cases consisting of domain and TLD of the URL behind each link (the exceptions are explained later). Note, these strings are the only links in the emails. Figure 1 depicts an example.

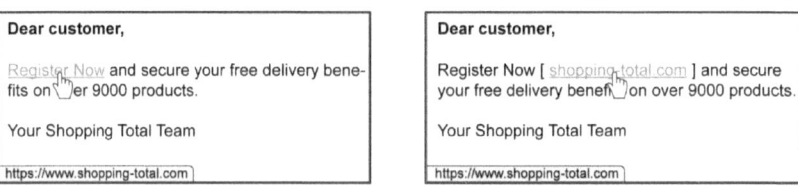

Fig. 1. Link in email, without (left) and with (right) our anti-phishing artifact.

Compared to the anti-phishing tooltip ideas, there are various advantages: (1) the relevant information to detect phishing URLs is displayed immediately, not only when hovering the link with the mouse. (2) We do not present the entire URL as a link, but only the transparent-string. Thereby, we thwart various URL obfuscation techniques such as subdomain-as-domain and path-posing. (3) It can be applied on both the server-side and the client-side. (4) It can be applied in the mobile context. (5) It may support visually impaired users in phishing detection, as the transparent-string is more easy to read aloud than longer URLs.

In this work, we evaluate our anti-phishing artifact in a between-subjects study with 109 Clickworker participants from the UK. We asked participants to distinguish between 28 screenshots of both phishing and legitimate emails. The study group saw the screenshots with the transparent-strings, while the control group saw unmodified email screenshots. Our results show that participants in the study group have an overall phishing recognition rate of 79.4%, against the control group's 60.57%. Thus, applying the Useful Transparency theory (see Vossing et al. [58]), our anti-phishing artifact results in significantly better phishing detection than the baseline. Further, the control group results confirm previous research results, i.e., that most people are not aware that they should check the URL in the statusbar and have problems reading URLs correctly. Improving the effectiveness in such cases is discussed as future work.

2   Research Design

Our overall research design is Design Science Research (DSR), as it allows to consider the theoretical and practical tasks necessary when designing and implementing IT artifacts (see [31]) and has proven to be an important and legitimate paradigm in IS research (see [19]). Acknowledging that different methodologies for design science exist (see [20,47,51]), in the style of Kühl et al. [26] we favor a clear differentiation between an abstract "suggestion" and a concrete, more programming-specific "development". Following Kuechler & Vaishnavi [25] a DSR project should cover: Awareness of problem (Sect. 3), suggestion (Sect. 4), development (Sect. 5) and evaluation (Sect. 6).

Our design process is informed by the kernel theory of *Useful Transparency*, from Hosseini et al. [21], who define "useful transparency" as the ability of users "to make decisions based on the provided information and act upon them" (p. 258). The theory and its relation to our approach are explored in Sect. 4.

3   Awareness of the Problem

Phishing definitions focus on two aspects: (1) phishing deceiving victims to click a link and share sensitive information (e.g., passwords, personal data, bank details) through authentic-looking phishing messages (e.g., [24,29,40,44]) and (2) phishing spreading malware through links/attachments (e.g., [7,15,27,61].) We accept both (1) and (2) as valid, but focus our work on links contained in emails.

Phishing is not a new phenomenon, but is far from being solved or under control. Numbers and damage have rather increased than decreased: FBI [14] ranked phishing as 2020's most common cybercrime and IBM [22] as the second most expensive cause of breaches. Verizon [52] reports that 43% of all data breaches involve phishing and 95% of phishing is delivered via email. The Anti-Phishing Working Group [3] reports that the average wire-transfer loss from business email compromise in Q2 2021 is $106,000, up from $75,000 in Q4 2020.

As people still find phishing in their inbox, they remain one important piece of the anti-phishing measures. Simple phishing emails can be identified by checking the sender address or the plausibility of the content. Advanced attacks, however, are sent from spoofed email addresses and contain plausible content. This because the content is either obtained by re-using a legitimate emails or it is based on credible information collected, e.g., from webpages and/or social networks.

Thus, the only reliable indicator to recognize a phishing email is the URL behind the links, as shown in Garera et al. [16] and Ma et al. [30]. However, the URL is only displayed once the link is hovered with the mouse. In many desktop contexts, the URL behind a link is displayed in a statusbar in the browser window lower-left corner, not where the users' focus is. Often, phishing emails abuse the link text as a means to disguise the real URL, e.g., by showing a seemingly correct URL as link text. Very advanced phishing emails may have clickable elements (e.g., form and formaction elements) that do not show any URL in the statusbar, visible only in the email source code. Phishers also use short URL and redirect services to hide the final destination, completely hiding it and requiring to reach the final destination without actually opening the webpage.

Researchers have shown in Wash [60] that users are not aware of the need to check the URL behind a link. When they do, they have difficulties judging them, e.g., as shown in Albakry et al. [1]. Thus, to decrease phishing risks, email receivers need to be further supported. We do so with our anti-phishing artifact, that simplify the decision making on whether a link is safe to click or directs to a phishing page. Based on the Useful Transparency theory from Hosseini et al. [21], the anti-phishing artifact provides the information needed to judge a link in the email text, without users' actions or reading the source code.

4   Suggestion

In this section we introduce a short overview of our artifact. A full description of its working is presented in Mossano et al. [37].

We apply the Useful Transparency theory, from Hosseini et al. [21] to increase the *effectiveness* of email receivers in distinguishing between legitimate and phishing emails. We do so by enhancing the transparency of the relevant information, showing it in easy-to-read and easy-to-judge text-based links with the *transparent-string* available whenever an email is opened, without further users' actions. Thus, the relevant (and only the relevant) information is provided just-in-place, i.e., where users' focus is just before clicking a link.

The transparent-string is in most cases the domain and TLD of the original URL behind the link or, for short URLs and redirect URLs, of the final destination URL. Depending on the URL, the transparent-string can also be an IP address or, for cloud service URLs, include some subdomains to indicate that the corresponding account owner is in charge of the content, not the organization in the domain (e.g., docs.google.com). The transparent-string only provides the minimum information required to decide on the URL legitimacy. Note, the statusbar is left untouched and it shows the entire URL on mouse hover. An example of an email modified by our anti-phishing artifact is in Fig. 1.

Our design has two main reasons: no extra user action is needed to get the relevant information to judge a link, as the indicator (transparent-string) is in the email text, i.e., just-in-place, as recommended in Petelka et al. [40]. Besides, the transparent-string reduces the amount of wrong decisions, as phishers can no longer trick users with subdomain attacks or the path attacks (e.g., "amazon.com.host749.com" becomes "host749.com"). Fairly, if a webpage legitimate URL is unknown or if the difference between the legitimate and phishing URL is minimal (e.g., "shop-total.com" instead of "shopping-total.com"), seeing the transparent-string would not help much. However, this would be true also without our artifact, which in turn helps those users that know the legitimate URL.

5   Development

The proposed anti-phishing artifact can either be applied centrally or locally. We decided to implement it locally as an extension for either a web browser or an email client that modifies the email right before displaying it. Although mobile email client apps could be extended too to apply our anti-phishing artifact before displaying an email, the focus of our current research is on the desktop context.

Clickable Elements in Emails. Various HTML elements can create links in emails: anchor-elements, form-elements, formaction-elements and area elements. From the users' point of view, there is no difference between form-elements and formac tion-elements. Note, "link" usually indicates only anchor elements, but we use it for all four types for simplicity. JavaScript could also be used to create links, but our artifact does not address it as the common email clients and web mail services block such elements. We call *link-types* how links appear to users, i.e., images, URL-like (e.g., "www.amazon.com" or "facebook.com"), and text (e.g., "Click here"). Each one could also look like a button (see Fig. 2).

| | Image Type | | URL-Like | | Misc | | Area Map |
	Generic	Button-like	Generic	Button-like	Generic	Button-like	
Unmodified		Start Now	Register now at https://example.com/register	example.org/path	Register now and secure benefits.	Start Now	
Artifact	Image Link: [example.org]	Image Link: [example.org] Start Now	Register now at [example.com]	[example.org]	Register now [example.com] and secure benefits.	Start Now example.org	Area Link [example1.com] Area Link [examplg2.com]

Fig. 2. Before and after applying our anti-phishing artifact

Abstract Algorithm. Our anti-phishing artifact deals with all the different elements and link-types. First it resolves the transparent-string for all URLs in an email. Then, it proceeds based on how the link is integrated (see Fig. 2). As HTML and CSS are relatively rich languages, emails can be very complex and we cannot rule out that the anti-phishing artifact makes them unreadable. Hence, we implemented a toggle function to undo all substitutions on demand.

Resolving the Transparent-String. Using short URL services or a redirect services the original URL is not the final destination. Thus, we first check whether such services were used. If so, we apply the functionality proposed in Volkamer et al. [56] to reveal the final destination URL without loading the corresponding web page. Afterwards, the final destination URL is treated as the original URL. Next, we extract the host from the URL with the functionality proposed in Volkamer et al. [56] and check whether it is an IP address. If yes, the IP address is displayed as the transparent-string. If not, the transparent-string is the domain and the TLD of the URL, using the Mozilla Foundation's Public Suffix list to do so (see Mozilla [38]), as proposed in Volkamer et al. [56]. Last, the transparent-string is checked against potential homographic attacks, handling non-ASCII characters by replacing them in the transparent-string with so-called puny code. Note, this is the approach adopted by programs such as Google Chrome 51+.

Specific Attack Strategies. If our approach is adopted, phishers may adapt their strategies to it. Hence, we asked several security researchers to think of potential attacks. They proposed what we call the *doctored-pruned-URL*: phishers could try to confuse users by putting the link only on parts of a URL-like text, e.g., "amazon.com". This link would be modified to "amazon.com [book-657.jp]".

6   Evaluation

6.1   Methodology

Our main goal is to evaluate the usability of our proposal in the private context. With respect to *effectiveness* in distinguishing between legitimate and phishing emails, our anti-phishing artifact is based on the Useful Transparency theory. Correspondingly, we want to confirm the following hypothesis:

H-effective. Our anti-phishing artifact helps participants to significantly *better* distinguish between legitimate and phishing emails than without.

Furthermore, we investigate efficiency and satisfaction by answering the following research questions:

RQ-efficient. How efficient are participants with and without our anti-phishing artifact in distinguishing between legitimate and phishing emails?

RQ-satisfaction. How do participants rate our anti-phishing artifact on the System Usability Scale (SUS) compared to the statusbar?

Study Design. We designed a between-subjects study with two groups: one *study group* (SG) and one *control group* (CG). The SG saw emails with our artifact, i.e., the complete URLs are displayed in the statusbar and the transparent-string is added to the email text. The CG saw unmodified email, i.e., the complete URLs are displayed in the statusbar and the email text is unmodified. We choose a between-subject design to avoid the *Carry-over effect* described in Keren [23], i.e., the performance in one treatment influence the other. In a within-subject design, participants would have seen the emails in both interfaces. As the emails differed only in the way links are displayed, but not in content or appearance (as described in Sect. 6.1), participants might have judged an email in one interface based on how they judged the same email in the other interface.

We used a *role-play approach*: participants were asked to answer according to a specific scenario (details in paragraph "Scenario"). We combined this role-play with a *quiz-like approach*: participants saw email screenshots and were asked to distinguish whether it was a phishing email or not. A binary choice is representative of private users' real world judgment conditions. There are questionnaires to measure security awareness, e.g., Vishwanath et al. [53]. Yet, they are not focused on phishing and target awareness, rather than decision making in realistic situations. Hence, we believe that a quiz-like approach is more appropriate for our research goal. The participants saw static screenshots, with the cursor hovering over the link and displaying the browser's statusbar with the URL behind the link (as in Reinheimer et al. [42], see Sect. 6.1). We are aware that this makes security the participants' primary, if not only, task. Yet, this allowed us to evaluate various phishing attacks without running simulated phishing campaigns, avoiding the challenges shown in Volkamer et al. [57] and Pirocca et al. [41]. It also allowed us to run an online study, reaching a higher number of participants and avoiding issues with the COVID-19 restrictions on lab studies.

The emails are in the Chrome web browser, in MS Windows 10. This is the most common combination of desktop operating system and browser in the UK, according to Statcounter [45, 46]. The emails are seen in the Gmail web interface.

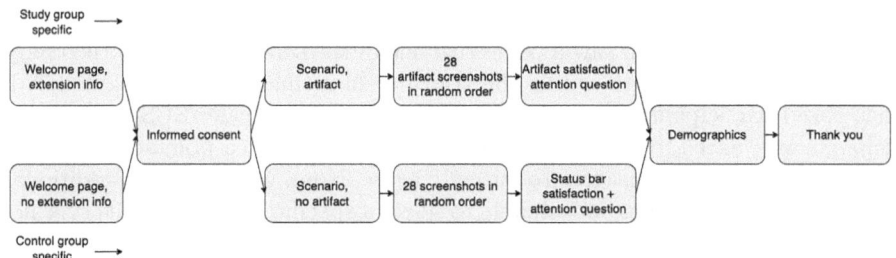

Fig. 3. Study procedure.

The *study procedure* is depicted in Fig. 3. The different steps are:

Welcome. The participants recruitment through SoSci Survey is detailed in Sect. 6.1. After clicking the SoSci Survey link, all participants saw one of two welcome pages. We explained the evaluation and what their task was. The SG read that we were evaluating a new browser extension[1] and how it helps distinguishing between legitimate and phishing emails; no explanation about the extension working was given. We told the CG that we were interested in determining their skill to distinguish between legitimate and phishing emails. Potential limitations caused by the security focus are addressed in Sect. 7.

Informed Consent. We asked the participants to not use external materials or help to limit external influences. We also explained them that a low performance had no negative consequence. We also informed the participants of the attention questions that, if answered incorrectly, would have barred them from continuing and be compensated. We added that they could have terminated the study at any time, without providing any reason, by closing the browser window. If this was the case, we would not have used their data. Lastly, we informed the participants that their data would have been processed and stored in Germany, not the UK.

Scenario. We decided to use a role-play approach, slightly different depending on the group. We told both groups to distinguish between phishing and legitimate emails as if they were a fictional persona named "David T. Jones", recently moved to the UK. Relevant information about David was provided. We again informed the SG that David installed a new browser extension to help him recognize phishing emails. No explanation about the extension working was given.

Judging Screenshots. We asked the participants to distinguish among 28 email screenshots, presented in random order, the phishing from the legitimate ones. Every email was for a service activation. The SG saw email screenshots with the transparent-links, while the CG saw the same images without modifications. More information on the emails and their selection is provided in Sect. 6.1.

Satisfaction. Each group saw a page with one of the screenshots from the study with either the statusbar or our the transparent-string being highlighted. We then asked participants to answer the System Usability Scale (SUS)[2]. The participants were asked to answer each item as themselves on a 5-points Likert scale, ranging from strongly disagree to strongly agree. Note, we added one additional attention question asking participants to select a specific item of the Likert scale.

Demographics. We asked our participants various question about themselves: Highest study degree and its field, which email provider they mainly use, which software they usually check emails with, whether they received any anti-phishing training or informed themselves on how to check detect malicious emails, what type of anti-phishing training/awareness material they used to learn, and how long ago did they receive the training or informed themselves last.

---

[1] We mentioned a browser extension to avoid confusion for the slightly different email appearance. We don't believe this biased the participants, as their primary task was distinguishing between phishing and legitimate emails.

[2] The SUS is a common tool used to evaluate the usability of systems and products, initially developed by Brooke [8]. We used the SUS version from Bangor et al. [5].

Thank You. We thanked them for their participation and clarified that we modified some of the legitimate emails to better fit the study, so they should not have considered the screenshots as perfect examples of official emails. We also provided our contacts again, in case they were needed.

Email Selection. We decided to show the same amount of phishing and legitimate emails. We only included advanced phishing emails, i.e., phishing emails only identifiable using the URL behind the link. We selected legitimate emails and changed the URL behind the relevant link to get a phishing email. We also modified the link type to equally cover the different UI cases from Sect. 5.

The following *three dimensions* are relevant for us to decide which phishing emails to include[3]: the different UI cases, the URL obfuscation technique, and the sending organization. As it can be seen in Fig. 2, there are seven different *situations from a user interface perspective*. However, the area-element one is related to the image-generic case and is only very rarely used in the email context. Therefore, we decided to focus on the remaining six situations (two per link-type – see Fig. 2) for the user study. Furthermore, we distinguish four *URL obfuscation techniques*[4]: arbitrary-URL (i.e., the URL domain is an arbitrary name or IP), subdomain-as-domain (i.e., the host name is placed in the subdomain part of the URL), path-posing (i.e., the host name is placed in the path of the URL), and typo-swapping (i.e., similar looking domain but, e.g., spelled with letters in different positions or similar looking characters, e.g., rn instead of m). Note, we decided to use URLs with HTTPS protocol for both phishing and legitimate email screenshots. This was done for three reasons: Firstly, nowadays most phishing websites use SSL/TLS, as reported in APWG [3]. Secondly, participants may judge URLs legitimacy on their protocol alone, as reported in Alsharnouby et al. [2]. For the same reasons, HTTPS-only was used in Albakry et al. [1], Volkamer et al. [56] and Peteleka et al. [40]. Ultimately, as shown in Oest et al. [39], almost 86% of successful phishing attacks use HTTPS.

Thus, we have *12 different phishing cases* to be considered (4 URL obfuscation techniques x 3 link-types). We decided to use different sending organizations for each of the 12, i.e., 12 different legitimate emails that were changed into phishing ones. Considering that the UK has a specific double format top level domain (.co.uk), we decided to include one such legitimate URL per obfuscation technique, i.e., ending with such top level domain. These 12 organizations were identified based on the top ALEXA UK pages. In addition to the four URL obfuscation techniques, we also considered *two additional attack cases*: mismatch attack and the doctored-pruned-URL attack. The mismatch attack was also studied in Chiew et al. [12] and Caputo et al. [11], and it was described as a link showing a URL address different than the one behind it. Ideally, all

---

[3] Note, for the user study, we do not consider form and form-action elements. This has two reasons: CG would have no chance to decide about phishing or not for those emails as the URL would not appear in the statusbar. Furthermore, for the UI/screenshots it does not make a difference which of the two elements is used.

[4] These are similar techniques to those studied in, e.g., [29,43,54,55].

URL obfuscation techniques in Table 1 should be studied in combination with these two attack cases. However, the resulting number of screenshots would be too high. Therefore, we decided to use the arbitrary URL obfuscation technique in combination with these two attack cases. For these two additional cases we use two new sending organizations, again identified based on the top ALEXA page for the UK. Thus, in total 14 phishing emails are studied. See Table 1 for a description of each of the *28 emails*.

Table 1. List of URLs used in the email screenshots used in the user study

Obfuscation technique	Link type	Organization	Legitimate URL	Phishing URL
Arbitrary URL	Image - Generic	BBC	https://www.bbc.co.uk	https://www.linkyzt.com
	URL-like - Generic	Netflix	https://www.netflix.com/browse? lnktrk=EMP& g=4F4D261316D39C280880331...	https://www.host745.com/browse? lnktrk=EMP& g=4F4D261316D39C280880331...
	Misc - Button-like	Spotify	https://wl.spotify.com/	https://129.13.152.9
Subdomain-as-Domain	Image - Button-like	Google	https://accounts.google.co.uk/ signin/v2/identifier? service=accountsettings...	https://accounts.google.co.uk. nimsky57.ru/identifier? service=accountsettings...
	URL-like - Button-like	Facebook	https://www.facebook.com/	https://www.facebook.com. host547.com/
	Misc - Generic	Instagram	https://www.instagram.com/ activate	https://www.instagram.com. 3nk317rc.com/activate
Path-Posing	Image - Generic	Ebay	https://rover.ebay.co.uk/rover/2	https://www.mppls.com/www. ebay.co.uk
	URL-like - Generic	Wikipedia	https://en.wikipedia.org/wiki/ Special:ConfirmEmail/ a784d79322cb80d4f1127...	https://www.host875.com/en. wikipedia.org/wiki/Special: ConfirmEmail/a784d79322...
	Misc - Button-like	Zoom	https://us05web.zoom.us/ activate?code=xTk7ww9F_p- zq4eTrrNExMcEGiD...	https://www.providershop58.com/ us05web.zoom.us/activate? code=xTk7ww9F_p...
Typo-Swapping	Image - Button-like	Amazon	https://www.amazon.co.uk/	https://www.amzaon.co.uk/
	URL-like - Button-like	The Guardian	https://profile.theguardian.com/ verify-email/q1fjo- KOUgAkzWwRpyPxS1...	https://profile.theguardain.com/ verify-email/q1fjo- KOUgAkzWwRpyPxS1...
	Misc - Generic	Microsoft	https://www.microsoft.com/en- gb/activate/ jjuP9kjj3uH78dhsuuy& 89klOhEyp9m	https://www.mircosoft.com/en- gb/activate/ jjuP9kjj3uH78dhsuuy& 89klOhEyp9m
Mismatch	URL-like - Generic	Daily Mail	https://www.dailymail.co.uk/ registration/activate.html? email=jones.t.david88%40...	https://www.jiorlikniski.cn/ registration/activate.html? email=jones.t.david88...
Doctored-Pruned-URL	Misc - Generic	UK Government	https://www.gov.uk/confirm	https://www.uhszhiklo.cz

Recruitment, Data Protection, and Ethics. We recruited UK participants using the panel service "Clickworker". According to Cohen [13], without sufficient information – as it is the case for our study – a medium effect size helps not to over- or underestimate the expected effect size. Therefore, we decided to plan for medium effect size. We assumed to use a T-test for independent groups, for the test strength analyses with G*Power. In addition to the effect size, we set the test power to 0.8 and the alpha error to 0.05. Hence, we calculated a sample size of 51 participants per group. To avoid falling below this limit due to exclusion, we set the number of participants per group to 60 to have a buffer[5].

Based on pre-tests, we expected the study to be finished in 30 min. We wanted to pay the participants based on the UK minimum wage. However, there is no unified minimum wage, rather the remuneration is based on age and role, as shown in GOV.UK [18]. Since the participant selection was random and no age groups where pre-defined (other than participants had to be 18 or above), we decided to use the latest (at the time, the one from April 2020) minimum wage for the oldest age group (25+): £8,72/hour. Once considered the time required to complete the study, the participants received £4,36 (8,72: 60 = 4,36: 30).

We used SoSci Survey to collect the data, as they are compliant with the *European Data Protection Regulation* (GDPR). However, in the UK the GDPR principles were added to the *Digital Act* of 2018, creating what is now known as UK-GDPR. We informed the participants that their data is stored and processed in Germany. We provided them with a link to the privacy policy of SoSci Survey and a contact person among the researchers. The study description was submitted for consideration and approved by the ethical board of our university. as part of the review, the data protection officer of our university checked and approved both the informed consent and the overall study design.

6.2   Results

Participants and Data Cleaning. We have 126 complete datasets (not considering the participants that were directly excluded because they failed the attention question). We performed the following data cleaning steps: we excluded three participants because they judged 100% of the screenshots as either all legitimate or all phishing. We removed one outlier in sensitivity. We removed, for the same reason, nine participants in criterion[6]. Lastly, we removed four outliers because of the time. These were removed because they excessively skewed our results by violating the 1.5 times interquartile range distance in both directions (see [49]). This left us with an overall dataset of 109 participants, 53 in the CG and 56 in the SG. The average age for the CG was 36.94 with SD 9.1, ranging from 20 to 57 years and for the SG was 36.98 with SD 11.7, ranging from 18 to 67 years. The education of the CG versus the SG was 11 versus 18 high school, 27 versus 26 with a bachelor, both ten with a master, two versus none PhD, and three versus two other. Table 2 shows, on the left, the email services the participants used and, on the right, the web clients usually used to read their emails. 18 CG participants and 24 SG ones stated that they previously participated in an anti-phishing training or informed themselves about it.

---

[5] The legitimate mismatch for the CG contains a typo in the link-text dddaily-mail.co.uk. The legitimate doctored-pruned-URL only has "confirm" as a link.

[6] The signal detection theory used to measure effectiveness considers sensitivity and criterion (see Sect. 6.2).

Table 2. Users email services (left) and clients (right) used by participants.

Email Service	CG	SG
Gmail	43	48
Yahoo	3	4
BT	3	1
iCloud	2	0
Own server	0	1
Other	2	2

Clients	CG	SG
Chrome	34	42
Outlook	12	17
Apple Mail	8	4
Firefox	5	6
Edge	4	5
Thunderbird	2	1
Other	2	4

Table 3. Descriptive statistics for both groups.

		CG		SG	
		Mean	SD	Mean	SD
Effectiveness	Phish	50.0%	19.4	71.7%	21.7
	Legit	71.2%	14.4	87.1%	13.1
	Overall	60.6%	12.3	79.4%	13.3
	Sensitivity	0.6	0.7	2.3	1.5
	Criterion	0.3	0.3	0.4	0.6
	Efficiency	511.7 s	241.6	533.4 s	275.7

Analysis Methods

H-effective. We employed the Signal Detection Theory (SDT) to measure our participants' skill to distinguish between phishing and legitimate emails. SDT have already been used in various studies on phishing identification (e.g., in [9,10,32,33,36,42]). SDT uses two variables, signal (phishing emails) and noise (legitimate emails), to calculate various outputs. In line with the aforementioned researches, we decided to look for two values: sensitivity (d') and criterion (C). We defined sensitivity as the skill to successfully distinguish between phishing emails (signal) and legitimate ones (noise). The large d', the higher the participants' skill is. We use criterion (C) to determine the participants' tendency while distinguish emails. The closer C is to 0, the less tendency in the answers in direction of either phishing or legitimate emails exists. On the one hand, the more positive C is, the more a participant was over-cautious, and identified legitimate emails as phishing one (more false positives). On the other hand, the more negative C is, the more a participant showed over-confidence, identifying more phishing emails as legitimate (false negatives).

We calculated assumptions relevant for the SDT parameters, i.e., equal variance and Gaussian distribution. For sensitivity ($F = 13.848, p < 0.001$) and criterion ($F = 11.523, p = 0.001$) the assumption of equal variances is violated and therefore we report the results for the Welch t-test. We then calculated the parameters for sensitivity and criterion per participants. Afterwards, we calculated the mean values per measurements. To evaluate *h-effective*, we used independent t-tests to check the differences among participants' sensitivity and criterion. For each t-test, we checked the assumptions for sensitivity and criterion.

Efficiency. We used the average time spent on all screenshots. To evaluate efficiency, we started with an exploratory analysis looking at the descriptive data. As we had no knowledge about a potential difference between the SG and CG for such a "short" evaluation, we tested the hypothesis that there might be a significant difference between both groups (without a clear trend). We calculated assumptions relevant for the efficiency, i.e., equal variance ($F = 1.628, p = 0.205$) and Gaussian distribution. Therefore we tested two-tailed and used an independent t-test to check the differences among participants' efficiency.

Satisfaction. Regarding the SUS (described in Sect. 6.1), we followed the guidelines on how to score it shown in Lewis [28]. We started off with an exploratory analysis looking at the descriptive data. As we had no previous knowledge about a potential difference between the SG and CG for such a "short" evaluation, we moved on with testing the hypothesis that there might be a significant difference between both groups (without a clear trend). We calculated assumptions relevant for the satisfaction, i.e., equal variance ($F = 0.616, p = 0.434$) and Gaussian distribution. Therefore we tested two-tailed and used an independent t-test to check the differences among participants' satisfaction.

Analysis Outcome. All the descriptive results are provided in Table 3.

Effectiveness. The SG participants (M = 2.29, SD = 1.45) demonstrated significantly better sensitivity scores, $t(107) = 7.682$, $p < 0.0001$, when compared to the CG participants (M = 0.62, SD = 0.73). The effect size for this analysis ($d = 1.448$) was found to exceed Cohen's convention for a large effect ($d = .80$) (see [13]). The participants in the SG (M = 0.37, SD = 0.58), when compared to the participants in the CG (M = 0.31, SD = 0.35), demonstrated no significantly difference for the criterion scores, $t(107) = 0.683, p = 0.491$. However, as the criterion of the SG is almost neutral, demonstrating no significant difference between both groups means we can accept *h-effective*.

We also looked at the participants' performance for the individual email screenshots. The descriptive results are provided in Table 4. The Google phishing email has the worst performance for the CG (subdomain-as-domain, 17% correct answers). In comparison, the Microsoft phishing email was the worst-performing screenshot for the SG with about 34% (typo-swapping). The Facebook phishing email showed the best performance with 77% (subdomain-as-domain) for the CG. For the SG, the best result is the Dailymail phishing screenshot with 91% (mismatch) and Facebook with 89% (subdomain-as-domain). The doctored-pruned-URL attack achieved better results in the SG (77%) than in the CG (53%). Of the legitimate email screenshots, the Dailymail one achieved by far

Table 4. Percentage and standard deviation of correct judgments per example.

Obfuscation technique	Link type	Organization	Control Group Legit		Phish		Study Group Legit		Phish	
			Mean	SD	Mean	SD	Mean	SD	Mean	SD
Arbitrary URL	Image - Generic	BBC	94%	23	45%	50	96%	18	71%	46
	URL-like - Generic	Netflix	81%	40	60%	49	95%	23	79%	41
	Misc - Button-like	Spotify	77%	42	36%	48	84%	37	75%	44
Subdomain-as-Domain	Image - Button-like	Google	83%	38	17%	38	91%	29	73%	45
	URL-like - Button-like	Facebook	64%	48	77%	42	79%	41	89%	31
	Misc - Generic	Instagram	62%	49	47%	50	84%	37	59%	50
Path-Posing	Image - Generic	Ebay	59%	50	60%	49	73%	45	84%	37
	URL-like - Generic	Wikipedia	62%	49	64%	48	95%	23	80%	40
	Misc - Button-like	Zoom	66%	48	55%	50	79%	41	86%	35
Typo-Swapping	Image - Button-like	Amazon	83%	38	40%	49	89%	31	59%	50
	URL-like - Button-like	The Guardian	89%	32	40%	49	96%	19	46%	50
	Misc - Generic	Microsoft	60%	49	38%	49	86%	35	34%	48
Mismatch	URL-like - Generic	Daily Mail	32%	47	68%	47	82%	39	91%	29
Doctored-Pruned-URL	Misc - Generic	UK Government	81%	40	53 %	50	91%	29	77%	43

the lowest score for the CG with 32%. For the SG, the eBay email screenshot scored the lowest with 73%. The screenshot that performed worst in the CG for legitimate examples had a strange sender email address (registration@and.co.uk for dailymail.co.uk). Note, this was not due to our modifications. Without the artifact and without checking the statusbar, this might have caused a wrong judgment, as a common recommendation is to check for strange email addresses.

Efficiency. The SG took slightly longer ($M \approx 533$ s) to judge all screenshots compared to the CG ($M \approx 511$ s). We checked for significant difference between both groups and there is none, $t(107) = 0.436$, $p = 0.663$.

System Usability Scale (SUS). Based on Bangor et al. [5,6], a SUS value above 71.4 on adjective ratings scale is considered at least "good". The SG (M = 72.54) is on average slightly below the CG (M = 77.88). However, the artifact is sufficient usable. We checked whether there is a significant difference between both groups and there is none, $t(107) = 1.812$, $p = 0.073$.

7   Discussion

Effectiveness. Our study results show that participants with the artifact perform significantly better when distinguishing between legitimate and phishing emails containing a dangerous link. An unexpected positive outcome is the large effect size. As stated in Sect. 6.1, we decided for a medium effect size due to the absence of information on the novel artifact. However, we found that the distance between SG and CG (d = 1.44 95% CI [–1.868 to –1.022]) not only exceeded our conservative approach, but also Cohen's large effect size of 0.8. Hence, the difference between the groups' performances is highly significant. This is very positive, as the study design we used is not favorable to the artifact: The idea behind the Useful Transparency theory (and our the artifact) is to have the critical information integrated into the email body so that the transparent-string is visible before deciding to click on a link. However, in our study design, the users did not interact with the email screenshots by themselves, i.e., the URL was already displayed in the statusbar for the CG too, without participants moving the mouse to the link. For future work, we plan to study if the difference between the two groups increases further when participants need to interact with the email to see the URL in the statusbar.

Our study shows that the artifact supports users in particular in both mismatch cases: (1) when phishers use the mismatch obfuscation technique to trick users into clicking a trustworthy looking URL in the email body. (2) When senders accidental cause a mismatch as an honest mistake – with 68% in the CG to 91% in the SG for (1) and with 32% in the CG to 68% in the SG for (2). Our findings also confirm past research results from [2]: Some of the worst performing examples were ones with the typo-swapping obfuscation technique. While we could argue that this obfuscation technique is not very realistic, as big services such as Google or Meta are continuously searching for domains similar to the legitimate ones (see [17,34,35]), it is worth improving the performance rate further as future work, e.g., by displaying the transparent-string differently, e.g., "a r n a z o n . c o m".

One results that can be inferred is that adding the relevant information just-in-place, i.e., next to the link, help users distinguishing between legitimate and phishing emails, as shown in Petelka et al. [40]. We plan to investigate further this effect as future work, e.g., checking if tooltips have similar results.

Efficiency and System Usability Scale. The results show that there is no significant difference between both groups with regard to efficiency. For our study setting this seems not to be that surprising, as the screenshots already show the URL behind a link, putting the CG in nearly the same starting position as the SG, i.e., the relevant information is available without first moving the mouse to a link. Furthermore, participants have not received any explanations about our anti-phishing artifact. Whether a transparent-link is more efficient, in particular after having received some explanations and/or after having used it for some time, is left for future work. Participants' SUS rating of the artifact is good, if we consider that it is a novel approach and that they have not received any explanations. The perceived usability is comparable to the one of the status quo (having the URL displayed in the statusbar).

Limitations. Our study design has security as its primary goal, an unlikely situation in real life. However, considering that our focus was to test a new approach's effectiveness, we argue that having security as the primary focus still bears useful results. The first step is to perform better in such a situation; the next one is – as soon as it is allowed due to the COVID-19 restrictions – to replicate the study in a lab environment, with a cover story and fewer phishes to make it more realistic. Furthermore, it is worth noticing, that although participants primary task was security, the CG did not perform much better than guessing (60% overall hit rate and 50% phishing detection). This confirms past research results that users lack awareness of the importance of checking the URL in the statusbar before clicking the link (see Wash [60]), and that people struggle with URLs in general (see Albakry et al. [1]). This also underlines the need for approaches like our anti-phishing artifact. Also, we acknowledge that the emails were all confirmations of new accounts. Giving the fact that phishes could only be detected when checking the URL and the transparent-string respectively. Thus, for the purpose of the study the actual content of the email was not that important. The emails were realistic, given the scenario presented. Furthermore, such emails lack the emotional pressure that, e.g., a fake bill would deliver. Similar to Reinheimer et al. [42], we use emails twice: As a phishing email and a legitimate one. Like Reinheimer et al. [42], we also believe that the impact of this choice is limited, as they were shown in random order. We choose email from organizations in the Alexa UK top webpages to reduce the effect of unknown services – and their legitimate URLs – on the results. Admittedly, we could not be sure of the familiarity of each participant with them, as we did not interviewed them about this. A possible solution to this could have been to use organizations created *ad-hoc* for this study. We believe, although, that this would not have solve the issue, as fictitious organization would have extended the unfamiliarity to every single participant, instead of some of them. We could have add the legitimate URL above each email, so that the participants could have compared those with the one showed. However, this would have greatly diminished the difficulty of the task and it would have been completely unrealistic (i.e., no legitimate URL is shown in real-life situations). We decided to use only one link for each email to help control for interfering factors. However, in real-life it is normal to received emails with multiple links, which might cause disruption when our artifact is applied. This could be solved by the toggle function, as it would return the email to its intended, original layout. Such evaluation, however, was besides the scope of this study and it will be covered in future works.

8   Conclusion

We developed a novel anti-phishing approach based on the Useful Transparency theory from Hosseini et al. [21]. The idea is to substitute all links present in an email with what we call a "transparent-string". Thereby, the artifacts presents the relevant information (and only that) about the link where the users' focus is. Furthermore, it enables checking the destination of the link also in case of form-elements and formactions-elements (in which no URL is displayed in the statusbar), as well as in case of short URLs and redirect URLs (without putting users at risk). We conducted an online survey with UK participants to evaluate our approach with respect to effectiveness in distinguishing between phishing and legitimate emails, efficiency and perceived usability. Our results show that by incorporating the Useful Transparency theory into our artifact, we were able to propose an approach which supports users in significantly better distinguishing between phishing and legitimate emails. Furthermore, the artifact does not lead to a delay in decision making (and, thus, has no negative impact on the users' performance) and does not decrease the perceived usability of emails.

A   System Usability Scale

(See Table 5).

Table 5. System usability scale used with research question. The italics is what the study group saw. Capitalized is the attention question added to the scale.

SUS scale used
I think that I would like to use this feature/*extension* frequently.
I found this feature/*extension* unnecessarily complex.
I thought this feature/*extension* was easy to use.
I think that I would need assistance to be able to use this feature/*extension*.
I found the various functions in this feature/*extension* were well integrated.
PLEASE, FOR THIS QUESTION, SELECT STRONGLY AGREE - 5.
I thought there was too much inconsistency in this feature/*extension*.
I would imagine that most people would learn to use this feature/*extension* very quickly.
I found this feature/*extension* very awkward to use.
I felt very confident using this feature/*extension*.
I needed to learn a lot of things before I could get going with this feature/*extension*.

References

1. Albakry, S., Vaniea, K., Wolters, M.K.: What is This URL's Destination? Empirical Evaluation of Users' URL Reading, pp. 1–12. ACM, NY, USA (2020). https://doi.org/10.1145/3313831.3376168
2. Alsharnouby, M., Alaca, F., Chiasson, S.: Why phishing still works: user strategies for combating phishing attacks. Int. J. Hum. Comput. Stud. **82**, 69–82 (2015). https://doi.org/10.1016/j.ijhcs.2015.05.005

3. APWG: Phishing Activity Trends Report (2021). https://docs.apwg.org/reports/apwg_trends_report_q2_2020.pdf
4. Arachchilage, N.A., Flechais, I., Beznosov, K.: A game storyboard design for avoiding phishing attacks. In: SOUPS '14, p. 2 (2014)
5. Bangor, A., Kortum, P., Miller, J.: An empirical evaluation of the system usability scale. Int. J. Hum.-Comput. Int. **24**(6), 574–594 (2008). https://doi.org/10.1080/10447310802205776
6. Bangor, A., Kortum, P., Miller, J.: Determining what individual sus scores mean: adding an adjective rating scale. JUX **4**(3), 114–123 (2009)
7. Benenson, Z., Gassmann, F., Landwirth, R.: Unpacking spear phishing susceptibility. In: FC '17 (2017). https://doi.org/10.1007/978-3-319-70278-0_39
8. Brooke, J.: SUS: a "quick and dirty" usability. Usability Eval. Ind. **189**(3), 189–194 (1996)
9. Butavicius, M.A., Parsons, K., Pattinson, M.R., McCormac, A., Calic, D., Lillie, M.: Understanding susceptibility to phishing emails: assessing the impact of individual differences and culture. In: HAISA'17, pp. 12–23 (2017). http://www.cscan.org/openaccess/?paperid=354
10. Canfield, C., Fischhoff, B., Davis, A.: Using signal detection theory to measure phishing detection ability and behavior. In: SOUPS '15 (2015)
11. Caputo, D.D., Pfleeger, S.L., Freeman, J.D., Johnson, M.E.: Going spear phishing: exploring embedded training and awareness. IEEE Secur. Priv. **12**(1), 28–38 (2014). https://doi.org/10.1109/MSP.2013.106
12. Chiew, K.L., Chang, E.H., Sze, S.N., Tiong, W.K.: Utilisation of website logo for phishing detection. Comput. Secur. **54**, 16–26 (2015). https://doi.org/10.1016/j.cose.2015.07.006
13. Cohen, J.: Statistical Power Analysis for the Behavioral Sciences. Routledge, NY, USA (2013)
14. FBI: 2020 Internet Crime Report (2021). https://www.ic3.gov/Media/PDF/AnnualReport/2020_IC3Report.pdf
15. Filipczuk, D., Mason, C., Snow, S.: Using a game to explore notions of responsibility for cyber security in organisations. In: CHI '19, pp. 1–6 (2019). https://doi.org/10.1145/3290607.3312846
16. Garera, S., Provos, N., Chew, M., Rubin, A.D.: A framework for detection and measurement of phishing attacks. In: WORM '07, p. 1 (2007). https://doi.org/10.1145/1314389.1314391
17. Google: Report domain name abuse - Google Domains Help (2021). https://support.google.com/domains/answer/10093434?hl=en
18. GOV.UK: National Minimum Wage and National Living Wage rates (2020). https://www.gov.uk/national-minimum-wage-rates
19. Gregor, S., Hevner, A.R.: Positioning and presenting design science research for maximum impact. MIS Q. **37**(2), 337–356 (2013). https://doi.org/10.25300/MISQ/2013/37.2.01
20. Hevner, A., Chatterjee, S.: Design science research in information systems. In: DESRIST '12, pp. 9–22 (2010). https://doi.org/10.1007/978-1-4419-5653-8_2
21. Hosseini, M., Shahri, A., Phalp, K., Ali, R.: Four reference models for transparency requirements in information systems. Requir. Eng. **23**(2), 251–275 (2018). https://doi.org/10.1007/s00766-017-0265-y
22. IBM: Cost of a Data Breach Report 2021 (2021). https://www.ibm.com/security/data-breach
23. Keren, G.: Between or within Subjects Design: A Methodological Dilemma, pp. 257–273. Lawrence Erlbaum, New Jersey (1993)

24. Kirlappos, I., Sasse, M.A.: Security education against phishing: a modest proposal for a major rethink. IEEE Secur. Priv. **10**(2), 24–32 (2012)

25. Kuechler, W., Vaishnavi, V.: A framework for theory development in design science research: multiple perspectives. JAIS **13**(6), 395 (2012). https://doi.org/10.17705/1jais.00300

26. Kühl, N., Mühlthaler, M., Goutier, M.: Supporting customer-oriented marketing with artificial intelligence: automatically quantifying customer needs from social media. Electron. Mark. **30**(2), 351–367 (2020). https://doi.org/10.1007/s12525-019-00351-0

27. Kumaraguru, P., Rhee, Y., Acquisti, A., Cranor, L.F., Hong, J., Nunge, E.: Protecting people from phishing: the design and evaluation of an embedded training email system. In: CHI '07, pp. 905–914 (2007). https://doi.org/10.1145/1240624.1240760

28. Lewis, J.R.: The system usability scale: Past, present, and future. Int. J. Hum.-Comp. Int. **34**(7), 577–590 (2018). https://doi.org/10.1080/10447318.2018.1455307

29. Lin, E., Greenberg, S., Trotter, E., Ma, D., Aycock, J.: Does domain highlighting help people identify phishing sites? In: CHI '11, pp. 2075–2084 (2011). https://doi.org/10.1145/1978942.1979244

30. Ma, J., Saul, L.K., Savage, S., Voelker, G.M.: Beyond blacklists: learning to detect malicious web sites from suspicious urls. In: KDD '09, pp. 1245–1254 (2009). https://doi.org/10.1145/1557019.1557153

31. March, S.T., Smith, G.F.: Design and natural science research on information technology. Decis. Support Syst. **15**(4), 251–266 (1995). https://doi.org/10.1016/0167-9236(94)00041-2

32. Martin, J., Dubé, C., Coovert, M.D.: Signal detection theory (SDT) is effective for modeling user behavior toward phishing and spear-phishing attacks. Hum. Factors **60**(8), 1179–1191 (2018). https://doi.org/10.1177/0018720818789818

33. Mayhorn, C.B., Nyeste, P.G.: Training users to counteract phishing. Work **41**(Suppl 1), 3549–52 (2012). https://doi.org/10.3233/wor-2012-1054-3549

34. Meta: Protecting People from Domain Name Fraud (2020). https://about.fb.com/news/2020/03/domain-name-lawsuit/

35. Meta: Protecting People From Imposter Domain Names (2020). https://about.fb.com/news/2020/06/imposter-domain-names/

36. Moreno-Fernndez, M.M., Blanco, F., Garaizar, P., Matute, H.: Fishing for phishers. improving internet users' sensitivity to visual deception cues to prevent electronic fraud. Comput. Hum. Behav. **69**(C), 421–436 (2017). https://doi.org/10.1016/j.chb.2016.12.044

37. Mossano, M., et al.: SMILE - smart email link domain extractor. In: SPOSE '21, pp. 403–412 (2022). https://doi.org/10.1007/978-3-030-95484-0_23

38. Mozilla Foundation: Public Suffix List (2020). https://publicsuffix.org/

39. Oest, A., et al.: Sunrise to sunset: analyzing the end-to-end life cycle and effectiveness of phishing attacks at scale. In: CSS '20, pp. 361–377 (2020)

40. Petelka, J., Zou, Y., Schaub, F.: Put your warning where your link is: improving and evaluating email phishing warnings. In: CHI '19, pp. 1–15 (2019). https://doi.org/10.1145/3290605.3300748

41. Pirocca, S., Allodi, L., Zannone, N.: A toolkit for security awareness training against targeted phishing. In: ICISS '20, pp. 137–159 (2020). https://doi.org/10.1007/978-3-030-65610-2_9

42. Reinheimer, B., et al.: An investigation of phishing awareness and education over time: when and how to best remind users. In: SOUPS '20, pp. 259–284 (2020)

43. Reynolds, J., et al.: Measuring identity confusion with uniform resource locators. In: CHI '20, pp. 1–12 (2020). https://doi.org/10.1145/3313831.3376298
44. Sheng, S., et al.: Anti-phishing phil: the design and evaluation of a game that teaches people not to fall for phish. In: SOUPS '07, pp. 88–99 (2007)
45. Statcounter: Desktop Browser Market Share United Kingdom (2020). https://gs.statcounter.com/browser-market-share/desktop/united-kingdom
46. Statcounter: Desktop Operating System Market Share United Kingdom (2020). https://gs.statcounter.com/os-market-share/desktop/united-kingdom
47. Teixeira, J.G., Patrício, L., Tuunanen, T.: Advancing service design research with design science research. J. Serv. Manag. **30**(5), 577–592 (2019). https://doi.org/10.1108/JOSM-05-2019-0131
48. Tschakert, K.F., Ngamsuriyaroj, S.: Effectiveness of and user preferences for security awareness training methodologies. Heliyon **5**, e02010 (2019). https://doi.org/10.1016/j.heliyon.2019.e02010
49. Upton, G., Cook, I.: Understanding Statistics. Oxford University Press, Oxford, UK (1996)
50. Vance, A., Jenkins, J.L., Anderson, B.B., Bjornn, D.K., Kirwan, C.B.: Tuning out security warnings: a longitudinal examination of habituation through fMRI, eye tracking, and field experiments. MIS Q. **42**(2), 355–380 (2018). https://doi.org/10.25300/MISQ/2018/14124
51. Venable, J., Pries-Heje, J., Baskerville, R.: Feds: a framework for evaluation in design science research. Eur. J. Inf. Syst. **25**(1), 77–89 (2016). https://doi.org/10.1057/ejis.2014.36
52. Verizon: Data Breach Investigations Report (2021). https://enterprise.verizon.com/resources/reports/2021-data-breach-investigations-report.pdf
53. Vishwanath, A., et al.: Cyber hygiene: the concept, its measure, and its initial tests. Decis. Support Sys. **128**, 113–160 (2020). https://doi.org/10.1016/j.dss.2019.113160
54. Volkamer, M., Renaud, K., Canova, G., Reinheimer, B., Braun, K.: Design and field evaluation of passsec: raising and sustaining web surfer risk awareness. In: TRUST '15, pp. 104–122 (2015). https://doi.org/10.1007/978-3-319-22846-4_7
55. Volkamer, M., Renaud, K., Gerber, P.: Spot the phish by checking the pruned url. Inf. Comput. Secur. **24**(4), 372–385 (2016). https://doi.org/10.1108/ICS-07-2015-0032
56. Volkamer, M., Renaud, K., Reinheimer, B., Kunz, A.: User experiences of torpedo: tooltip-powered phishing email detection. Comput. Secur. **71**, 100–113 (2017). https://doi.org/10.1016/j.cose.2017.02.004
57. Volkamer, M., Sasse, M.A., Boehm, F.: Analysing simulated phishing campaigns for staff. Comput. Secur. 312–328 (2020). https://doi.org/10.1007/978-3-030-66504-3_19
58. Vössing, M., Kühl, N., Lind, M., Satzger, G.: Designing transparency for effective human-ai collaboration. Inf. Syst. Front. 1–19 (2022). https://doi.org/10.1007/s10796-022-10284-3
59. Wang, J., Li, Y., Rao, H.R.: Overconfidence in phishing email detection. JAIS **17**(11), 1 (2016). https://doi.org/10.17705/1jais.00442
60. Wash, R.: How experts detect phishing scam emails. Proc. ACM Hum.-Comput. Interact. **4**(CSCW2), 160:1–28 (2020). https://doi.org/10.1145/3415231
61. Wash, R., Cooper, M.: Who provides phishing training? In: CHI '18 (2018). https://doi.org/10.1145/3173574.3174066

62. Wright, R.T., Jensen, M.L., Thatcher, J.B., Dinger, M., Marett, K.: Influence techniques in phishing attacks: an examination of vulnerability and resistance. Inf. Syst. Res. **25**(2), 385–400 (2014). https://doi.org/10.1287/isre.2014.0522

63. Zhu, E., Chen, Y., Ye, C., Li, X., Liu, F.: OFS-NN: an effective phishing websites detection model based on optimal feature selection and neural network. IEEE Access **7**, 73271–73284 (2019). https://doi.org/10.1109/ACCESS.2019.2920655

Work in Progress – Brick by Brick: Using a Structured Building Blocks Method to Engage Participants and Collect IT Security Insights

Uta Menges[1]([✉]) [ID], Jonas Hielscher[2] [ID], Annette Kluge[1] [ID],
and M. Angela Sasse[2] [ID]

[1] Faculty of Psychology, Ruhr-University Bochum, Bochum, Germany
{uta.menges,annette.kluge}@ruhr-uni-bochum.de
[2] Ruhr-University Bochum, Horst-Görtz-Institute of IT-Security, Bochum, Germany
{jonas.hielscher,mangela.Sasse}@ruhr-uni-bochum.de

Abstract. Qualitative research methods from psychology and social sciences are feasible tools to gain deep understandings of people's IT security behaviour, knowledge, sentiments and routines. One of these methods, individuals' own expression in the form of drawings, sketches, charts and other visual representations, are important to understand deep knowledge and mental models. However, those methods are, to some degree, dependent on the *artistic skills* of the participants – those that are not confident in their handwriting and drawing might engage less. Building Blocks (sets of interlocking bricks) require less artistic ability and it is very easy to engage participants – they can *just start building*. IT security researchers already used such bricks to model participants thoughts, but in heterogeneous ways. We on the other hand used the LEGO© SERIOUS PLAY© (LSP) method – that describes a structured way on how to build models – to conduct four workshops (with $n = 48$ participants in total), in which the participants were asked to build multiple models of everyday IT security in different contexts. We performed a first initial coding of the pictures we took during the workshops. In this paper we report our research method, what we did to improve the workshops and data collection and what we learned so far by using LSP.

Keywords: Building Blocks Workshop · Building Blocks in IT-Security · Qualitative Research Methods · Human-Centred Security · Security Workshops

1 Introduction

To collect and analyse knowledge and to understand the mental models of people in IT security, researchers often use well established methods from social science and psychology like interviews [20], diary studies [8], questionnaires [11], interactive group sessions [1], or even ethnographic observations in the field [14]. Those

M. Mehrnezhad and S. Parkin (Eds.): STAST 2022, LNCS 13855, pp. 134–145, 2025.
https://doi.org/10.1007/978-3-031-83072-3_8

methods have been established for decades but they do not necessarily encourage participants to fully engage in the research process. Here, more interactive and game-based methods come into play. LEGO© SERIOUS PLAY© (LSP) is used in different areas and for diverse purposes, such as individual coaching or in an organisational context to promote team building or to develop the corporate culture [13]. It defines a strict way of using interlocking bricks to collect thoughts and knowledge of participants. The advantage over more traditional methods, like drawing on boards or creating mind maps, is the low hurdle for active participation.

Interlocking bricks were in different forms already used in previous IT security studies, foremost by Coles-Kemp et al. [6,7,9,10]. The used building methods were heterogeneous (e.g. modelling by coloured bricks, modelling based on communication flows) as were the data collection and analysis methods (coding of participants explanations, video and audio transcripts of the workshops). In this paper we outline a new, more structured way of using those bricks for qualitative data collection: by using the LSP method that has a clear pathway and set of rules on how to build models and engage participants. We organised 4 independent in-person workshops with $n = 48$ participants, where we tasked the participants to build and explain models of bricks that describe different forms of everyday security. In a first attempt we coded the pictures we took of the models. In this paper we report our work-in-progress with this method and how far we came to answer our research question: *Q1: Can LSP be used to generate qualitative in-depth knowledge of IT security from workshop participants, to learn more about their everyday and work-related experiences and challenges in the context of IT security measure, and to activate them to approach and deal with the topic of IT security in a creative and cooperative way?*

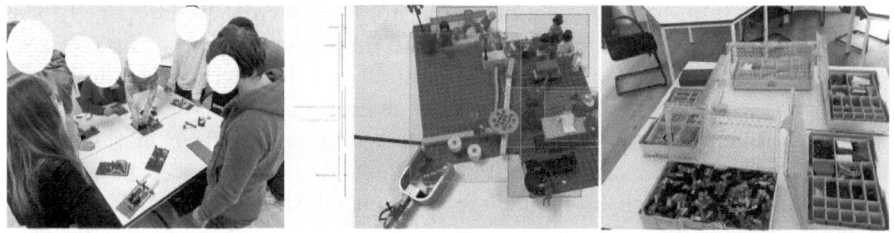

Fig. 1. (I) Participants discussing a group model, (II) the coding process in MaxQDA, (III) the LSP bricks arranged at a central table.

2 Related Work and Background

2.1 IT Security and Interlocking Bricks

Interlocking bricks were used in IT security research but we are the first to use the structured LSP method to collect qualitative data. Among other things, Coles-Kemp [6] developed a study approach based on "creative security", described as a technique for participatory and playful engagement. A total of 55 security practitioners used kits of interlocking bricks to model technical, security and social impacts of IoT surveillance. Data analysis was based on handwritten annotations and photos of the models. Heath et al. [10] describe that these creative methods include participatory physical modelling for co-creation and representation. By having participants build models with coloured bricks, it is possible to model relevant issues into tangible scenes. In another study aimed at better understanding the conditions under which a smart city brings benefits to citizens, Heath et al. [9] again used a methodology based on creative safety. In addition to a standardised protocol, modelling components in the form of Lego were introduced. The study participants worked with interlocking bricks on scenarios and questions related to smart technologies. To address the difficulties that the human dimension is often glossed over in the context of cybersecurity studies and that different degrees of trust and solidarity lead to different perceptions of security, the authors [7] describe that a four-stage case study was undertaken. During the last two stages of this process, participants were given interlocking bricks selected so as to encode the movement of shared information and data, actors and devices.

2.2   LEGO© SERIOUS PLAY©

Hillmer describes the LSP method in his practice guide as a format that follows a clear process [13]. Participants have the opportunity to present their thoughts, concepts and feelings. At the heart of each process is a specific question or problem that relates to the topic of IT and information security in the workshops described here. Participants are "forced" to radically simplify in the LSP process, as they have to present complex models and concepts with the Bricks. This is especially helpful to prioritize and structure their own thoughts [13]. In this case, the simplification can primarily serve to make the seemingly abstract subject area of IT security more tangible. In addition, this method is suitable for a more reserved group member, since they share their models with the others. The flow state also plays a crucial role in connection with the LSP method. Zenk et al. [23], investigated whether LSP workshops lead to improved flow experience components as well as higher creative output than traditional meetings. Their results show that two components of the individual flow experience were significantly higher in LSP and the group experience component – continuous communication – was significantly lower, as expected. In terms of creative output, their study showed that LSP teams outperformed traditional meeting teams. A crucial role is assigned to the LSP moderator since, in addition to the tasks of preparation, follow-up and implementation, they also take on the role of support and mediator during the process. In the case of the workshops described here, the two authors assume this role. They have familiarised themselves with this method in advance, in particular through literature, and have prior experience in the counselling context with individuals and groups. At the beginning of the LSP process there is skill building, which serves to familiarise oneself with the method and the material. This is followed by the main part, which consists of two required and a third optional building stage.

A few authors report how they used LSP for scientific purposes, but only to transfer knowledge. Mccusker [17], presents her findings on the LSP method in the educational domain. In order to identify hazardous situations in group models, exchange ideas and discuss alternative proposals, the LSP method of Cerezo-Narváez et al. [5] was used by student engineers as a tool for teaching industrial risk prevention skills. In their exploratory study, Kranawetleitner et al. [15] addressed the problem that the digitisation process in organisations is often dependent on the size of the organisation and the sector. The majority of the 21 participants did not know the LSP method and had never used it before. The playful element of LSP was adopted by the clear majority of participants. The method also helped employees become aware of the practical implications of digitalisation, with some even learning through their participation. Furthermore, Uslar and Hanna [21] discuss how they have applied the LSP method in the context of domain-specific requirements engineering in industrial projects. Similar to the authors of this article, Asprion et al. [2] approached the topic of cybersecurity using LSP and used the method to teach core topics of cybersecurity and resilience in higher education. The initial results of their study indicate that LSP has a positive impact on learning and increases student engagement.

3   Method

We conducted 4 workshops, where the in total $n = 48$ participants were asked to solve IT security tasks with the LSP method. We then did a first initial coding.

3.1   Workshops

All 4 workshops were embedded in other events. Workshop I, II and IV were part of lectures or seminars at our university. Workshop III was part of a security training event we co-organised with a large European industrial corporation with more than 25,000 employees where we are currently performing research about Human Centred IT security. The participants were informed beforehand about the LSP method and our intent to use the results for our research. The workshops differed from each other in the type of participants and in the tasks given to the participants (see also Table 1). The general structure was a short introduction by the researchers (also acting as moderators – or as they are called in LSP: *Facilitators*), followed by the task to build a (I) model of a tower or bridge, (II) an abstract model of an IT security concept (e.g. VPN, phishing, ransomware, firewall), (III) models of workshop specific tasks – which were all created around the topic of **everyday IT security the participants faced themselves or were in a given case study** – that are end-user routines like authentication processes, VPN usage but also the communication with the IT security department or the prevention of tailgating. We did not define what we

understood as IT security and left it open to the interpretation of the participants. With this task we aimed to get insights into the mental models that
participants have about the interplay of security (department) and users, e.g.
whether they would model *security friction*? The participants created the models individually, in pairs, or in bigger groups. We used 1,5 full sets of LSP bricks[1]
that were arranged at a central table all participants had access to.

During each workshop we collected three types of data: (I) We took pictures
of every model the participants built. (II) We took notes on the participants'
explanations of their models. (III) We asked the participants for feedback in
a short online survey directly after three of the workshops. From the second
workshop on the participants also had to explain their models on small cards,
which we included in the data collection.

3.2 Coding

Our coding process is still in progress. So far we have used MaxQDA to code
the pictures we took of the models built during the main tasks, following [19].
We have also used MaxQDA to partially code the participants' notes as well
as our own and the pictures of the warm-up tasks. We deductively defined the
following categories of codes: (I) persons, (II) everyday security, (III) structures
and (IV) technologies. The data was then inductively coded by two researchers
(two workshops per researcher). We are planning to rerun our coding process
and try to follow Kuckartz's [16] approach, which is more collaboratively on
the one hand (including the calculation of the intercoder reliability), and on
the other hand we then will create code-sets that span all the workshops. We
have not done that so far, as we wanted to focus first on the improvement of the
workshops and the respective data collection between the workshops. In order to
evaluate the workshops and improve them for the following workshops, we used
the evaluations and feedback from the online surveys and took the comments –
if possible – into account in the design and implementation.

3.3 Ethics and Data Privacy

Our institution does not yet have an institutional review board (IRB) nor an
ethics review board (ERB) that we could consult for our study. We got consent from all participants to take pictures of their models and use them in our
research. In the first workshop we took pictures of the participants themselves,
for what we got their consent (see Fig. 1). Except these pictures, no personal
data of the participants was collected at any time.

3.4 Limitations

Our study has several limitations. Foremost, we report work in progress, especially regarding the coding strategy, therefore all results should be taken with

---

[1] Each consisting of thousands of interlocking bricks.

care. The tasks were changed slightly between each workshop to match the participants' context, which reduces the comparability between the results. The time we had available per workshop made amendments to the LSP method necessary, therefore we reduced the warm-up phase to two tasks each. Our participant sample is in no way representative and hence, generalisation of our results is not possible. Within the framework of the evaluation, it would have been desirable to also go into conversations as well as discussions of the participants during the individual construction phases. However, since we as facilitators had to respond to the participants' questions during the construction phases, accompany the process and prepare the other phases, it was not possible to include this aspect in the documentation. Furthermore, we did not want to create an impression of control and and evaluation of the discussions among the participants.

4 Results

4.1 Demographics

We did not ask the participants for demographic data. What we can report, based on the context of the workshops, is that all participants were less than 35 years of age, more than 1/3 were female, all were German speaking and all had a connection to IT security (either due to their education or due to their interests). The educational backgrounds of the participants are tied to the respective workshops (see also Table 1).

4.2 Workshops

All 4 workshops conducted have a common basic structure: The bricks were arranged on a central table, warm-up tasks had to be solved by participants individually and in teams and the main tasks were designed around the topic of everyday security (see also Table 1). We selected the main tasks in each workshop according to the background of the event and prior knowledge. In the following we report the results drawn from our coding process of the main-task model. The participants' explanations of their models and/ or individual bricks are summarised by us in a descriptive way based on our notes.

Workshop 1. The first workshop was conducted in April 2022. It was part of a graduate school program. The $n_1 = 8$ participants were PhD students with interdisciplinary research areas related to IT security topics. The workshop lasted 90 min. In total five building tasks had to be completed, with the main task being: *Build a model that shows how IT security should work in your everyday life.* Despite this positive framing, some participants showed how IT security does not work for them: crumbling (fire-)walls, multiple different path for attackers to reach assets, no help by IT security experts (modelled as an user left alone in the rain) and unintended data leaks. IT security was exclusively understood as a technique to protect either communication channels (by tunnelling them or placing guards at the entrance points) or assets (data or money). Attackers were in all cases modelled as outsiders that try to circumvent the security measures. One participant showed that IT security is a bottomless pit at the moment: just throwing more money on security will not improve the level of security. In two cases the users were shown on lonely islands together with their assets, where attackers will not reach them.

Workshop 2. The second workshop was conducted in May 2022 with $n_2 = 19$ IT security master's students as part of a lecture series. In the lecture series the students worked with a case study in a hospital setting. We used this case study to model the primary task of the workshop: *Build a model that shows how IT security does work/ does not work in the hospital.* Firewalls and gates were the most frequently used concepts appearing on 6 and 7 occasions, respectively. In all models where defenders were represented the defence was exclusively represented as a task for security specialist, never for employees. On the other hand, in 7 models the employees (doctors and nurses) circumvented security in some regard (password sharing, RFID card sharing, single account usage). None of the models described that this might be the case due to task overload, as was described in the case study – a typical form of an exhausted compliance budget [3]. Only once was the blame put on the security staff when technical problems with the hospital IT were displayed. Overall, participants exclusively chose to show problems with IT security routines in the hospital, despite the task description being open to positive examples as well. Attackers were in all cases modelled as outsiders (behind walls or in front of gates) that would use tools to infiltrate the hospital. Only in some cases did the models show the intention of the attackers (e.g., to disturb a surgery or steal assets – in form of money bricks). In one case, the attacker was modelled as a spy, overseeing the hospital routine from a "watchtower". In another case, the hospital's CISO was sitting on a throne and was unreachable for other hospital employees. And in a third case, the IT department was stealing time from employees through useless technological innovations.

Table 1. The 4 workshops differ in their context and in the models the participants had to build.

	Workshop 1	Workshop 2	Workshop 3	Workshop 4
n	8	19	17	4
Setting	Graduate school	Lecture	Inter-Organisation	Seminar
Participants	PhD researchers (different disciplines)	IT security students	MA multidisciplinary apprentices	Psychology BA Students
Duration	1.5h	1.5h	1h	3h
Content	IT security in every day life	IT security in a case study (hospital)	IT security in the participants organisation	IT security at work and/or at university

Workshop 3. The third workshop was also conducted in May 2022. It was organised within a 3-day, in-person workshop hosted by a German corporation that partners with us. At this workshop apprentices were educated on different aspects of corporate information security. $n_3 = 17$ apprentices participated in our workshop. The group was divided into two groups. Both groups participated in our workshop one after another independently. Both sessions lasted 60 min. The task considered for this evaluation was the following: *Build a model of IT and information security as it should work in your everyday working life.* The participants focused their models on generic IT security measures, but also on specific measures including two-factor authentication, passwords, password managers, virus scanners, firewalls and face recognition. In addition, the coding process revealed that they built different types of data worth protecting. IT security staff and attackers were also frequently represented in the models. A participant in the second group tried to show, through his model, that IT security departments that are slow in their responses lead to delayed learning and working in the organisation. Another participant from group one presented as desirable in his model that IT security should be a simple and linear means to achieve the goal of "secure behaviour". In his model, he used several figures to show that this goal could only be achieved as a group. In another model, it was impressively shown how employees stand waiting behind the wall (firewall) and neither know nor understand what is actually happening in the context of IT security.

Workshop 4. The fourth and last workshop was held with $n_4 = 4$ psychology students as part of a seminar in which they dealt with the topic of IT security in organisations in the beginning of July 2022. The LSP workshop took about three hours. The main task of a total of five consisted of: *Build a model that shows how IT security should work in your everyday work/ study life.* These students dealt with the topic of IT security in an organisational context for the first time. Among other things, they were familiarised with the security learning curve [12] as part of a theoretical introduction. None of the participants had previously been involved with LSP or gone through an LSP workshop. The coding process showed that the participants mainly chose IT security staff, employees, users and animals (for attackers or protection) for their models. Generic IT security measures, firewalls and (organisational) data requiring special protection were represented especially often. In the group model, the participants built a model that contained parts from all four individual models. Threats were presented in the form of attackers who were placed in front of the organisation. Security measures were presented in both generic and detailed forms (anti virus, password manager, etc.). They used connecting elements to show that the different security mechanisms must "work together" and not interfere with each other. A gap in the "corporate wall" was built to show that an organisation can never experience 100% security, as technology is always evolving and so are attackers. The students used green bricks to depict a room with two employees, symbolising that it is important and helpful to have a protected place to talk to each other in peace about the topic of IT security, to ask questions and to be able to talk about challenges. A comprehensive IT security/ awareness training was presented on a black board and concrete instructions for the employees were symbolised with the help of a white board. It was shown that only three out of four employees represented can undergo a security training. One employee is not able to do so because he is busy following a security measure.

4.3   Post-workshop Survey Results

Of the $n = 48$ participants, 38 took part in the post-feedback online survey. Some of the participants reported back that by approaching the topic of IT security through the LSP method, they had become aware that the reason some employees do not participate in awareness and IT security training may be that they cannot, because they are not given the necessary time by their employer. Some have also noticed that the model they have built presents IT security in organisations in a very positive way.

5   Discussion

Here we discuss a) substantive results: the models the participants created, and b) methodological results: what we learnt about conducting model workshops.

What We Learned about IT Security from Participants' Models. Having a background in IT security does not necessarily lead to a deeper understanding of everyday security (routines). For example, did the IT security master's students in the second workshop had a very narrow perspective on how security works for security staff (defender at the walls of the fortress) versus employees (bad guys circumventing security) and those differ not from models from the other groups. In multiple models, communication problems between different security stakeholders were shown – something we want to investigate in more detail in future rounds of coding and further workshops. Interestingly, independent of whether the task was formulated negatively or positively, the majority of models showed problems with security: Flaws in the security itself, blaming of others (e.g. employees) and communication problems between security staff and users/employees. This fits into the image that IT security is rarely seen as an enabler and with a positive connotation [18].
    The evaluation also showed that in several models, the topic of interaction and collaboration – on different levels – was taken into account and considered relevant. This relates firstly to the technical side: the individual security mechanisms should function together. Furthermore, this concerns the human-technology interaction, as individual models emphasised the relevance of the fact that the IT security mechanisms and the IT security staff must also "work together". On the other hand, the human level was presented and it was shown that both users and organisations are only protected if the IT security staff and the employees communicate and work together.

Learnings from the Method. Comparing results from the four workshops, it becomes clear that having enough time is an important factor for the success of LSP. As there was more time available at the fourth, the participants were able to share and reflect on the individual and group models in more detail. It was very helpful to introduce the rules for sharing the models in detail (do not tell a story but explain the model; tap the bricks you are telling about beforehand, etc.) and to repeat them during the process. These insights made the authors aware of the central role of the facilitator – already described in the literature [13] – who is responsible for the process.

The quality of our data collection is limited to the pictures and our notes. It seems promising to also record the complete workshop with a camera as in [10], where individual interactions and discussions among participants could be analysed as well. We decided not to record these sessions because we did not want to put off participants concerned about privacy; the company of the participants in Workshop 3 only agreed on the condition that individual participants remained anonymous.

Without explanations and notes by the participants it is hardly possible to reconstruct the content later. We found that the models are not self-explanatory. Therefore, the focus of the evaluation was not exclusively on the representational value of the models, but rather on observing and recording the participants' explanations about their models and the exchange about them.

The Chances of LSP. LSP has the advantage to be a structured method – compared with so many other (creative or brick-based) methods. This makes (I) the single steps and results reproducible (like we did between the four workshops), (II) the method teachable to other researchers (like we thought ourselves based on the description by Hillmer [13]), (III) it easier to transfer it back to the industry, where it already used for teaching purposes.

In our workshops even participants who did not previously know each other quickly interacted with each other through the LSP method, and a productive working atmosphere characterised by mutual respect was established in a very short time. Even participants who had not previously dealt with the topic of IT security were able to approach this topic under these conditions with the help of this method. This means it works as a communication focus as intended in participatory design [4, 22].

6   Conclusion and Further Work

We report work-in-progress from qualitative research with LSP. So far we conducted four workshops with $n = 48$ participants. We coded the collected data, but are still in the process of improving this strategy and will report the final coding strategy. Our preliminary results show that participants model IT security as a hurdle for users/employees – independently of whether they have an IT security background. LSP is a promising research method than engages most people and could serve as an alternative to focus group or as a method in action research. To be able to answer our research question, we still need to compare LSP with other qualitative data collection methods. We are planning to perform workshops with the same tasks but other creative methods (like drawing, creating mind maps, etc.) and then compare the coding results.

Acknowledgments. We want to thank all participants of our Lego workshops. Many thanks also to Mary Cheney, Marco Gutfleisch and Markus Schöps for their proof-reading as well as to the anonymous reviewers for their helpful feedback. The work was supported by the PhD School "SecHuman - Security for Humans in Cyberspace" by the federal state of NRW, Germany and also by the Deutsche Forschungsgemeinschaft (DFG, German Research Foundation) under Germany's Excellence Strategy - EXC 2092 CASA - 390781972.

References

1. Ashenden, D., Lawrence, D.: Security dialogues: building better relationships between security and business. IEEE Secur. Priv. **14**(3), 82–87 (2016). https://doi.org/10.1109/MSP.2016.57

2. Asprion, P.M., Schneider, B., Moriggl, P., Grimberg, F.: Exploring cyber security awareness through LEGO serious play Part I: the learning experience. Management **20**, 22 (2020)

3. Beautement, A., Sasse, M.A., Wonham, M.: The compliance budget: managing security behaviour in organisations. In: Keromytis, A., Somayaji, A., Probst, C.W., Bishop, M. (eds.) Proceedings of the 2008 Workshop on New Security Paradigms, p. 47. Association for Computing Machinery, New York (2008). https://doi.org/10.1145/1595676.1595684

4. Bodker, S.: Through the Interface: A Human Activity Approach to User Interface Design. Taylor & Francis Group, Milton (1990)

5. Cerezo-Narváez, A., Córdoba-Roldán, A., Pastor-Fernández, A., Aguayo-González, F., Otero-Mateo, M., Ballesteros-Pérez, P.: Training competences in industrial risk prevention with lego® serious play: a case study. Safety **5**(4), 81 (2019)

6. Coles-Kemp, L., Jensen, R.B., Heath, C.P.R.: Too much information: questioning security in a post-digital society. In: Bernhaupt, R., et al. (eds.) Proceedings of the 2020 CHI Conference on Human Factors in Computing Systems, pp. 1–14. ACM, New York, NY, USA (2020). https://doi.org/10.1145/3313831.3376214

7. Hall, P., Heath, C., Coles-Kemp, L.: Critical visualization: a case for rethinking how we visualize risk and security. J. Cybersecur. tyv004 (2015). https://doi.org/10.1093/cybsec/tyv004

8. Hayashi, E., Hong, J.: A diary study of password usage in daily life. In: Proceedings of the SIGCHI Conference on Human Factors in Computing Systems, pp. 2627–2630 (2011)

9. Heath, C.P.R., Crivellaro, C., Coles-Kemp, L.: Relations are more than bytes: re-thinking the benefits of smart services through people and things. In: Proceedings of the 2019 CHI Conference on Human Factors in Computing Systems, pp. 1–12. CHI '19, Association for Computing Machinery, New York, NY, USA (2019). https://doi.org/10.1145/3290605.3300538,

10. Heath, C.P., Hall, P.A., Coles-Kemp, L.: Holding on to dissensus: participatory interactions in security design. Strateg. Des. Res. J. **11**(2), 65–78 (2018). https://doi.org/10.4013/sdrj.2018.112.03

11. Herbert, F., Farke, F.M., Kowalewski, M., Dürmuth, M.: Vision: developing a broad usable security & privacy questionnaire. In: European Symposium on Usable Security 2021, pp. 76–82 (2021)

12. Hielscher, J., Kluge, A., Menges, U., Sasse, M.A.: Taking out the trash: why security behavior change requires intentional forgetting. In: New Security Paradigms

Workshop, pp. 108–122. ACM, New York, NY, USA (2021). https://doi.org/10.1145/3498891.3498902

13. Hillmer, D.: PLAY! Der unverzichtbare LEGO SERIOUS PLAY Praxis-Guide für Trainer, Coaches und Moderatoren (German). Hanser, München (2021)

14. Kocksch, L., Korn, M., Poller, A., Wagenknecht, S.: Caring for it security: accountabilities, moralities, and oscillations in it security practices. Proc. ACM Hum.-Comput. Interact. **2**(CSCW), 1–20 (2018)

15. Kranawetleitner, T., Krebs, H., Kuhn, N., Menner, M.: Needs analyses with LEGO serious play. In: Ma, M., Fletcher, B., Göbel, S., Baalsrud Hauge, J., Marsh, T. (eds.) Serious Games, LNCS, vol. 12434, pp. 99–104. Springer International Publishing, Cham (2020). https://doi.org/10.1007/978-3-030-61814-8

16. Kuckartz, U.: Qualitative Text Analysis: A Guide to Methods, Practice & Using Software. SAGE, Los Angeles and London and New Delhi and Singapore and Washington, DC (2014)

17. McCusker, S.: Lego, seriously: thinking through building. Int. J. Knowl. Innov. Entrep. **2**(1), 27–37 (2014)

18. Menges, U., Hielscher, J., Buckmann, A., Kluge, A., Sasse, M.A., Verret, I.: Why IT Security Needs Therapy. In: Computer Security. ESORICS 2021 International Workshops. Springer (2022). https://doi.org/10.1007/978-3-030-95484-0

19. Rädiker, S., Kuckartz, U.: Videodaten, Audiodaten und Bilder codieren (German). In: Rädiker, S., Kuckartz, U. (eds.) Analyse qualitativer Daten mit MAXQDA, pp. 85–94. Springer Fachmedien Wiesbaden, Wiesbaden (2019). https://doi.org/10.1007/978-3-658-22095-2

20. Redmiles, E.M., Acar, Y.G., Fahl, S., Mazurek, M.L.: A summary of survey methodology best practices for security and privacy researchers (2017)

21. Uslar, M., Hanna, S.: Teaching domain-specific requirements engineering to industry: applying lego serious play to smart grids. In: 1st Workshop on Innovative Software Engineering Education (2018)

22. Winograd, T.: Bringing design to software. ACM (1996)

23. Zenk, L., Primus, D.J., Sonnenburg, S.: Alone but together: flow experience and its impact on creative output in lego serious play. Eur. J. Innov. Manag. (2021)

Author Index

M. Mehrnezhad and S. Parkin (Eds.): STAST 2022, LNCS 13855, p. 147, 2025.
https://doi.org/10.1007/978-3-031-83072-3